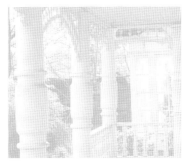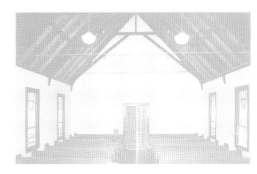

ARCHITECTURAL PERSPECTIVES OF

CLEVELAND COUNTY

NORTH CAROLINA

Historical Inventory by BRIAN R. EADES

Edited by J. DANIEL PEZZONI

ARCHITECTURAL PERSPECTIVES OF
CLEVELAND COUNTY
NORTH CAROLINA

Cleveland County Historic Preservation Taskforce
Shelby, Cleveland County, North Carolina

© 2003 Cleveland County Historic Preservation Taskforce
311 East Marion Street, Shelby, N.C. 28150
P.O. Box 1210, Shelby, N.C. 28151
All rights reserved.

Printed in Canada by Friesens Corp.
Design and production by Julie Allred, B. Williams and Associates,
Durham, North Carolina.

Front endsheet: Murray Cotton Gin, Cleveland County. Ca. 1950 photo courtesy of the Cleveland County Historical Museum.
Back endsheet: Cora Mills, Kings Mountain. Ca. 1920 photo courtesy of the Kings Mountain Historical Museum.
Frontispiece: Cleveland County Courthouse Square, Shelby. Ca. 1940 photo by Willis courtesy of the Cleveland County Historical Museum.
Art source key: Brian R. Eades is credited as "BRE"; Thomas J. Forney, Jr. is credited as "TJF"; J. Daniel Pezzoni is credited as "JDP"

The survey on which this book is based was financed in part with federal funds from the National Park Service, Department of the Interior. The contents and opinions here do not necessarily reflect the views or policies of the Department of the Interior, nor does the mention of trade names and commercial products constitute endorsement or recommendation by the Department of the Interior.

Library of Congress Cataloging-in-Publication Data
Eades, Brian R. (Brian Russell), 1971–
Architectural perspectives of Cleveland County, North Carolina / historical inventory by Brian R. Eades ; edited by J. Daniel Pezzoni.
    p. cm.
Includes bibliographical references and index.
ISBN 0-9740507-0-9 (cloth : alk. paper)
1. Architecture—North Carolina—Cleveland County.
I. Title: Cleveland County. II. Pezzoni, J. Daniel, 1961– III. Title.
NA730.N82C584 2004
720'.9756775—dc22   2003062572

The Cleveland County Historic Preservation Taskforce dedicates this book to the memory of four of our original members whose enthusiasm inspired us and whose knowledge of Cleveland County's history and architectural heritage greatly influenced this project.

Ruby Alexander of Kings Mountain
Elva Thompson Gheen of Shelby
Albert Glenn of Boiling Springs
Jackie Rountree of Grover

The Rogers Theatre and a biplane face off in this circa 1940 photograph by Floyd M. Willis. The Shelby theater and the little WACO airplane were apparently posed as a stunt to promote ticket sales for the 1938 20th Century Fox movie Test Pilot. *Photo courtesy of the Lloyd Hamrick Collection.*

CONTENTS

Preface   ix

Acknowledgments   xi

Cleveland County: A Historical and Architectural Essay, *by J. Daniel Pezzoni*   1

Featured Properties   59

Selected Inventory   221

References:

Appendix: National Register and Study List Properties   283

Glossary   285

Bibliography   295

Index   299

PREFACE

A concerted effort to document and preserve Cleveland County's historic architecture was begun in 1994 by the Cleveland County Historic Preservation Taskforce. The Taskforce was an outgrowth of the preservation recommendations of the Cleveland Tomorrow study prepared for the county by the Urban Institute of the University of North Carolina Charlotte. Operating under the auspices of the Cleveland County Economic Development Commission, the Taskforce originally consisted of Jeanne Kincaid, Mooresboro, chairman; Ellie Buse, Brownie Plaster, Kay Archer Price, Cindy Cook, Elva Gheen, Thurman Brooks, Robert Borders, Ginny Hughes, and Keaton Fonvielle, Shelby; Jackie Rountree, Grover; Jack Hoyle, Belwood; Hill Carpenter, Waco; Ruby Alexander, Johnsie Reavis, and Mary Neisler, Kings Mountain; Libby Sarazen, Lattimore; Albert Glenn, Boiling Springs; and Betty Hord and John Rudisill, Lawndale. Joining the Taskforce later were Carole Ann Hudson, Betty Rose Heath, and Tommy Forney, Shelby; Lansford Jolley, Boiling Springs; David Neisler, Kings Mountain; Claude Lavender, Earl; Bobby Warlick, Lawndale; Jean Francis, Grover; and Cindi Cannon, taskforce coordinator.

With the support of these dedicated individuals, donations from civic-minded local citizens and groups, and funding from the North Carolina Department of Cultural Resources and Cleveland County, the Taskforce hired architectural historian Brian R. Eades to conduct an extensive survey of the county's historic properties. Brian's 1997–98 survey documented over 900 properties and led to the placing of many individual properties and potential historic districts on the state's Study List of sites that warrant consideration for the National Register of Historic Places. The original products of this survey, consisting of property files, photographs, maps, inventory entries, and a manuscript history and architectural history, are permanently housed at the Division of Historical Resources Western Office in Asheville (a branch of the state Department of Cultural Resources), and copies are available at the Cleveland County Chamber of Commerce office in Shelby. In 2002 the Taskforce hired architectural historian J. Daniel Pezzoni to edit and supplement the inventory entries, draft a historical and architectural essay, and prepare the survey products for publication.

Following this introduction is an essay that traces the county's architectural development with reference to broader historical trends. The principal source for the essay was Brian Eades's manuscript "The History and Architecture of Cleveland County, North Carolina." The essay provides context for two sections that present architectural and historical information on individual properties, titled Featured Properties and Selected Inventory. Most of the property entries were written by Brian Eades and edited by Dan Pezzoni; most entries for Shelby and for post–World War II properties were written by Dan Pezzoni. The property entries are followed by an appendix that lists properties in the National Register of Historic Places and the state Study List, a glossary of architectural terms, a bibliography, and an index. Photographs by Brian Eades are identified with the initials *BRE*; those by Dan Pezzoni are identified with *JDP*; those by Thomas J. Forney, Jr. are identified with *TJF*; and those taken or provided by other individuals and institutions are appropriately credited. In property entry headings and elsewhere in the text, the abbreviation "ca." stands for "circa," a Latin word meaning "about" that indicates a date is approximate or conjectural. For those readers who wish to seek out the properties profiled in this book, the Historic Preservation Taskforce asks that they view properties from public thoroughfares and otherwise respect property rights.

In the words of Taskforce member Betty Hord, it is hoped that this book "will encourage an appreciation of our county's history and its architectural heritage and serve as a catalyst for efforts to preserve the places we call home." In this spirit, the Taskforce congratulates the City of Kings Mountain for establishing the Kings Mountain Landmarks Commission in 1999. The Taskforce encourages other municipalities to follow suit and supports the establishment of a County Landmarks Commission.

ACKNOWLEDGMENTS

The Cleveland County Historic Preservation Taskforce extends its appreciation to the many property owners and others who assisted the survey on which this publication is based. Individuals and organizations that assisted the project during the publication phase include Lane Alexander, W. Ted Alexander, Andre Studio, O. Stanhope Anthony, Carole Arey, Jack Arey, Beverly F. Barnes, Fred B. Blackley, Helen Borders, Ladley Burn, Nellie Carpenter, the Cleveland County Historical Museum, Tim Demmitt, Carl J. Dockery Jr., Robert Falls, Nicholas Galizia, O. Max Gardner III, Angela M. Greenfield, Lisa Griffin, Larry Hamrick Sr., Rita Harris, Mabeline Haynes, Betty Rose Heath, June Hadden Hobbs, Roger Holland, Mike Hoyt, Jack Hunt, Lee Jensen, Cothenia J. Jolley, the Kings Mountain Historical Museum, Ariel Lambert, Gail Langston, the Lawndale Historical Museum, Dennis Lee, Keith Longiotti, Louisville Free Public Library, Bill McCarter, Vic McCord, Esther M. Muench, Andy Neisler, U. L. "Rusty" Patterson, Preservation North Carolina, Betty Ross, the Shelby Star, Rush Hamrick Sherman, Fred M. Simmons, Suzanne Simmons, Joe Stockton, Cassie Tarpley, Wanda Taylor, Uptown Shelby Association Inc., Harold Watson, Jack Weller, Lamar Wilson, and Mike Wright. Tommy Forney and Lamar Wilson were especially helpful in gathering images for the book.

Present and past staff members of the Office of Archives and History of the North Carolina Department of Cultural Resources who assisted the project during the survey and publication phases include Claudia R. Brown, Chandrea Burch, Jannette Coleridge-Taylor, Bill Garrett, Clay Griffith, John Horton, Nick Lanier, Jennifer Martin, Michelle Ann Michael, Michael T. Southern, and Ann Swallow. Nick Lanier was especially helpful in printing most of the photographs used in the book. Julie C. Allred and Barbara Williams at B. Williams and Associates produced the book, and Christi Stanforth copyedited the manuscript. A special acknowledgment is extended to Cindi Cannon, administrative assistant of the Economic Development Commission, whose able assistance helped make this publication a reality.

1996 CONTRIBUTORS

The Cleveland County Historic Preservation Taskforce thanks the following for their financial contribution to this publication.

Benefactor

Michael and Patsy Cheng
Dover Foundation
O. Max Gardner Foundation, Inc.
Historic Shelby Foundation
Kings Mountain Historical Museum Foundation, Inc.
Charles A. and Mary S. Neisler
C. Andrew and Sylvia M. Neisler, Jr.

Patron

BB&T
Mr. and Mrs. George Blanton, Jr.
Mr. and Mrs. Wayne Brunnick
Cindi Cannon
Carolina State Bank
Cleveland County Chamber
DM&E Corporation
Dicey Mills, Inc.
Mr. and Mrs. Hugh M. Duncan
First National Bank of Shelby
Keaton Fonvielle
Mr. and Mrs. Robert Forney
Elva T. Gheen
Mr. and Mrs. Marvin Hamrick
Mr. and Mrs. Charlie Harry
Milton Holloman
R. Michael and June P. Miller
Steven G. and Linda W. Nye
Mr. and Mrs. Jack Palmer, Jr.
Dr. and Mrs. Harold E. Plaster, Jr.
Dr. and Mrs. Harold E. Plaster, Sr.
Kay and Kim Price
Reliance Electric/Rockwell Automation
Shelby Savings Bank, SSB
J. L. Suttle, Jr.
J. L. Suttle Jr. and Co., Inc.

Sponsor

Alexander Realty
Dr. and Mrs. Michael W. Alexander
Mr. and Mrs. Robert J. Arey
Mr. and Mrs. William Jackson Arey
Mr. and Mrs. Thomas B. Austell
AZDEL, Inc.
Mr. and Mrs. John Barker
Mrs. Herman A. (Ellen) Beam
Dr. T. R. Blackburn
Chip Blackley
Mr. and Mrs. Fred Blackley
Gary and Jo Boggs
Yvonne and Jim Boggs
Boiling Springs Lions Club
Dr. and Mrs. Richard Bowling
Dr. and Mrs. Douglas R. Boyette
Robin Brackett
Eleanor B. Buse
Mr. and Mrs. Charles S. Byers, Jr.
Joe E. Cabaniss
Mr. and Mrs. R. J. Callahan
CellularOne
Mr. and Mrs. George Clay, Jr.
John W. Cline
Cindy Cook
Sam and Sallie Craig

Sponsor

Jim and Marcie Crawley
Mary Jane Darr
Cecil Dickson
Mr. Charles L. Elliott
Edwin C. Ford
Maxine F. Forrest
Mr. and Mrs. Arnold Gibbs
Mr. and Mrs. Albert Glenn
Mr. and Mrs. Joe A. Goforth
Richard and Linda Goforth
William and Virginia Greene
Mr. and Mrs. Edgar B. Hamilton
Mr. and Mrs. C. Rush Hamrick, Jr.
Gordon G. Hamrick
Mr. and Mrs. Harvey B. Hamrick
Mr. and Mrs. Larry D. Hamrick, Sr.
Mr. and Mrs. Julian Hamrick
Mr. and Mrs. David L. Harry, Sr.
Betty Rose Heath
Mr. and Mrs. Wade Hendricks
Robin and Roger Holland
Mr. and Mrs. Alton M. Hopper, Jr.
Richard and Betty Hord
Jeri J. Horn
Jack and Wilma Hoyle
Mr. and Mrs. W. Hill Hudson III
Mr. and Mrs. R. Alan Hughes
Mr. and Mrs. Jay Teddy
Miss Burnette Hunt
Dr. and Mrs. Jack Hunt
S. W. Jackson, Jr.
Jeanne Woolbert Kincaid
Kings Mountain Association of Realtors, Inc.
Dobbin Lattimore
Leasing Services, Inc.

June C. Lee
Mr. and Mrs. R. T. LeGrand, Jr.
Mr. and Mrs. Frank Love
Gerald and Frances Lutz
John R. McBrayer
Dorothy P. McIntyre
Dr. and Mrs. Avery W. McMurry
Elizabeth Mauney
Town of Mooresboro
David C. Neisler
Joe and Jessi Ogburn
Hazel W. Olsby
Personnel Services Unlimited, Inc.
Mr. and Mrs. Ali Paksoy
Ellen Taylor Palmer
Johnny and Johnsie Reavis
Lester "Les" Roark
Royster P&M Warehouse Co.
Jackie Rountree
John Rudisill, Sr.
Dr. and Mrs. Paul Sarazen
Mr. and Mrs. Paul M. Sarazen III
Newlin and Rachel S. Schenck
Mrs. Jack (Ruth) Schweppe
Barbara T. Simpson
Becky and Loyd Smith
Eloise Young Spangler
Mr. and Mrs. Linton Suttle
Dr. and Mrs. L. Steve Thornburg
Rita and Hubert Toney
Wade Tyner
Bobby Bryan Warlick
Dr. and Mrs. M. Christopher White
Lamar and Carol Wilson
Mr. and Mrs. Thomas Wood

Contributors

Mr. and Mrs. Shem K. Blackley, Jr.
DeVane Interiors
Mr. and Mrs. Mason Gaston
Marilyn and Bill Jack
Laura and Chuck Lampley

Magnolia Garden Club
Mrs. Charles K. Padgett
Adelyn Parker
Upper Cleveland County Chamber of Commerce

2002 CONTRIBUTORS

The Cleveland County Historic Preservation Taskforce thanks the following for their financial contribution to this publication.

Benefactor

Dover Foundation, Inc.

Patron

Anonymous
Adelaide and Dick Craver
First National Bank
Dr. and Mrs. Harold E. Plaster, Jr.

Sponsor

Dr. and Mrs. Michael W. Alexander
Mr. and Mrs. Ted Alexander
Mr. and Mrs. Robert J. Arey
Mr. and Mrs. William Jackson Arey
Mary and Frank Beam
Mrs. George Blanton, Jr.
Robert and Helen Borders
Virginia Falls Bost
Dr. and Mrs. Richard Bowles
Robin Brackett
Tom and Ada Bridges
Doug Brown
Mr. and Mrs. Wayne Brunnick
Ann and Rob Deaton
Mr. Charles L. Elliott
Mr. and Mrs. Bob Elmore
Keaton and Betsy Fonvielle
Mrs. Robert Forney
Ray and Darlene Gravett
C. Rush Hamrick, Jr.
Mr. and Mrs. Larry D. Hamrick, Sr.
Max J. and Jane B. Hamrick
Ronald J. Hawkins
Mr. and Mrs. Wade Hendricks
Dr. and Mrs. William R. Henshaw

Doris and Milton Holloman
Home Realty Co., Inc.
Mr. and Mrs. Alton M. Hopper, Jr.
Mr. and Mrs. Charles A. Horn
Mr. and Mrs. Lansford Jolley
James (Jim) Kunkle
Dobbin and Mary Ann Lattimore
Mr. and Mrs. R. T. LeGrand, Jr.
Mrs. Ray Webb Lutz
Ron and Shirley Mauney
Clifford B. and Doris H. McCurry
Dr. Avery W. McMurry
Mrs. Dan (Bettye) Moore
Marilyn and Henry Neisler
Steve and Judy Padgett
Adelyn and Bill Parker
Dr. and Mrs. William R. Plaster
Kim and Kay Price
Lester "Les" Roark
Mr. and Mrs. R. H. Rogers, Jr.
Clemmie and Margaret Royster
Will and Tina Rucker
Mr. and Mrs. Phil Rucker
Mrs. Paul Sarazen
Mr. and Mrs. Paul M. Sarazen, III

Sponsor

Michael and Joanne G. Schenck
Newlin and Rachel Schenck
Mr. and Mrs. John V. Schweppe, Jr.
Shelby Savings Bank
Ralph and Clevie Spangler
Mr. and Mrs. Linton Suttle
Mr. and Mrs. David R. Teddy
Dr. and Mrs. John L. Thompson, Jr.

Jill and Mason Venable
Mr. and Mrs. Henry Lee Weathers
Lou Alice Whisnant
David M. Wilkison
Mr. and Mrs. Lloyd Williams, Sr.
Mr. and Mrs. Michael Wood
Mr. and Mrs. Stough A. Wray, Jr.
Lamar Young

Contributor

Shem K. Blackley, Jr.
Dr. and Mrs. Thomas R. Blackburn
Terry and Larry Brown

Sam and Sallie Craig
Eloise and Dave Gallagher
Betty Rose Heath

CLEVELAND COUNTY:
A HISTORICAL AND
ARCHITECTURAL
ESSAY

THE AIM OF THIS BOOK is to acquaint the reader with Cleveland County's remarkable architectural heritage. Much can be learned about the county through an understanding of its buildings. The settlement period is recalled by log cabins, simple country churches, and family cemeteries. The prosperity of railroads and King Cotton is manifested in the Victorian residences that filled the newly established towns and revitalized countryside of the late nineteenth century. The Industrial Revolution arrived late in the county, but when it did it ushered in cotton mills and mill villages, key elements of town life in the twentieth century. Affluence and urbanization introduced new building types and styles, including some of the state's best examples of Egyptian Revival and domestic Mission-style architecture. The county's architectural evolution continues to the present with inspired examples of modern design.

Cleveland County is located in the western North Carolina Piedmont, the gently rolling region bounded by the coastal plain on the east and the Appalachian Mountains on the west. The 466-square-mile county is adjoined by Gaston and Lincoln counties on the east, Burke County on the north, Rutherford County on the west, and Cherokee County, South Carolina, on the south. Charlotte, North Carolina's largest city, is located approximately thirty miles east of the county's border.

The county's northern edge is defined by the South Mountains, an outlying range of the Blue Ridge. The South Mountains have several peaks that are almost 2,000 feet in height, including Covington Mountain (1,960 feet) and Paine Mountain (1,920 feet). The First Broad River rises in these mountains

previous pages: Merchant R. L. Hunt in front of the Hunt & Hewitt Store, Lattimore. Early 1920s photo courtesy of Burnette Hunt.

right: The Broad River near Boiling Springs. Photo by Broad River Council.

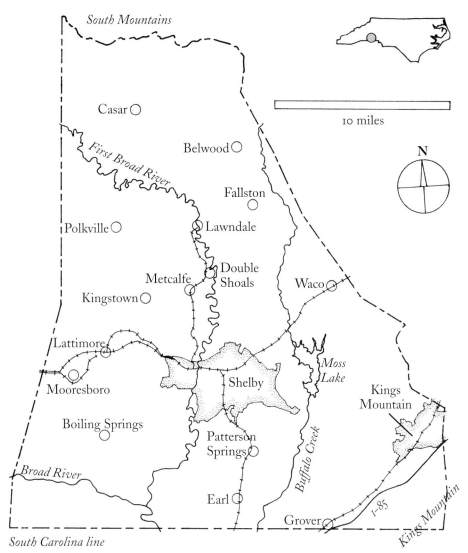

and flows southward the length of the county to join the Broad River, which crosses the county's southwest corner. Buffalo Creek, another tributary of the Broad, drains the southeast quadrant of the county. The relatively level character of the county's southern end is broken by the flanks of Kings Mountain, a solitary height that lies mostly across the border in South Carolina.

Cleveland County has a population of approximately 100,000 people (the 2000 census figure was 96,287). Its most populous community is Shelby, the county seat, which had a population of 19,477 in 2000. Next in population are Kings Mountain (9,693) and Boiling Springs (3,866). Other communities include Earl, Grover, and Patterson Springs south of Shelby; Lattimore and Mooresboro near the county's west border; and Belwood, Casar, Fallston, Kingstown, Lawndale, Polkville, and Waco in the county's northern portion. The county is served by two federal highways: Interstate 85, which clips the

Mural by Clive Haynes of the Kings Mountain area during the Revolutionary War era, Kings Mountain

southeast corner near Kings Mountain, and Highway 74, which passes through Kings Mountain, Shelby, and Mooresboro. The Southern and Seaboard Air Line railroads operated in the county in the late nineteenth and twentieth centuries; today this trackage is largely controlled by the CSX Corporation.

The first visitors to Cleveland County were Native Americans. Archaeological evidence points to Native American use of the land's natural resources as far back as the Archaic Period (8,000 B.C. to 500 B.C.). There is speculation that the area later served as a buffer zone or common hunting ground between the Cherokee and Catawba peoples. European settlers began to arrive in the 1750s. Largely Scots-Irish and German, these settlers traveled to the Carolina backcountry from Philadelphia via the Great Wagon Road, and they quickly established farms, small-scale industries such as mills and distilleries, and, later, churches and communities. They also built houses.[1]

Little is known about domestic architecture in Cleveland County's colonial and early national periods, but the broad outlines can be inferred from regional

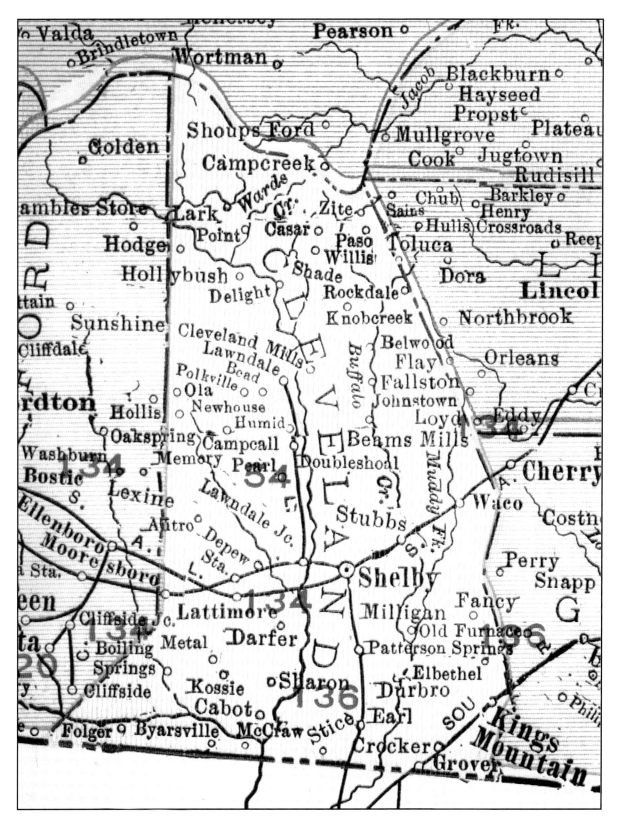

Map of Cleveland County from 1915 Rand McNally Commercial Atlas

A batten shutter with wrought-iron strap hinges, left; half-dovetail notching, right. Both on Dr. Hamilton's Office, Hamilton-McBrayer Farm, Mooresboro vicinity (BRE)

architectural usage and from the few surviving houses that date to the first century of settlement. The county's early houses were generally small in scale and were built using indigenous materials such as wood, earth, and stone. Many residents of the eighteenth-century Carolina backcountry relied on log construction because of the abundance of timber and the minimal cost and effort required. Typical features included fieldstone or wooden foundations; stone, log, or mud-and-stick chimneys; unglazed shuttered windows; and board or wood-shingle roofs. Most houses had one-room interiors, with or without wood floors; some of the finer residences boasted the hall-parlor plan, with a partition dividing the interior into unequal halves. Presumably aspects of the form and construction of these houses reflected the British or German cultural inheritance of the settlers. In log construction a type of corner notching known as the half-dovetail notch prevailed locally.

Perhaps the earliest surviving house in the county, and one that is representative of early construction, is the Irvin-Hamrick House. The half-dovetail log cabin is thought to have been built by Revolutionary War veteran James Irvin (1765–1845) shortly after he purchased his home site in the Boiling Springs vicinity in 1794. Notable features of the house include a gable-end fieldstone chimney and evidence that the windows were originally unglazed (one window is fitted only with a batten shutter). The house has been preserved by descendants of the Hamricks, who acquired it in 1850, and a description of life here in the late nineteenth century has been handed down. Another early example is the half-dovetail log core of the Lattimore House, dating to the first quarter of the nineteenth century. The one-room-plan house possesses simple refinements such as remnant beaded weatherboard siding, beaded ceiling joists, and six-panel doors hung on strap hinges with bulbous ends. Later still but in the spirit of early settlement is the mid-nineteenth-century Phifer House, with standard dimensions of approximately 20 by 24 feet but locally rare V-notched corners. The Phifer House is one of the most accessible of Cleveland County's early dwellings, as it was carefully disassembled at its original location in the Bethlehem vicinity and reerected at the Broad River Greenway.[2]

The county's wealthiest individuals were not content to live in log cabins and instead built larger frame and masonry houses with stylish details. About

Irvin-Hamrick House, Boiling Springs vicinity. 1895 photo courtesy of Ruth Hamrick Sherman.

Interior of the Lattimore House, Polkville vicinity. Photo by Michael T. Southern courtesy of the North Carolina Office of Archives and History.

1814, Benjamin Ellis, owner of a ferry on the Broad River near the South Carolina line, built a two-story frame residence now known as the Ellis Ferry House or the Grambling House. The dwelling's two brick chimneys were considerably finer than the stone or wood chimneys that were typical of the period; one is laid in Flemish bond with patterned glazed headers in the stack. The numerous and large windows of the house were another improvement over the small shuttered holes of the commoner dwellings. The windows on the first story have nine-over-six sash, those on the second story are six-over-six, and a four-light transom spans the front entry. The three-room-plan interior combines elements of the Georgian style—the classically inspired style of eighteenth-century Britain and the colonies—with the lighter Federal style of the early nineteenth century. Brick construction was more costly than frame, and its expense and its greater strength and durability made it prized by the elite. The oldest surviving brick dwelling is the Ramseur-Sarratt House, a two-story house of Flemish-bond construction located near Earl and thought to date to about 1800. Local tradition maintains that the house was built by its owner Phillip Ramseur, a brick mason and carpenter.

Steady population growth in the Cleveland County area during the early nineteenth century bolstered efforts to create a new county out of western Lincoln County and eastern Rutherford County. In January 1841 the state legislature passed the bill forming the new county, which was initially named Cleaveland in honor of Battle of Kings Mountain hero Benjamin Cleaveland (the name was changed to Cleveland during the administration of President Grover Cleveland). Land was donated for a county seat, named Shelby after

Ramseur-Sarratt House, Earl vicinity (BRE)

Isaac Shelby, another patriot who established his reputation at the Battle of Kings Mountain. The county seat grew slowly during the antebellum period. According to some accounts, the first private dwelling was not built until 1847, and at the time of the Civil War the town was described as "just a wide place in the road, mostly woods and all frame buildings." At first the county court met elsewhere—in the commodious two-story house of William Weathers, which formerly stood at the intersection of Zion Church Road and Cornwell Road north of Shelby—but in 1845 the government moved into a brick courthouse erected by builders George Smith and John Dameron on the public square in Shelby.[3]

The 1845 courthouse was a stoutly proportioned Greek Revival building with offices on the street level below a main courtroom level reached by double flights of steps on the east and west fronts. The steps met at porticoes with heavy masonry columns, painted white or stuccoed, on arched platforms. The building featured pedimented gables with small lunettes, entries with sidelights and transoms, and a pair of chimneys on each gable end. In form and finish the courthouse could be taken for one of the grand plantation houses built by the

Cleveland County Courthouse, 1845. Photo, circa 1898, courtesy of the Cleveland County Historical Museum.

region's more prosperous antebellum planters. The 1845 courthouse stood until 1907–8, when a much larger Classical Revival replacement was constructed.[4]

The Greek Revival style of the 1845 courthouse was the most popular style of the mid-nineteenth century, nationally and locally. Its simple forms, inspired by the column and lintel construction of ancient Greek temples, struck a chord with Americans who revered the culture and government of ancient Greece. The style was more robust than the delicate, almost fussy Federal style, but despite their differences the two styles were often hybridized. A representative example of the Greek Revival style is the 1840s Joshua Beam House, located on Buffalo Creek near Shelby. The two-story heavy frame house was built for the entrepreneurial Joshua Beam, who owned gold mines, mills, an ironworks, and a mercantile firm. The house features a symmetrical five-bay facade with a center two-tier porch, a nod to the pedimented porticoes of classical architecture. Greek Revival influence is most evident in the mantels of the center-passage-plan interior, which have fireplace openings in symmetrically molded frames with turned corner blocks. The finishes of the Joshua Beam House call to mind designs published in the pattern books of American architect Asher Benjamin and others that served as sources of inspiration for country carpenters.[5]

By the end of the antebellum period, Cleveland County's countryside had matured into its present form: a landscape of farms with a supporting infrastructure of wagon roads, mills and other small industries, country stores, churches, and a handful of villages, including the struggling county seat. The farms revolved around the main dwelling, and their operation depended on a host of domestic and agricultural outbuildings. These were generally small in scale and simple in construction. Nearest the house was the kitchen, often detached because of the danger posed to the main dwelling by cooking fires. The kitchen might double as a residence for a slave cook, if the white farm family was prosperous enough to own one. Slave houses undoubtedly existed in antebellum Cleveland County, but few if any survive.

Smaller outbuildings housed functions associated with food storage: meathouses for the curing of hog flesh, ventilated dairies and water-cooled springhouses for the preservation of milk products, and corncribs and granaries for storing Indian corn, wheat, oats, and rye. Many of the earliest surviving corncribs are unchinked log, a form of construction that was ideal for holding and ventilating the contents. Stock barns appear to have been relatively rare until the late nineteenth century, as cattle often ranged freely through the countryside.

Many items were produced on the farm for family use. Country folk wore "homespun," and cloth-making, washing, food preparation, and child rearing filled the days of farm women. Luxuries and staples such as coffee and sugar that could not be produced on the farm were supplied by general stores located at crossroads, mills, and other frequented places. General stores only survive in number from the late nineteenth and early twentieth centuries in the county, but these later stores are probably representative of earlier ones. They are typically frame buildings, one to two stories in height, with characteristic gable fronts that distinguish them from most dwellings. The storefronts have large display windows—a lure to prospective customers—and often recessed entries. Shelves line the walls, separated from the public by rows of counters, an arrangement that gave the storekeeper control over the merchandise (self-service did not come in until the supermarkets of the post–World War II era). One of the county's oldest country stores is the Oates Store, which may date to shortly after the Civil War.

Country stores made convenient locations for post offices, which multiplied with the establishment of the star route delivery system in the late nineteenth century. Often the post office occupied a small cubicle in a front or rear corner of the store. Post offices were also sometimes located in houses. The 1888 house of George H. Simmons near Polkville contained the Pearl Post Office at the end of the nineteenth century, and the ca. 1900 residence of J. W. Brackett housed the Belwood Post Office from 1918 to 1932. Perhaps the earliest post office in the county is the one at the vanished community of Durbro near Patterson Springs, which may date to before 1886 and is now used for farm storage.

Churches were another important component of rural communities. In Cleveland County, as elsewhere in Piedmont North Carolina, the religious outlook was essentially Protestant; the largest congregations belonged to Baptist, Presbyterian, and Methodist churches. Sandy Run Baptist Church is thought to be the county's oldest congregation (1772), followed by Shiloh Presbyterian Church (1780). Many congregations that formed before about 1900 originally worshiped in simple log chapels, and some, including the Zion and Ross Grove Baptist congregations, met first in temporary brush arbors or "stands" constructed of log posts driven into the ground and roofed over with boughs and foliage. A brush arbor also served the Capernaum Baptist congregation near Waco until it was replaced by the present permanent arbor in 1919. Arbors and tabernacles (an alternate name) are typically associated with rural areas, but the Shelby Tabernacle stood in town on Warren Street in 1900. As congregations grew in size and affluence, frame and brick buildings were erected. Churches, like stores, were traditionally gable-fronted, an arrangement that focused the in-

Capernaum Arbor, Waco vicinity. Photo courtesy of the Cleveland County Historical Museum.

Elliott Chapel, Polkville vicinity. Photo by Forrest Ellis courtesy of the Cleveland County Historical Museum.

terior space on the altar and pulpit at one end. Some antebellum churches featured galleries that provided additional seating for whites or segregated seating for blacks.[6]

Elliott Chapel, a Methodist church built near Polkville in 1871, is representative of the county's early frame churches, with its plainly detailed weatherboard exterior, nine-over-nine windows with louvered shutters, and double front entries. By the end of the nineteenth century many newly constructed churches incorporated details from the Gothic Revival style, notably the pointed lancet arch used for door, window, and belfry openings. The lancet arch and stained glass windows, also popular, referenced the Gothic ecclesiastical architecture of medieval Europe. In the twentieth century, the Colonial Revival style largely replaced the Gothic Revival, and some churches added multistory educational, office, and fellowship hall wings to their rear or side elevations.

Rural churches were favored locations for the establishment of graveyards, as were farms, with their numerous family burial plots. The majority of early graves received crude memorials such as fieldstones or wooden headboards; rows of fieldstone markers survive in the Collins Cemetery near Grover, in use from the late eighteenth century onward. A few local stonecarvers fashioned more permanent memorials before 1800. Among the earliest dated gravestones in the county is that of Elizabeth Dover in Shiloh Presbyterian Church Cemetery near Grover, with a death date of 1788 (it is possible the stone is back dated, that is, carved after the death date). The Dover gravestone has a disc-shaped head on a rectangular trunk, a form known as an effigy marker for its stylized

A Historical and Architectural Essay 13

Shiloh Presbyterian Church Cemetery, Grover vicinity (BRE)

resemblance to the human body. Effigy markers were common in rural areas of North Carolina through the mid-nineteenth century.

The Charlotte region supported a number of prolific gravestone workshops, beginning with the Bigham family workshop of Mecklenburg County in the 1760s. Several Cleveland County gravestones appear to be the work of a South Carolina workshop that was operated by members of the Crawford and Caveny families. The headstones of Elijah Spurlin (d. 1845) in the El Bethel United Methodist Church Cemetery and Lydia Martin (d. 1847) in Shelby's Sunset Cemetery feature crudely rendered willow tree carvings that are similar to the work of William N. Crawford (1808–94). Another stone from about the same period, located in the Shiloh cemetery, has quarter sunbursts in its upper corners and an eight-pointed star centered above the inscription. This stone is also similar to the work of William Crawford and to headstones carved by his brother, Robert M. Crawford (1803–65). The decorative motifs of these

stones have a number of sources and associations. The weeping willow was a conventional symbol of mourning on nineteenth-century tombstones nationwide. The quarter sunbursts call to mind decoration in Federal-style furniture and architectural carving, and the star was a popular motif in British and German folk art.[7]

The Civil War did not visit the kind of devastation on Cleveland County that it did on other areas of the South, but the conflict did drain the area of resources, impede development, and bring personal loss to many families. On the eve of the war, according to the federal census of 1860, slaves numbered 2,131 (approximately 17 percent) of the county population of 12,348. After the war the freedmen established homes, farms, churches, and schools, but political equality was not achieved for another hundred years. Another important event of the era was the coming of the railroad. The first line to reach the county was the Piedmont Air Line, later known as the Atlanta & Charlotte Air Line. Construction began in 1869; the line opened to Kings Mountain on December 1, 1872, and to Grover about the same time. The Atlanta & Charlotte came under the control of the Richmond & Danville in the early 1880s, and in 1894 it was incorporated into the newly created Southern Railway system. The citizens of Shelby had opposed a referendum to build a railroad to the town in 1857, but in 1874 the Carolina Central Railroad connected Shelby to Charlotte via Lincolnton. The Wilmington, Charlotte & Rutherford Railroad operated the line in 1884. In 1900 Shelby was served by the Southern Rail-

Lydia Martin headstone, Sunset Cemetery, Shelby (JDP)

Elizabeth Dover headstone, Shiloh Presbyterian Church Cemetery, Grover vicinity (BRE)

way and the Seaboard Air Line, which coalesced in the 1890s and was officially consolidated in 1900. From Shelby the two lines extended westward, roughly parallel, through Lattimore and Mooresboro.⁸

The northern two-thirds of the county was initially excluded from this surge of railroad construction. Henry Franklin Schenck (1835–1915), developer of Cleveland Mills and the community of Lawndale, was unsuccessful in convincing the major carriers to build a spur line to his enterprises, so in 1899 he bankrolled the construction of the Lawndale Railway. Officially known as the Lawndale Railway & Industrial Company line but locally nicknamed the Lawndale Dummy, the narrow-gauge railroad connected Lawndale to the other lines at Shelby. The cars made several stops along the route, including the marshaling yard at Metcalfe, and carried coal, raw materials, finished textiles, and passengers to and from Lawndale. Competition from automobiles and trucks forced the line to shut down in 1943, but two boxcars were saved from the scrap heap and have been restored and placed on exhibit at Metcalfe Station and at the Lawndale Historical Museum on the Piedmont School grounds.⁹

Enhanced rail connections stimulated agricultural production in the county, especially cotton cultivation, because farmers could more easily transport their

Lawndale Railway & Industrial Company Engine House (demolished), Lawndale. Early-twentieth-century photo courtesy of Tommy Forney.

Cotton warehouses such as the Shelby Bonded Warehouse were another architectural form associated with cotton cultivation. 1955 photo courtesy of the North Carolina Office of Archives and History.

Interior of a Cleveland County cotton gin. Circa 1950 photo courtesy of the Cleveland County Historical Museum.

products to market. Statewide, cotton production more than doubled during the 1870s; in Cleveland County the rise was exponential, from 520 bales in 1870 to 6,126 bales in 1880—nearly a twelvefold increase. An 1884 federal census report identified the southernmost section of the county, the area served by the Atlanta & Charlotte Air Line, as the principal cotton-production area: 10 to 15 percent of total land area was planted in the crop. By contrast, in the hilly northern quadrant of the county, which was farther from rail transport, cotton fields accounted for less than 1 percent of the landscape. The cotton boom translated into a wave of new home construction. Farmers channeled profits into richly ornamented Victorian houses that dwarfed the log cabins of previous generations.[10]

King Cotton introduced two common building types to the Cleveland County rural landscape, the cotton house and the cotton gin. The cotton house was a relatively undifferentiated building, one or two stories in height, used to store cotton before it was taken to gin and market. The cotton gin housed machinery for removing seeds from the cotton lint, a process known as ginning, and in the late nineteenth century steam power and mechanized baling were added to facilities. Twentieth-century gins are typically rectangular buildings, two stories in height, with wood or metal cladding and drive-through side sheds for wagons and trucks. The Boggs Cotton Gin near Fallston is a typical example, with corrugated metal siding, a gable roof, shed extensions, and an interior divided into rooms for the gins and their operating machinery.

An abundance of cotton and labor made conditions ideal for textile manufacturing. In this regard Cleveland County was also part of a statewide trend. Cheap labor gave the region an advantage over northeastern states, where the

A Historical and Architectural Essay 17

industry was more developed but where higher wage rates prevailed. In North Carolina the number of cotton mills increased from 49 in 1880 to 91 in 1890, 177 in 1900, and 281 in 1910. By the early twentieth century textiles had become the state's leading industry, and North Carolina surpassed all other states in the manufacture of cotton goods.[11]

H. F. Schenck was one of the first in the county to see opportunity in textile manufacturing. In 1873 he opened a small water-powered cotton mill on Knob Creek, and in the late 1880s he relocated to the First Broad River at what would become the town of Lawndale. Northern investors provided the funds for Schenck to build a large brick mill complex by 1888. Capitalists in Kings Mountain and Shelby were quick to follow. H. F. Schenck's son, John F., began Lily Mills in Shelby in 1905. Shelby was soon chosen as the site for three other mills as well: the Belmont Cotton Mills, begun about 1887; Shelby Cotton Mills, established in 1899–1900; and the Ella Mills, founded by John Randolph Dover in 1907. In Kings Mountain, the Kings Mountain Manufacturing Company (KMMC) was established in the late 1880s by William and Jacob Mauney and was soon joined by the Enterprise Mill (1892), the Dilling Mill (1892–94), and the Cora, Lula, and Bonnie Mills, all in 1900. The Bonnie Mills and two others in Kings Mountain—the Sadie and Mauney Mills—were offshoots of the KMMC. The Neisler family of Kings Mountain entered the field in the early twentieth century with the opening of the Pauline Mills (1910), Margrace Mills (1914), and Patricia Mills. Minette Mills was founded in Grover in 1919. The feminine names given to the mills honored wives and daughters of the mill owners. Minette Mills, for example, combined the names of two daughters of owner Charles F. Harry, Minnie and Jeanette. Margrace Mills was a tribute to mill founder Charles E. Neisler's daughters Margaret Sue and Laura Grace. John Randolph Dover named his Esther, Ora, and Ella Mills after female members of his family.[12]

Cleveland County's cotton mills of the late nineteenth and early twentieth centuries were impressive complexes. Long machinery halls of brick construction dominated the scene, with ranks of tall windows to supply ample light and ventilation for the millworkers. Key to the design of the buildings was the use of "slow burning construction." Steam engines, primitive lighting systems, and combustible materials created serious fire hazards. To counteract the danger, mill builders adopted brick construction; heavy timber framing and flooring that would char but not instantly ignite; and, in many cases, sprinkler systems. Attics were eliminated and ceiling joists were left exposed so that fires could not spread undetected. Multistory mills typically featured projecting elevator and stair towers that became the focuses of ornamentation, as did the office, usually treated as a separate building.[13]

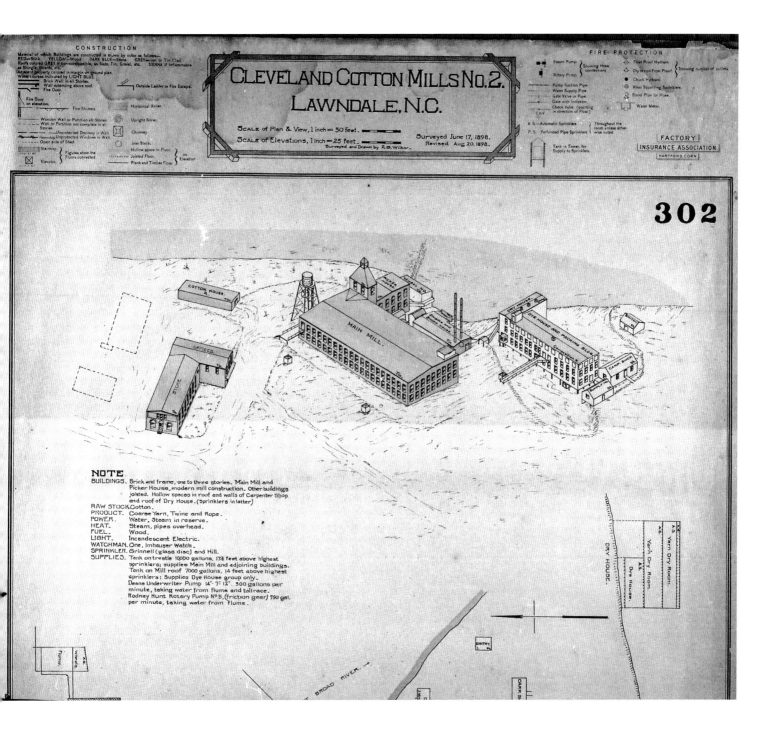

Detail from the 1898 A. G. Wilbor plan and isometric drawing of Cleveland Cotton Mills No. 2, Lawndale. Photo courtesy of the Lawndale Historical Museum.

Mill villages were important adjuncts to the county's textile mills. The practice of housing millworkers in company-owned residential enclaves developed in the nineteenth century as a practical response to the geographic and economic contexts of the state's textile industry. Before steam became the standard industrial power source, mills had to be built near water power, and these sites were sometimes far from existing communities: hence the need to create artificial communities nearby. Also, mill hands often could not afford to build

A Historical and Architectural Essay 19

their own housing, and simple but well-built mill houses became one of the enticements mill owners used to recruit workers. The mill villages were generally conventional in plan, with right-angle street layouts and uninterrupted rows of houses. An exception was the 1919 design of Shelby's Eastside Manufacturing Company Mill Village, by nationally known city planner Earl S. Draper of Charlotte and New York City (the Eastside Mill was later known as the Esther Mill). Draper's plan introduced curvilinear streets, park space, street trees, and other amenities so as to avoid a bleak, company-town appearance.[14]

Cleveland County's mill housing exhibited a range of forms. In Kings Mountain alone may be found the gabled houses of the ca. 1900 Dilling mill village and the ca. 1920 Phenix mill village, the hip-roofed houses of the ca. 1914 Margrace mill village, the pyramidal-roofed and multiple gable houses of the ca. 1900 Cora mill village, and the gable and hip-roofed houses of the ca. 1920 Sadie mill village. Most varied are the ca. 1910 Pauline mill houses, which mix gable, hip, pyramidal, and multiple gable roofs. Cotton mill houses were almost invariably one-story structures of light nailed frame construction. Some

Phenix Mill, Kings Mountain. Circa 1930 photo by Yates Studio courtesy of the Kings Mountain Historical Museum.

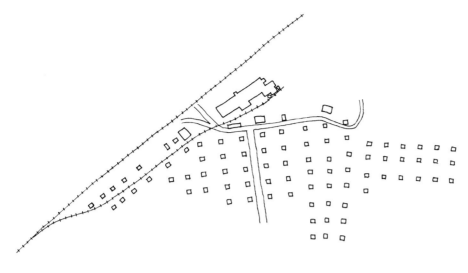

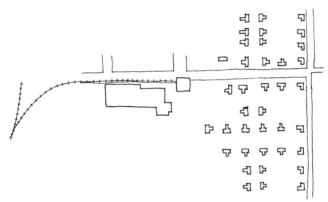

Schematic plans of the Dilling Mill Village, top, and the Bonnie Mill Village, bottom, in 1914, Kings Mountain

mill owners were careful to build a mix of houses with differing numbers of rooms to accommodate the needs of their renters. How-to manuals for mill owners such as Daniel A. Tompkins's *Cotton Mill, Commercial Features* (1899) featured mill house designs and likely contributed to the architectural development of the standardized mill village forms.[15]

Mills and mill villages were accompanied by other essential buildings, including company stores, which accepted the scrip with which millworkers were sometimes paid. Lawndale's Cleveland Mill & Power Company Store was an architectural showcase. The two-story brick building—probably a design of Charlotte architect Charles Christian Hook—featured a classical front with arched display windows, a pediment topped with an urn, and wing walls with painted signage that assured customers of a "complete line of general mdse." Historic photographs show its shelving-lined walls stocked with crockery, glass lamp chimneys, and other items. Another important Cleveland Mills structure was the mill chapel, remodeled with Gothic Revival touches in 1923. The church (torn down in 1977) was shared by the Baptists and Methodists of the mill community. For its workers, Minette Mills in Grover operated not

clockwise from top left:

Cleveland Mill & Power Company Store, Lawndale. Early-twentieth-century photo courtesy of the Lawndale Historical Museum.

Union Church at Cleveland Mills (demolished), Lawndale. Photo courtesy of Tommy Forney.

Lily Mills Clubhouse, Shelby (BRE)

Pauline Mills Clubhouse, Kings Mountain (BRE)

only a company store but also a bowling alley and a pool room. Clubhouses were amenities offered by several mills. The ca. 1920 Pauline Mills Clubhouse in Kings Mountain features a fieldstone exterior; the ca. 1940 Lily Mills Clubhouse in Shelby is brick.[16]

The mill village housing, with its light frame construction and ornamental roof forms, was indicative of a new approach in the county's domestic architecture. The coming of the railroad and of large-scale industry coincided with advances in building technology that were reflected in county dwellings, both rural and town. Steam-powered circular-saw sawmills, in limited use before the Civil War, became common afterward, as did mechanized "sash and blind" factories that mass produced building components for rail shipment. The greater availability of mill-sawn dimensional lumber combined with the spread of light nailed frame construction to encourage greater creativity in house design. Before the change the county's houses adhered to simple, boxlike forms with unembellished gable or sometimes hip roofs. By the end of the nineteenth

A rare interior view of a late-nineteenth-century architectural woodwork manufacturing plant, the W. H. Thompson Factory, Belwood. Photo courtesy of the Cleveland County Historical Museum.

century a wide range of new house forms had been introduced, the most flamboyant with towers, bay windows, complex hip-and-gable roofs, enveloping verandas, and an exuberant variety of sawn, turned, incised, and molded wooden "gingerbread" detail.

The early stages of the transformation occurred during the third quarter of the nineteenth century with the introduction of new nationally popular styles to the county, in particular to the growing town of Shelby. The Italianate style, loosely modeled on the architecture of Italian country houses and characterized by bracketed cornices, arched window heads, and a generally freer approach to form, enjoyed great popularity nationwide beginning in the late 1850s and locally after the Civil War. Italianate cornices and window heads appear in local farmhouses through the end of the nineteenth century, and the style was the inspiration for much commercial architecture of the period as well.

Slightly later, and less common than the Italianate, was the Second Empire style, named for the reign of Napoleon III (1852–70) and identified by the French mansard roof. The 1868 Graham House at 609 S. Washington in Shelby is believed to have had elements of the style before a twentieth-century remodeling. Better known and impeccably preserved is the Banker's House at 319 N. Lafayette, which has been home to a succession of Shelby bankers since its construction about 1875, beginning with original owner Jesse Jenkins. The

Porch detail from the Victorian house Rose Hill, Shelby (BRE)

George C. Herndon House, Kings Mountain. Photo courtesy of the Kings Mountain Historical Museum.

stuccoed two-and-a-half-story brick house is distinguished by its projecting front tower, mansard roofs with decorative dormers on the tower and house proper, and patterned slate roof shingles. The house's bracketed cornice and arched window heads are points of similarity between the Second Empire and Italianate styles. In addition to being a premiere example of the Second Empire style in North Carolina, the Banker's House is probably one of the first known works of an outside "big name" architect in Cleveland County. The house is attributed to architect G. S. H. Appleget, a leading practitioner of the Second Empire style in cities across North Carolina, who located in Charlotte in 1875. (Another Charlotte architect, W. Phillip, advertised in a Shelby newspaper in 1875.) Second Empire houses were also built in Kings Mountain. The spectacular ca. 1878 George Carruth Herndon House stood on Bethlehem Road until it was demolished in 1969, but the 1874 I. Walton Garrett House at 100 N. Piedmont survives. An exceptionally late example of the style is the mansarded 1910 Waters Library on the Piedmont School campus in Lawndale.[17]

The Italianate and Second Empire styles and one other, the Gothic Revival style, rare in Cleveland County domestic construction but present regionally, paved the way for the Victorian architecture of the latter part of the nineteenth century and the beginning of the twentieth. The term "Victorian" is a broad one; some of the finer houses, characterized by such elements as two-story bay windows, hip-and-gable roofs, wraparound porches, and variegated sidings, are more properly referred to as Queen Anne. One of the more elaborate residences of the period is the Victor and Esther McBrayer House at 507 N. Morgan in Shelby. Built in 1893, the one-story frame house juxtaposes an assemblage of gabled elements that are unified by a long front porch with chamfered posts on paneled bases, brackets and a sawn fringe under the cornice, and a balustrade with turned balusters alternating with turned pendants that hang from the handrail. The gables contain three-part round-arched vents with shaped louvers that create a highly decorative effect. Similar shaped-louver vents appear on houses of the same period throughout southern Cleveland County; perhaps they are the signature of a single (unidentified) builder. Also notable are the gabled ventilation dormers, which have scalloped openings on their front faces that create a fishscale pattern—an imaginative take on the fishscale wood-shingle sheathings of the era.[18]

Another inspired example, one more identifiably Queen Anne in character, is the 1899–1900 Calton-Martin House in Lattimore. The most distinctive feature of the house is its wraparound porch with glassed-in corner gazebos. Open gazebo-like elements were sometimes appended to Queen Anne porches; here the builder modified these elements for use as greenhouses. The enclosures have octagonal plans, concave roofs with wooden finial spikes, and beaded matchboard panels under and

Ventilation dormers similar to those on the Victor and Esther McBrayer House appear on other Cleveland County residences such as the C. J. and Sarah Hamrick House, Boiling Springs (BRE)

Glassed-in porch gazebo of the Calton-Martin House, Lattimore (JDP)

A Historical and Architectural Essay 25

over the multiple four-over-four windows. The concave roofline extends to the main house gables, which are sheathed with decorative wood shingles and have unusual oval vents (oval panes were popular in mail-order doors of the era). Also idiosyncratic are the ungainly drumlike porch supports, considerably heavier than the slender turned posts typical of the era. The original owner of the house, William T. Calton, operated a lumber yard; perhaps his residence served as a sort of "sample house" for his products, a strategy used by others in the trade.

Cleveland County houses from the late nineteenth century and the early twentieth were often built with an ingenious feature that occurs almost exclusively in Cleveland County: a small wing, typically about 5 or 6 feet square, that projects from the side of the kitchen and rises several feet above the kitchen roof. This wing contained the cookstove, and small windows or operable vents at the top served to draw heat away from the stove and kitchen. (A secondary benefit may have been the venting of smoke, as even stoves with stovepipes were sometimes prone to smoking.) Cleveland County's stove towers are known by several names, including kitchen flues, Dutch flues, Deutsch chimneys, German chimneys, heat standoffs, and setbacks. Secondary features include a brick or metal flue to vent the stove, a rope or lever to operate the vents at the top of the tower, and windows at stove level to provide light and additional ventilation. The best-preserved stove tower in the county belongs to the kitchen of the late 1890s John and Vertie Lattimore House near Polk-

Stove tower of the Newton House, Casar vicinity (BRE)

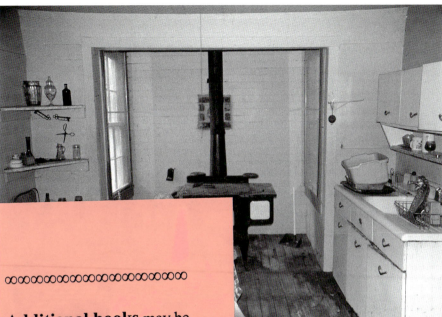

...kstove in place. The frame Osborne-... ...ve tower of brick as a fire-prevention... ...nces Forney House (now gone). Ar-... ...ple appear to have stopped building... ...he New Deal and World War II eras...

...'s kitchens in the nineteenth century... ...hough the excess heat produced was... ...Civil War inventors patented a host... ...on, and experts on home economics... ...book *All Around the House*, Eunice... ...o the Cleveland County stove tower:... ...part of the kitchen to prevent over-... ...gh for the cook-stove." Since excess... ...tionwide, the question remains why... ...ut apparently not elsewhere. Perhaps... ...helby was a factor. Benjamin Boyer... ...omas operated a foundry in Shelby... ...ddition to its mainstay, cotton mill... ...M. S. Worthington was associated... ...builder Michael Rudisill.[20]

...nsformation as profound as that ex-... ...th century large community ceme-...

A stove tower interior in the John and Vertie Lattimore House, Polkville vicinity (BRE)

Stove tower of the Osborne-Carpenter House, Lawndale vicinity (JDP)

∞∞∞∞∞∞∞∞∞∞∞∞∞∞∞∞∞

Additional books may be purchased at the following locations:
- First National Bank
  Shelby – main office
  Kings Mountain
  Boiling Springs
  Lawndale
- The Gallery
- Cleveland County Arts Center
- Kings Mountain Historical Museum
- Cleveland County Memorial Library
- Spangler Branch Library in Lawndale

Book Signing
Feb. 28 at Cleveland County Arts Center, 10 a.m. to 2 p.m. with Brian Eades & Dan Pezzoni

Pride in Preservation Tour
Watch for the next Tour in late Spring.

For more information, contact Cindi Cannon
Cleveland County Chamber
704-487-8521

A small family graveyard with professionally carved marble monuments: the Poston Cemetery, Polkville vicinity (BRE)

Mauney Mausoleum, Mountain Rest Cemetery, Kings Mountain (JDP)

teries were laid out adjacent to Shelby (Sunset Cemetery) and Kings Mountain (Mountain Rest Cemetery). Professionally surveyed, nondenominational, and fee-based, these cemeteries were a far cry from the family burial grounds of earlier generations. (A portion of Sunset Cemetery, earlier known as the Shelby City Cemetery, apparently dates to the antebellum period, but overall the cemetery is later in character.) Grave memorials changed too, from local stone and wood to imported marble in the second half of the nineteenth century and imported granite by the middle of the twentieth century. A marble works for the carving of marble monuments stood near the southwest corner of Warren and Lafayette streets in Shelby in 1885. At the turn of the twentieth century, D. J. Hamrick—first mayor of Boiling Springs, merchant, stonemason, and grandfather of writer W. J. Cash—carved tombstones at a shop near where the Boiling Springs Methodist Church now stands. Many Hamrick tombstones can be seen in the Boiling Springs Baptist Church Cemetery.[21]

County residents also experimented with other materials for gravemarkers. In the shared Methodist/Baptist cemetery in Double Shoals stand two small cast-iron gravemarkers with arched tops. One features the molded figure of a dove, the other a recumbent lamb. The blank midriffs of the markers would have received painted or adhered inscription panels, but those panels are now missing (or were never provided). The Double Shoals iron gravemarkers are similar to metal markers patented by several inventors in the 1880s and 1890s and used for the display of inscription panels or images.

In the early twentieth century, concrete came into vogue for building and highway construction, and its affordability made it an attractive gravemarker material for the county's poorer residents. Several concrete markers survive in the Eastside Cemetery on Lineberger Street in Shelby; those of Robert L. McCombs and Sam Froneberger mimic the form of the more costly stone monuments of the period, with rough textured sides that evoke quarry-faced stonework and smooth inscription panels. The latest phase in cemetery evolution began in the early 1950s with the creation of Cleveland Memorial Park, which featured an octagonal fountain pool and a Garden of Memories. The management assured lot purchasers that "every grave and lot will receive the same attention and care forever."[22]

Innovation also characterized county farms, and in the late nineteenth century a new set of specialized agricultural buildings was added to the traditional suite of corncribs, granaries, and stables. The new emphasis on cotton cultivation prompted the construction of cotton houses, described above. Mules were favored for cotton farm work, and the larger farmers built sizable mule barns to shelter their teams. Weatherboard claddings were typical for farm buildings, as they were for houses and other buildings, and farm building construction followed the same transition from mortise-and-tenon heavy frame construction to light, nailed frame construction during the late nineteenth century. At the same time, agricultural reformers began to promote new, more efficient, and more sanitary building forms. The best-known of these forms is the gambrel-roofed barn, a form that is well suited to material-conserving light frame construction and allows for hay storage without obstruction from structural members. One of the county's earliest surviving gambrel-roofed barns is the 1928 John McBrayer mule barn near Boiling Springs.

Cleveland County was an early center of the dairy industry in North Carolina. Two creamery businesses were established in the county in 1909, and in 1918 Coleman Blanton's Brushy Creek Dairy Farm began delivering milk in glass bottles. The greatest growth in dairying occurred between 1939 and 1951, when the number of dairy farms rose from 18 to 115. Local dairy historian Frank Spencer explains that many cotton farmers converted to dairy because of devastation by the boll weevil, which swept through the area in the late 1940s. Increased consumption of dairy products during World War II was also likely a factor. The Brushy Creek Dairy Farm is representative of the county's large dairy operations. Many buildings on the farm are constructed of concrete block: in the early twentieth century, health authorities promoted this

A cast-iron gravemarker in the Double Shoals Cemetery, Double Shoals (JDP)

Concrete gravemarker of Robert L. McCombs (d. 1919), Eastside Cemetery, Shelby (JDP)

Gambrel barn behind the George and Mary Jane Sperling House, Shelby vicinity. Photo by Sybil A. Bowers courtesy of the North Carolina Office of Archives and History.

novel material as a more hygienic alternative to wood. Silos for making ensilage (fermented feed) gradually appeared on county dairy farms; a locally early survival is the ca. 1940 brick silo on the Brackett Farm near Belwood. A few large operations, such as the Rufus and Kathleen Plonk Farm near Kings Mountain, which had a herd of 325 milk cows at its height, later added metal silos.[23]

Another lucrative agricultural specialization was poultry production. Urbanization spurred demand for poultry products, rail transportation and later trucking gave county farmers access to markets outside the area, and the county's large population of millworkers and their families provided a local market. One of the first large poultry operations was the Webber-Austell Farm near Earl. Bostick Austell purchased two chickenhouses in South Carolina and reerected them on his farm in the 1920s. About 1930 Austell added a concrete block egg-packing house, and by the late twentieth century the farm featured overhead pipes for mechanically supplying feed to the chickenhouses. Small, shed-roofed chickenhouses with banks of (usually) south-facing windows—a type championed by extension services and university agriculture departments—were built on many county farms beginning in the 1920s.[24]

Architectural diversification also occurred in the county's towns and vil-

Cleveland County dairy barn and chickenhouse interiors. Circa 1950 photos courtesy of the North Carolina Office of Archives and History.

lages. Early commercial buildings in the towns—gable-fronted and frame—were indistinguishable from their country kin. A rare first-generation survival is the diminutive rear wing of the Mauney House at 104 N. Battleground in Kings Mountain, built in the early 1870s as the store of William A. Mauney. The structure has been altered, yet it evokes the scale and raw simplicity of the county's incipient business districts. Wooden commercial buildings were susceptible to fire, especially in closely packed downtowns, and merchants eventually replaced their flammable starter buildings with larger, longer lasting, and more finely appointed brick commercial blocks. Because downtown space was at a premium, the new brick buildings often shared side party walls. Gable roofs were rejected in favor of rear-sloping shed roofs that channeled rainwater runoff to the back and, as an added benefit, made the street elevation taller and more imposing. Common features included stepped side parapets, side walls emblazoned (when exposed) with brightly painted advertising, and decorative front parapets, often with cornices, brackets, and crestings. As with the standard country store, the key element of the downtown commercial building was its glass storefront, often shaded by frame or canvas awnings that allowed merchandise to be displayed on the sidewalk.[25]

Gardner Drug Store interior, Shelby. 1900 photo by John C. McArthur courtesy of the Cleveland County Historical Museum.

A. V. Wray & 6 Sons Department Store in the 1940s. Photo courtesy of the Lloyd Hamrick Collection.

Shelby preserves the county's largest collection of late-nineteenth- and early-twentieth-century commercial buildings. Among the earliest survivals in Shelby's "Uptown"—as the commercial district has long been known—are two pre-1885 stores at 108 and 110 W. Marion and a run of one-story brick stores, numbers 119 through 125 N. Lafayette, constructed between 1870 and 1896. These latter buildings feature decorative brick parapets and window heads, and they formerly housed dry goods merchants, grocers, jewelers, and the like. After 1900 classical ornament was often added to upper levels of the facade, as in the 1910 Royster Building at 116 E. Warren and the 1911 facade of the Wray Building at 102 S. Lafayette. The Wray Building features windows of various forms accented with projecting brickwork and stone keystones, lintels, imposts, and sills. Beginning with the depression of the 1930s, in an attempt to boost flagging businesses with a more modern appearance, merchants added lustrous veneers of colored structural (or Carrara) glass to their storefronts. A striking example of the Moderne look is the former Loy's Mens Shop storefront at the east end of the Royster Building.[26]

The commercial life of the towns attracted multitudes of traveling salesmen, out-of-town businessmen, and others who needed short-term accommodations. The traffic supported the establishment of hotels during the mid- and late nineteenth century. One of the first was Shelby's 1840s Courtview Hotel, later known as the Commercial Hotel, which once overlooked the courthouse square from the corner of Marion and Lafayette Streets. The brick hotel—said to be Shelby's first brick building—featured a corbeled cornice, a

Uptown Shelby's East Warren Street with the Royster Building in the center, above; Loy's Mens Shop at the corner of the Royster Building, right. Both 1980s photos courtesy of the North Carolina Office of Archives and History.

34 Architectural Perspectives of Cleveland County

Courtview Hotel, Shelby. 1930s photo courtesy of Claude Hoke Thompson and the Cleveland County Historical Museum.

balcony with an ornamental iron railing, and nine-over-nine and twelve-over-twelve windows. A successor to the Courtview was the Central Hotel, which faced the southwest corner of the square. In the first decade of the twentieth century the three-story Central Hotel featured Classical Revival details such as pedimented window heads and quarry-faced stone storefronts on Lafayette Street with well-defined voussoirs in the arches over doors and windows. A one-story "sample rooms" building for the display of salesmen's samples stood behind the hotel proper. After a 1928 fire the Central Hotel was renamed the Hotel Charles and given a Mission-style makeover with ornamental iron balconies and a bracketed Spanish tile pent roof below a shaped parapet. Kings Mountain had its hotels too, including the frame Mountain View Hotel, which stood on the site of the 1948–49 Joy Theatre.[27]

Cleveland County developed as a resort destination in the late nineteenth century. Patterson Springs and Cleveland Springs welcomed visitors who came for health reasons or simply to relax and socialize. Springs-goers from the Carolinas and Georgia flocked to county watering holes to escape the heat and fever of the lowlands, and the celebrated Georgia poet Sidney Lanier is said to have imbibed the local lithia and sulfur waters. Beginning in the 1890s the water was piped to a spring pavilion on the courthouse square and sold for a penny a glass.[28]

William George Patterson developed the Epps springs as the Patterson Springs resort, where visitors had their pick of sulfur, iron, or freestone waters. A branch of the Atlanta & Charlotte division of the Richmond & Danville railroad reached the resort and its accompanying village in 1885. By the turn of the century a frame hotel with a fancy two-tier wraparound veranda had been erected. A more successful resort was Cleveland Springs, located east of Shelby. The first hotel there was built by Thomas Wilson in 1851 and burned in 1854. A second hotel, similar to the one in Patterson Springs, was built in 1866, and the grounds were developed with walkways, single and double-decker gazebos, and an open-sided bowling alley. A third hotel was erected in 1921 at about the same time Cleveland County was connected to the main New York–to–Jacksonville highway. The multistory brick hotel was designed

below: Patterson Springs Hotel, Patterson Springs. 1898 or 1899 photo courtesy of the Cleveland County Historical Museum.

opposite top: Cleveland Springs Hotel, Shelby vicinity. 1920s postcard courtesy of the Lawndale Historical Museum.

opposite bottom: Cleveland Springs spring gazebo with the hotel on the hill behind. 1920s photo courtesy of the Cleveland County Historical Museum.

CLEVELAND SPRINGS HOTEL, SHELBY, N. C.

Kings Mountain Military School, Kings Mountain. Late-nineteenth-century photo courtesy of Philip Baker and the Cleveland County Historical Museum.

by Charlotte architect Louis H. Asbury and boasted a monumental Doric portico and a full-length sitting porch. Scattered about the grounds were rustic log bridges and a spring pavilion of brick with a pergola roof. The third hotel burned in the late 1920s, and its columns stood as an evocative ruin until recent years.[29]

The hundred years from the Civil War to integration in the 1960s encompassed dramatic change in the county's educational architecture. In the nineteenth century education was largely the responsibility of the local community, and the "old field schools" of the era were often poorly constructed and equipped. Conditions began to improve toward the end of the century, when private academies were established in Shelby, Kings Mountain, and other smaller communities. The 1876 Kings Mountain Military School, also known as Captain Bell's Boys School, was of particular architectural interest. The two-story frame academy was distinguished by a castellated tower with dark vertical painted stripes—perhaps an attempt at evoking medieval half-timber construction—and toothy merlons around the top. Some private schools had a campuslike quality. The late 1880s Belwood Institute included a classroom building, boarding halls for boys and girls, a kitchen building, and a chapel. The Belwood schoolhouse was Queen Anne in style, with a complex hip-and-gable roof, a louvered octagonal cupola, and polychrome weatherboard and wood-shingle cladding. In Lawndale, the Piedmont School was established in 1896 and developed at its present site beginning in 1900. Students boarded at the Piedmont campus until the late 1920s.[30]

A statewide approach to public education existed as early as the 1830s, but it was not until the administration of "Educational Governor" Charles B.

38 Architectural Perspectives of Cleveland County

Belwood Institute, Belwood. Circa 1900 photo courtesy of Jack Hoyle.

Aycock in the first decade of the twentieth century that public schooling truly took root. Enabling legislation of the period required that county school boards erect schoolhouses from plans approved by the state Superintendent of Public Instruction. In 1903 Superintendent J. Y. Joyner issued an instructional pamphlet with school designs by the Raleigh architectural firm of Barrett & Thomson; an expanded edition was published in 1911. The 1908 Earl School was closely modeled on Barrett & Thomson Design No. 2, with an octagonal cupola and double front stoops that reflected the two-room plan within. Design No. 2 included coatrooms with lunch cupboards and a rolling partition that allowed the two classrooms to be combined into one for commencements and other functions. Schools such as Earl's were designed "in accordance with modern principles of ventilation, light and sanitation," according to Superintendent Joyner. The mostly one- to three-room frame schools of the era gave way to larger brick facilities during countywide consolidation in the 1920s and 1930s.[31]

above left: Earl's public school for white students. 1908 photo courtesy of the Cleveland County Historical Museum.

above right: Earl's public school for black students. Another early African American school was the Douglas Academy in the Lawndale vicinity, founded about 1900. In its last manifestation Douglas school became Central Cleveland Junior High School, which closed in 1983. The campus was sold to Lawndale First Baptist Church. Photo courtesy of the Cleveland County Historical Museum.

opposite top: Cleveland Elementary School on Hudson Street, once known as County Training School No. 2, has served Shelby's African American students since the original section was erected in the 1920s with assistance from the Rosenwald Fund (JDP)

opposite bottom: Polkville High School was representative of the consolidated schools of the 1920s until its recent demolition (BRE)

In Cleveland County as throughout the South, African American educational facilities lagged behind those of whites. To address this nationwide problem, southern black leader and educator Booker T. Washington teamed with Chicago philanthropist Julius Rosenwald to create the Rosenwald Fund. The fund offered matching grants to white-controlled school boards, and from the 1910s until the early 1930s it supported the construction of 5,357 schools and auxiliary buildings, approximately 800 of which were built in North Carolina. Twelve Rosenwald schools were erected in Cleveland County between about 1920 and 1930 according to standardized plans distributed by the fund, and one of them still stands. Many of the county's Rosenwald Schools were built by African American carpenter Haynes F. Jones.[32]

A notable exception to the trend from private to public schooling was the private Boiling Springs High School, founded with support from the Kings Mountain and Sandy Run Baptist Associations in 1905. The original high school, built in 1907–8 and known as the Huggins-Curtis Building, dwarfed all other school buildings in the county: this two-story brick edifice with a five-story bell tower contained forty-four dormitory rooms, multiple classrooms, a dining room, and a chapel. Local farmer John F. Moore appears to have been primarily responsible for the construction of this ambitious building. In 1928 the institution evolved into a junior college; later, in the 1940s, it gained firm footing as Gardner-Webb College (now University). The Huggins-Curtis Building incorporated details that were vaguely Colonial Revival in character, a style that would become dominant with the construction of Washburn Library in 1943 and the renovation of E. B. Hamrick Hall the same year. A late 1940s–1950s construction campaign added the O. Max Gardner Memorial

Huggins-Curtis Building, Gardner-Webb University, Boiling Springs. Circa 1910 photo courtesy of Lansford Jolley.

Student Union Building, which features the gable roofs and chimneys of a Georgian plantation house, and the John R. Dover Memorial Library, distinguished by an arcaded portico and an octagonal cupola with a belled roof. Recent university buildings in the Colonial Revival style include the 1993 Noel Hall, which contains the School of Divinity, and the 1996 Hollifield Carillon.[33]

High-profile projects such as the Gardner-Webb campus, as well as the many commercial buildings and large residences built during the era, provided work for a host of builders and architects, both local and from outside the area. By 1869 builder Mike Rudisill had established a planing mill in Shelby, and presumably many of the buildings built in Shelby during this period used materials from the Rudisill mill. The former Presbyterian Manse at 525 S. Washington in Shelby, built before 1883, is believed to have been Rudisill's work. Another builder of the era was Matthew Marcus Mauney (1844–1917) of the Polkville vicinity, who worked throughout the region and appears to have specialized in the construction of cotton mills. Mauney built Shelby Cotton Mills in 1899–1900 and is believed to have erected buildings for the Cleveland Cotton Mills at Lawndale. He also built dams, including a pegged timber-frame dam on Brushy Creek near his house, and constructed the steel bridge that spanned the Broad River on the road between Shelby and Boiling Springs (presumably assembled from components manufactured elsewhere).[34]

Until the 1930s, Cleveland County relied on outside architectural expertise. Many architects active in Shelby were based in the regional metropolis of Charlotte, including G. S. H. Appleget (noted above), Wheeler & Stern (First Baptist Church of Shelby, 1910–11), and W. G. Rogers (Masonic Temple Building, 1924). Charlotte architect J. M. McMichael completed a number of projects for Shelby physician Stephen S. Royster, including Royster's 1908–10 Classical Revival house at 413 S. Washington, the 1910 Royster Building at 116 E. Warren, and the 1920s Colonial Revival remodeling of the Andrews-Royster House at 417 S. Washington. McMichael also designed the Gothic-influenced Central United Methodist Church in 1924.[35]

The need for local architectural talent was filled in 1935 when Victor Winfred Breeze (1889–1961) opened an office in Shelby. Breeze had studied engineering at North Carolina State University and practiced architecture in Ashe-

Stephen S. Royster House, Shelby. Circa 1910 photo courtesy of the Cleveland County Historical Museum.

A Historical and Architectural Essay 43

Architect's rendering for the Shelby City Hall. Photo courtesy of Holland Hamrick & Patterson Architects.

Detail of the former Shelby Armory, built in 1941 with WPA funding (JDP)

ville in the 1920s. One of the more prominent works to emerge from his office is the 1939 Shelby City Hall at 300 S. Washington, a sophisticated Colonial Revival building with an open octagonal cupola, a scrolled pediment entry, and hyphen-connected side wings. The architect placed the building at an angle with respect to the corner of Graham and Washington Streets, thereby creating a small forecourt in emulation of the larger courthouse square a block away. Architect Fred Van Wageningen, who was educated at the Ecole des Beaux Arts in Paris, worked for Breeze and was involved in the design of the building.[36]

The Shelby City Hall was built with funding from the Works Progress Administration, a New Deal agency that assisted public works projects across the country, including many Cleveland County schools. Another WPA/Breeze collaboration is the 1937 former Shelby High School at 400 W. Marion, which features channeled piers in the Moderne style. This streamlined style, an early phase of the modernism that prevailed during the post–World War II era, was selected by Breeze for the 1939 Sterchis Store at 14 W. Marion and the 1939 Shelby Daily Star Building (now demolished) at 217 E. Warren. Domestic commissions of Breeze's include the 1937 Miller Apartments at 603 S. Washington and the 1938 remodeling of the LeGrand House at 614 S. Washington.

In 1954 V. F. Breeze formed the firm of Breeze, Holland & Riviere, which continues to the present day as Holland Hamrick & Patterson Architects.[37]

Like commercial and institutional building types, houses underwent considerable change during the first half of the twentieth century. The period was one of eclecticism in residential design, as the Victorian styles gave way to styles more closely associated with historical and exotic traditions. The related Classical Revival and Colonial Revival styles looked to classical and colonial American architecture for inspiration. The Tudor Revival style drew upon the traditional architecture of England, whereas the Mission style evoked the architecture of early California. The Craftsman style, popular for bungalows and Foursquare-form houses, prepared the ground for modern domestic architecture after World War II.

Rivaling in grandeur the Queen Anne houses of the late nineteenth century were the Classical Revival houses of the early twentieth. One of the best known is Webbley at 403 S. Washington in Shelby, a nineteenth-century house remodeled in the Classical Revival style in 1907 by attorney J. A. Anthony.

Webbley's front portico, left (JDP)

Webbley's study, above. Photo courtesy of the Gardner family.

Definitive of the style is Webbley's monumental front portico on fluted Ionic columns, flanked by more practical one-story sitting porches on Doric columns. Equally grand is the George Sperling House at 1219 Fallston Road in Shelby, built in 1927 by contractor Augustus Branton for agribusinessman George Sperling and his wife Mary Jane. The Sperling House portico, also supported on fluted Ionic columns, extends fully across the front of the house and has a center portion that bows out in a graceful curve. The Sperling House is constructed of yellow brick, as is another Classical Revival house of distinction, the 1923 J. G. Hord House at 100 S. Piedmont in Kings Mountain, which now serves as the Jacob S. Mauney Memorial Library. The Sperling and Hord houses share a secondary plan feature that is also typical of the style: symmetrically balanced side wings. These wings served a number of functions, as sitting porches (Hord house), porte cocheres (Sperling house), or glassed-in sunrooms (Hord and Sperling houses).[38]

Similar in many ways to the Classical Revival style was the Colonial Revival style, which shared an affinity for classical motifs and symmetrical compositions but was conceived as a revival of the architecture of the Colonial and Federal periods. The Colonial Revival proved more adaptable for smaller dwellings, which made it popular with home builders who wanted the dignity of the Classical Revival at an affordable price. This contributed to the style's longevity; many suburban Cleveland County houses built during the past half-century are Colonial Revival in inspiration. The sense of stability and propriety evoked by the Colonial and Classical revival styles also made them popular

Former Kings Mountain City Hall (demolished). Photo courtesy of the Cleveland County Historical Museum.

The front entries of two Tudor Revival houses: Shelby's Vauxhall on the left and Kings Mountain's Frank and Bonnie Summers House on the right (BRE)

for civic buildings. The Classical Revival was selected as the style for the 1907–8 Cleveland County Courthouse, and the Colonial Revival served for the 1930s city halls of both Shelby and Kings Mountain. The Colonial Revival style was employed for schools and churches, and it was also used for the 1927 Cleveland Country Club at 1360 E. Marion in Shelby.

The Tudor Revival and Mission styles were also popular during the early twentieth century. Tudor Revival details include false half-timbering, shallow Tudor arches, and quarrel-paned windows. The historically redolent style was popular with affluent home builders of the 1920s and 1930s. A prominent example is Vauxhall, built in the late 1920s for businessman John Lineberger and his wife Nannie at 1215 E. Marion in Shelby. The manorial brick residence features castellated wings, false half-timbering in gables and dormers, and windows and a front entry under Tudor arches. The style was also suited for more modest dwellings, as illustrated by the 1929 Lee House in Lattimore, a brick cottage with a characteristic steep gable roof and front chimney. Like the Colonial Revival, the Tudor Revival remains a popular suburban idiom.

A Historical and Architectural Essay 47

El Nido, Shelby. Photo courtesy of the North Carolina Office of Archives and History.

The Mission style evoked the Baroque-influenced architecture of colonial California's mission churches. The style appealed to Shelby artist Maude Sams Gibbs, a devotee of California's Spanish heritage. El Nido, built for Gibbs at 520 W. Warren in 1920–21, is regarded as one of the state's leading examples of Mission-style domestic architecture. The house features Spanish roof tiles (metal rather than ceramic), heavy eaves brackets, shaped parapets, and thick masonry pillars that support a front porch and a side porte cochere. Elaborately shaped parapets also distinguish the 1930s Maurice and Annie Weathers House at 1440 E. Marion in Shelby, which has Spanish roof tiles and round-arched porch openings.

The most popular style of the era in Cleveland County and elsewhere was the Craftsman style, which was perfected in California at the beginning of the twentieth century and soon spread with the assistance of pattern books, mail-order plans and house kits, and magazine promotions. The definitive Craftsman-style house type was the bungalow, a snug one-story or story-and-a-half dwelling suited for cost-conscious suburbanites. Typical bungalow features include spreading gable roofs that engage front porches, large shed or gable dormers to expand upstairs living space, and characteristic porch supports with squat wood posts on masonry pedestals. Craftsman bungalows sprouted like mushrooms in Shelby and Kings Mountain residential neighborhoods of the 1910s and 1920s, and they were popular among small farmers in rural areas. The Craftsman style was also used for another house type of the period, the Foursquare house, named for its four-room plan and identifiable by its cubic massing and typically hipped roof.

One of the largest concentrations of Craftsman bungalows and other eclectic houses is found in Belvedere Park, a residential neighborhood laid out to the east of downtown Shelby in 1921. Shelby businessman William Lineberger (d. 1936) retained Charlotte landscape architect Leigh Colyer to design the subdivision, which like the Eastside Manufacturing Company mill village was characterized by curvilinear streets, although Belvedere Park and the associated East Marion Street development catered to a more affluent population. Belvedere Park featured a main axial thoroughfare (Belvedere Avenue) with a tree-lined median, lots mostly wider than 100 feet, and a riding club and stables. Horses notwithstanding, Belvedere Park was an automobile suburb—the county's first—and it established Shelby's east side as the city's most desirable residential area.[39]

Forrest and Ruby Carpenter House chimney detail, Belwood vicinity (BRE)

At the same time that the new eclectic styles held sway in domestic construction, an interesting architectural subgenre developed in the Belwood area. Dr. Forrest Edwards owned a quarry north of Belwood known as Acre Rock, and he marketed his stone to churches and home builders. To construct his own residence, Edwards hired Albert Bleynat, a stonemason from the Waldensian community of Valdese in neighboring Burke County. The Waldenses were a Protestant sect from the Cottian Alps of northern Italy; in 1893 twenty-nine Waldenses immigrated to Burke County, bringing with them a vibrant stoneworking tradition. Albert Bleynat also executed the stonework for the 1941 remodeling of St. Peter's United Methodist Church, using stone Edwards donated from his quarry. The church's distinctive front facade, with corner towers on either side of a segmental-arched entry recess, is repeated in other stone churches of the area, such as the 1935 Clover Hill United Methodist Church. Perhaps Bleynat was involved in the design of both buildings. Later, a stonemason named Willie Carpenter used Acre Rock stone to build his own 1948–49 house and his brother Forrest Carpenter's 1950 house. The facades of both Belwood-area Carpenter houses feature arches.[40]

The mostly ahistorical Craftsman style foreshadowed, in Cleveland County and elsewhere, the modern styles that began to appear locally in the 1930s. Shelby's two 1930s movie houses, the 1936 and later Rogers Theatre at 213–221 E. Marion and the 1939 State Theatre at 318 S. Washington, were prominent examples of the Art Deco style. The Rogers, the better preserved of the two, features geometric, floral, and wave motifs and facade piers ornamented with narrow vertical strips of black Carrara glass, an effect that evokes more typical Art Deco fluting. The influence of the Art Deco style and the related Moderne style, discussed before, continued into the 1940s as seen in such buildings as the 1941 former Shelby Armory at 308 Gardner, a heavy rendition of the style typical of federally funded projects of the 1930s and 1940s.

The county's modern architecture grew more sophisticated after World War II. Inspiration came primarily from two competing schools of thought: the techno-minimalism of the International style and the more organic architecture of Frank Lloyd Wright and his disciples. The 1953 building of the Shelby Waterworks at 801 W. Grover, a design of the prolific Charlotte engineering and architectural firm of J. N. Pease, shows International style influence in its simple blocklike massing and its vertical and horizontal expanses of window. Even more representative of the style is the pristine marble and glass box originally occupied by the Cleveland Savings & Loan Association at 131 N. Lafayette, built in 1962 to a design by Shelby architects Holland & Riviere.[41]

Breeze, Holland & Riviere (as the firm was known until 1961) was equally versed in Frank Lloyd Wright's brand of modernism, as illustrated by the 1961 Kings Mountain Country Club. With its clean brickwork, angular porte cochere, and anchoring chimney, the building evokes Wright's Usonian house designs of the 1930s and later. Projects from all periods of Wright's develop-

Shelby Waterworks (JDP)

ment appear to have been mined for inspiration by the Raleigh firm of Ralph Johnson Associates in its 1965 design for the Shelby Building & Loan Building at 224 E. Warren (now Shelby Savings Bank). A Mayan-like fretwork frieze at the top of the octagonal-plan bank's four main elevations calls to mind Wright's textile-block experiments of the 1920s, and square perforations in the roof cantilevers cast rhomboids of light onto the stone corner elevations, an effect reminiscent of Wright's Marin County Courthouse, completed in 1963. Wright's influence continues in recent designs such as the 1996–97 Cleveland Eye Clinic at 1622 E. Marion in Shelby, designed by Tim Demmitt of Overcash-Demmitt Architects of Charlotte. In the design of the Cleveland Eye Clinic, Wright's Prairie style was evoked as an alternative to the sterile character associated with some modern health facilities.[42]

Modernism and the automobile transformed the county's domestic and commercial architecture. Virtually universal car ownership after World War II permitted developers to move far beyond the confines of the towns. The most popular site-built house form in postwar suburbia and in the countryside as well was the Ranch house or "Rambler": the low-slung Ranch form often incorporated an attached garage or carport and usually took full advantage of the large house lots of the new subdivisions. Architecturally sophisticated Ranch houses in Shelby include the 1959 Harold and Mary Lou Causby House at 900 W. Warren and the Robert Falls House at 1308 Wesson, built in 1960 to a design by local architect Fred M. Simmons. Also numerous toward the end of the twentieth century were manufactured homes, which now account for ap-

Robert Falls House, 1308 Wesson Road, Shelby. Early 1960s photo courtesy of the Cleveland County Historical Museum.

proximately 70 percent of new house starts. Some recent home builders have explored alternatives to standard house types. Bill and Thelma Ellis used a geodesic dome for their house, built on Mount Sinai Church Road near Earl in the early 1980s. The geodesic form, composed of triangular panels, was developed by technological visionary Buckminster Fuller in the 1950s.[43]

Modernism flourished on Cleveland County's emerging commercial strips, where sleek new service stations, roadside eateries, and shopping plazas sprouted in profusion. Service stations were built to standardized plans disseminated by the major gasoline retailers. Their white enameled metal skins, bathed in the glow of neon and fluorescent lights, projected an aura of efficiency and reliability. Restaurants like Bridges Barbecue Lodge, originally based in downtown Shelby, and assorted chain burger joints planted themselves on the highways and erected illuminated signs to catch the attention of motorists. Downtown merchants also pulled up stakes and headed for the suburban frontier. The

Bridges Barbecue Lodge sign, Highway 74, Shelby (BRE)

This Phillips 66 Station, which stood in downtown Shelby until its recent demolition, is representative of the expressive modernist buildings built along the county's commercial strips after World War II (BRE)

52 Architectural Perspectives of Cleveland County

Modern warehouses, Kings Mountain vicinity (JDP)

Upper Cleveland Office of First National Bank, 103 Piedmont Drive, Lawndale. Designed by Shelby architects Martin Boal Anthony & Johnson, this Postmodern branch bank is typical of the small scale commercial architecture built in the county at the turn of the millennium. (JDP)

construction of the Cleveland Mall at the east Highway 74 Business/Bypass intersection in the early 1980s created in essence a new town focus to vie with existing central business districts in Shelby and Kings Mountain. Regional highways and paved secondary roads were key to suburban development, as they were, increasingly, to the county's industrial development. The construction of Interstate 85 through the southeast corner of the county created opportunities for manufacturers and distributors, and by the turn of the millennium vast steel-frame assembly plants and warehouses had been erected, principally in the Kings Mountain and Grover areas near the interstate. Occasionally, as with the 1997–98 AGI plant on US 29 near Grover, these installations present

A Historical and Architectural Essay 53

architectural fronts to the public, whereas side and rear elevations are more utilitarian in character.⁴⁴

The shift of development to the suburbs during the second half of the twentieth century had a negative effect on established downtowns. In the early 1980s, as the Cleveland Mall neared completion, the City of Shelby took action to maintain the vitality of its central business district. Through the Shelby Economic Development Commission the city participated in the National Main Street Program, and Shelby was named one of the nation's first Main Street communities. Main Street participation led in turn to the creation of the Uptown Shelby Association (USA) and the Historic Shelby Foundation, both in 1982. The two organizations have a "hand-in-glove working relationship,"

Hamrick Family Reunion at the Irvin-Hamrick House, Boiling Springs vicinity. 1950s photo courtesy of the North Carolina Office of Archives and History.

according to present USA director Ted Alexander, and they have played a role in most Uptown Shelby revitalization projects from the 1980s on, including rehabilitations of the Masonic Temple Building, the Hotel Charles (First National Bank), and the Belk-Stevens Building. A recent and ongoing project of the USA and other groups is the rehabilitation of the Rogers Theatre, which has received planning funding from the National Trust for Historic Preservation. Shelby's revitalization initiatives were enhanced in 1983 by the listing of the Central Shelby Historic District in the National Register of Historic Places, a designation that qualifies property owners for participation in federal and state rehabilitation tax credit programs.[45]

The preservation ethos is shared by citizens throughout Cleveland County. Recent work in Kings Mountain includes the rehabilitation of the Joy Theatre as a performing arts center and the careful restoration of the Mauney House, one of the community's oldest residences. The Boiling Springs public high school continues to serve its community as office space for the town government and Gardner-Webb University. In Lawndale, preservation efforts have focused on rescuing the Piedmont School campus and its landmark Waters Library, and in Lattimore the Ambassador Baptist College has found new uses for a number of buildings that might otherwise have been neglected. The stewardship of rural historic properties has been the focus of individuals and families for many decades; witness the rehabilitation of the Irvin-Hamrick House by the Cameron Street Hamrick Memorial Association in the 1950s. Nevertheless, many challenges remain. The county's farms have suffered from the relentless expansion of suburbia. Cotton mills that were once the lifeblood of towns are today threatened by the decline of the region's textile industry, and some are being scavenged for materials. Losses will still occur, but hopefully more of Cleveland County's irreplaceable architectural heritage will be saved for the use and enjoyment of future generations.

NOTES

1. Eades, "History and Architecture of Cleveland County," 5.
2. Cross and Southern, "Irvin-Hamrick Log House"; Hutchison and Cross, "John Lattimore House."
3. Eades, "History and Architecture of Cleveland County"; Keller and Keller, "Central Shelby Historic District," 8.1–8.3; Patterson and Hambright, *Shelby and Cleveland County*, 7, 10.
4. Patterson and Hambright, *Shelby and Cleveland County*, 11; 1885 Sanborn map of Shelby.
5. Cross and Southern, "Joshua Beam House."

6. Tarpley, *A History of Faith*, 3, 93; Poston, *History of Zion Church*, 4; Robert Borders, personal communication; 1900 Sanborn map of Shelby.

7. Little, *Sticks and Stones*, 109, 126–39.

8. Eades, "History and Architecture of Cleveland County," 9, 30–32; Davis, *Southern Railway*, 26–29, 191; Smith, *Building a Railroad*, 19; Keller and Keller, "Central Shelby Historic District," 8.6; Lefler and Newsome, *North Carolina*, 488; Hilgard, *Report on Cotton Production*, Plate 12.

9. Eades, "History and Architecture of Cleveland County," 31; Bumgarner et al., *Lawndale Railway & Industrial Company.*

10. Eades, "History and Architecture of Cleveland County," 37; Powell, *North Carolina*, 417; and Hilgard, *Report on Cotton Production*, 591, Plate 13.

11. Copeland, *Cotton Manufacturing Industry*, 34; Webb, "Development of Industry," Appendix D; Lefler and Newsome, *North Carolina*, 548.

12. Eades, "History and Architecture of Cleveland County," 37; Bumgarner et al., *Lawndale Railway & Industrial Company; Our Heritage;* "Pictorial Review of Shelby and Cleveland County"; Perrin, "Kings Mountain Historic Inventory"; Land and Community Associates, "City of Shelby Architectural and Historic Inventory," 26–30; Patterson and Hambright, *Shelby and Cleveland County*, 70–71.

13. Hargrove and Hammond, "Dan River Basin Cultural Resources Study," 58.

14. Herring, *Welfare Work*, 15, 23; Rhyne, *Some Southern Cotton Mill Workers*, 21; Draper, "Village Plan for Eastside Mfg. Co."

15. Perrin, "Kings Mountain Historic Inventory."

16. Eades, "History and Architecture of Cleveland County"; Michael, "Rise of the Regional Architect in North Carolina," 113; Bumgarner et al., *Lawndale Railway & Industrial Company;* Patterson and Hambright, *Shelby and Cleveland County*, 86, 87, 91; Tommy Forney, personal communication.

17. Keller and Keller, "Central Shelby Historic District," 7.4; Survey and Planning Unit, "Banker's House"; *Shelby Aurora*, May 22, 1875; Kings Mountain Historical Society Collection; Eades and Eades, "Central School Historic District."

18. Southern, Sumner, and Best, "Dr. Victor McBrayer House."

19. Eades, "History and Architecture of Cleveland County"; Tommy Forney, Fred M. Simmons, and Lamar Wilson, personal communication.

20. Brewer, *From Fireplace to Cookstove*, 192; Keller and Keller, "Central Shelby Historic District," 8.5–8.6; *Heritage of Cleveland County*, 87; *Shelby Aurora*, May 22, 1875.

21. June Hadden Hobbs, personal communication; Clayton, *W. J. Cash*, 5, 19; Morrison, *W. J. Cash*, 17; Perrin, "Kings Mountain Historic Inventory," 25; 1885 Sanborn map of Shelby.

22. "Pictorial Review of Shelby and Cleveland County."

23. Eades, "History and Architecture of Cleveland County," 89; Spencer, "Cleveland County Dairy History."

24. Eades, "History and Architecture of Cleveland County," 89–90.

25. Mary Neisler, personal communication; Bridges, "Historic Treasures."

26. Patterson and Hambright, *Shelby and Cleveland County*, 48, 49; Land and Community Associates, "City of Shelby Architectural and Historic Inventory," 5, 6, 10, 21.

27. Cleveland County Historical Museum Collection; Patterson and Hambright, *Shelby and Cleveland County*, 27, 67; 1926 Sanborn map of Shelby.

28. Howe, "Folks Still Swear by Lithia Water"; "County's Mineral Springs Recall Colorful Era"; 1896 and 1900 Sanborn maps of Shelby.

29. Eades, "History and Architecture of Cleveland County"; Ebeltoft, "Shelby as Resort"; Cimino, "Area Got Its Start as a Resort Town"; Cleveland County Historical Museum Collection; Patterson and Hambright, *Shelby and Cleveland County,* 98–101; Rusty Patterson, personal communication.

30. Lefler and Newsome, *North Carolina,* 380–81; Hoyle, "Belwood School," 2–3; Cleveland County Historical Museum Collection.

31. Lefler and Newsome, *North Carolina,* 555–56; Joyner, *Plans for Public Schoolhouses,* 2, 12, 37–38.

32. Bridges and Jolley, "2002 Search in Cleveland County for the Works of Julius Rosenwald"; Hanchett, "Rosenwald Schools and Black Education in North Carolina," 387–88, 424, 431.

33. Lansford Jolley, personal communication; Jolley, *Dreaming, Daring, Doing,* 17–18, 57–59, 135, 140–41; "Pictorial Review of Shelby and Cleveland County"; Morrison, *Governor O. Max Gardner,* 207.

34. Keller and Keller, "Central Shelby Historic District," 8.5–8.6; Land and Community Associates, "City of Shelby Architectural and Historic Inventory," 34; Simmons, "Remembering Matthew Mauney"; *Heritage of Cleveland County,* 415–416; Fred M. Simmons and Tommy Forney, personal communication.

35. Keller and Keller, "Central Shelby Historic District," 7.9; Land and Community Associates, "City of Shelby Architectural and Historic Inventory," 30.

36. V. W. Breeze exhibit, Cleveland County Historical Museum Collection.

37. Ibid.; Land and Community Associates, "City of Shelby Architectural and Historic Inventory," 10, 12, 18, 21, 27, 35, 36.

38. Cross and Southern, "Webbley"; Bowers, "Sperling, George, House and Outbuildings."

39. Bowers, "East Marion–Belvedere Park Historic District."

40. Eades, "History and Architecture of Cleveland County"; Tarpley, *A History of Faith,* 76.

41. Roger Holland, personal communication.

42. Tim Demmitt, personal communication.

43. Bill McCarter and Robert Falls, personal communication; Eades, "History and Architecture of Cleveland County," 215–17.

44. Eades, "History and Architecture of Cleveland County," 210.

45. Ibid.; Ted Alexander, personal communication; Glisson, "Main Street," 71–72.

Joshua Beam House, Shelby vicinity. Circa 1930 photo by Floyd M. Willis courtesy of the Cleveland County Historical Museum.

FEATURED PROPERTIES

IRVIN-HAMRICK HOUSE

348 Beaver Dam Church Road (SR 1153)
Boiling Springs vicinity
Ca. 1794

Revolutionary War veteran James Irvin (1765–1845) was probably the builder of this half-dovetail log cabin. In 1794 Irvin purchased the 200-acre tract on which the house stands. Irvin married Rebecca Hardin of Lincoln County, and the couple raised ten children here. The property passed to James and Rebecca's children, who sold it to Cameron Street Hamrick in 1850. Hamrick (1822–1900) and his wife Elmira (1822–97) raised six sons here. Shortly before the Civil War the Hamricks began construction on a frame rear addition, but completion was postponed until after the war.

Years later a granddaughter of Cameron and Elmira recalled life in the house during the late nineteenth century:

> In the large front room of the house a log fire was always burning in the huge fireplace. Grandfather and grandmother sat on each side [and] she was busy making things with her hands. Tantalizing odors came from the kitchen. Aunt Frankie was mixing golden molasses and flour into gingerbread. It was rolled into great sheets and baked in large pans. Wonderful fruit pies were stacked one on top of the other.

The log section is a small, rectangular, gable-roofed dwelling on stone piers. Weatherboards survive on some elevations and may originally have covered the entire house. A crude fieldstone chimney rises on the west gable end. The windows have never been glazed; one is fitted with a batten shutter. The frame addition encloses a single room finished with flush vertical sheathing. Early on the interior of the log section had a hall-parlor plan with a vertical board partition; this partition has since been removed. The log walls are covered with wide vertical boards, and a simple mantel with flat pilasters frames the fireplace. An enclosed winder stair to the right of the fireplace rises to a garret. Cedars, hardwoods, and memorial oak trees shade the grounds.

Irvin-Hamrick House, left; interior, above. Both 1980 photos by Michael T. Southern courtesy of the North Carolina Office of Archives and History.

JOHN WELLS HOUSE

160 Stewart Road (SR 2286)
Kings Mountain vicinity
Late 18th or early 19th century

According to tradition, this log cabin may be the oldest surviving structure in Cleveland County. Some believe the cabin was used as a hospital for wounded soldiers following the Battle of Kings Mountain. The one-room log portion of the dwelling measures about 16 by 19 feet and is attached to a larger frame addition. The front and side doors are sheltered by a wraparound porch. A red-painted stone chimney rises on the east elevation. The house is associated with John Wells (ca. 1740–1819), who according to family tradition built it in 1780 after settling in the area around 1770. Later family members included John's son Isaac Wells (1782–1857), a blacksmith, hatter, and horse blanket maker; Isaac's wife, Ann Gladden Wells (1785–1857); and Isaac and Ann's son Robert H. Wells (1810–79) and daughter-in-law Lucinda Gladden Wells.

John Wells House (BRE)

RAMSEUR-SARRATT HOUSE

Brickhouse Road (SR 1137)
Earl vicinity
Ca. 1800

The Ramseur family is credited with the construction of this transitional Georgian-Federal-style dwelling, but whether it was built by David Ramseur (b. 1733) or his son Philip Ramseur (1784–1842) is uncertain. According to Ramseur descendants, the house was built in 1799; if so, it seems likely that someone other than the fifteen-year-old Philip was the builder. Philip Ramseur was a planter, tanner, brick mason, carpenter, and prominent Baptist preacher. His tannery was situated across the road from the house, and he is said to have used one of the downstairs rooms for preaching. Ramseur is said to have fired the brick for the house on the property and to have performed the carpentry and masonry work. Following Philip Ramseur's death, the property passed to his son Frederick Ramseur (1811–90) and then to his daughter Leonora Ramseur (1842–1920) and her husband Obadiah Sarratt (1840–1932). Their son Wellington Sarratt

Interior (BRE)

(1871–1949) operated a cotton gin and sawmill here. By 1910 Wellington lived in Earl and the house became the main residence for a large tenant farm. Sarratt's daughter Lucille Sarratt Haas, interviewed in 1984, recalled that the second floor was used as a play area when she was a child, and the yard was planted with boxwoods, roses, and crape myrtles.

The two-story three-bay dwelling is constructed of Flemish-bond brick with jack arches over the doors and windows. The house stands on a stone foundation with iron-barred cellar windows. The second-story windows once had nine-over-six sash; surviving window sash are two-over-two. The small gable windows once contained stained glass. The estimated date of the first rear kitchen is ca. 1832; the present kitchen with its metal sheathing dates to about 1940. The plastered interiors have chair rails and angled fireplaces with Georgian architrave mantels. The roof slates were reused from the 1845 Cleveland County Courthouse, which was demolished in 1907.

Ramseur-Sarratt House (BRE)

LATTIMORE HOUSE

Five Points Road (SR 1373)
Polkville vicinity
Early 19th century

The original log section of this unaltered nineteenth-century house appears to have been built for Daniel Lattimore (1775–1833), although he did not reside in it himself. The one-room half-dovetail log dwelling was apparently standing when Daniel sold 210 acres to his son "Big John" Lattimore (1801–77). John married Isabella Carson (d. 1875) in 1830, and the couple extended the house on its gable end and added rear shed rooms and a front porch bracketed by porch rooms, all frame. Since roughly half of John and Isabella's eleven known children were born during the 1830s, it is likely the additions were made then. By 1860 Lattimore had enlarged his holdings to nearly 1,000 acres. He employed the able-bodied among his twelve slaves in the production of grains, cotton, and tobacco, the last an unusual crop for the area. A son, Confederate veteran John L. Lattimore (1836–1905), acquired the home tract in 1870, and the house remains in the family although it was vacated in the late twentieth century.

The plain exterior is characterized by weatherboard siding, metal-sheathed gable and shed roofs, and brick gable-end chimneys. The front porch stands on chamfered posts with simple hand and foot rails, and the house wall under the porch has a horizontal flush board sheathing. Crude fieldstone foundation piers, six-panel doors on strap hinges, and remnants of wood-shingle roofing are other exterior features. The spartan interior has flush board walls and ceilings, beaded ceiling joists, and a Federal mantel with a two-panel frieze. Beaded weatherboards survive on the formerly exterior gable end of the log dwelling now covered by the frame addition. The Lattimore family cemetery lies nearby.

Lattimore House rear elevation. 1977 photo by Greer Suttlemyre courtesy of the North Carolina Office of Archives and History.

ELLIS FERRY HOUSE (GRAMBLING HOUSE)

150 Old Ferry Road (SR 1214)
Boiling Springs vicinity
Ca. 1814

Tryon County records reveal that in 1773 James Ellis purchased from Edward Dickson 230 acres on the south side of the Broad River near the South Carolina line. By 1800 Ellis had established a ferry at the location, and that year the community of Burrtown (later Irvinsville) was laid off just to the east of the ferry. In 1814 Ellis sold the ferry enterprise and 40 acres, including a landing, to his son Benjamin Ellis. The two-story heavy timber frame Ellis Ferry House was built about this time. Additional improvements were made to the complex as the nineteenth century progressed. A general store was located across the old post road that ran in front of the house. Prior to the Civil War, Benjamin's son Willis operated a doggery (tavern) here. Recognizing the ferry's importance to the local economy, in 1852 county officials required Benjamin to post bond to keep the ferry in good condition. In 1860 Benjamin Ellis sold the ferry, the house, and 300 acres to his son Rick Ellis. Prior to this time, Benjamin added to the rear of the house using locally fired brick. Several outbuildings appear to have been built about the same time.

The Ellis Ferry House stands on a brick foundation and has a gable roof. A one-story front porch shelters the three-bay facade. The front entry has a four-light transom, and there were nine-over-six windows on the first story and six-over-six windows on the second story. Double-shouldered stepped brick chimneys rise on the gable ends. The Flemish-bond south chimney has an unusual glazed header design that replicates the shoulder outline. A one-story kitchen ell extends to the rear.

The first floor has a three-room plan with a main hall on the north side and two smaller rooms on the south side separated by a partition. The main hall features a transitional Georgian-Federal mantel adorned with fluted pilasters resting on square blocks and capped with rectangular elements with rounded motifs. Projecting trapezoidal capitals top the pilasters, and a large capital rests on a center plate. A band of plain and reeded triangular carvings forms the border of the mantel. The second floor has been altered from the original three-room plan and now has an irregular four-room layout.

Ellis Ferry House (Grambling House) (TJF)

HAMILTON-MCBRAYER FARM

4315 West Dixon Boulevard (US 74)
Mooresboro
Early 19th century, ca. 1885

The origins of this property can be traced to 1807, when Dr. Joseph Hamilton purchased the 372-acre tract from John Moore, who had been granted the property in 1798. Hamilton built the original part of the house about 1823 and practiced medicine here until his death in 1831, whereupon his widow and daughter moved to England and the property was sold to Robert McBrayer. The McBrayers specialized in horse and mule trading, purchasing the animals in Tennessee and driving them over the mountains to their farm. About 1885 John E. McBrayer made Victorian additions to the house, more than doubling its size. The property remains in the McBrayer family, who lease it for the production of cattle, soybeans, cotton, and wheat.

The two-story frame house has a full-length two-tier Victorian porch, a large addition on the east side, and an enclosed back porch. Inside there is evidence for a former center-passage plan with a staircase in the passage. Flush board walls in the upstairs indicate early-nineteenth-century construction, and diagonal beaded matchboard sheathing and a carved Victorian mantel in one second-floor bedroom date to the ca. 1885 enlargement. One feature of note is an ice room located in the hallway between the kitchen and the dining room. The room has a thick wooden door that helps keep its interior temperatures low.

The oldest outbuilding on the farm is probably the half-dovetail log structure that served as a store and as Dr. Hamilton's doctor's office. It may have been built as early as the late 1810s. A frame smokehouse stands conveniently near the kitchen. There are a saddle-notched log stock barn and a ca. 1885 barn of frame construction with diamond-shaped cutouts in the siding for ventilation. Other outbuildings include a well-house with a roof extension over the well, a frame garage, and the grave of Joseph Hamilton.

top to bottom: Hamilton-McBrayer House; mantel; Dr. Hamilton's Office (all BRE)

TWIN CHIMNEYS (SMITH-SUTTLE HOUSE)

2160 Twin Chimneys Road (SR 1126)
Shelby vicinity
Early 19th century

According to tradition, English immigrant Minor W. Smith (1784–1847) and his wife Jane Berry Smith (d. 1852) had this evolved two-story house or a section of it built about 1817, the year their daughter Caroline Jane Smith is said to have been born here. There is also a tradition that the lumber and windows for the house were hauled to the site from Charleston, South Carolina. Greek and Gothic revival details suggest a later date, perhaps in the 1830s or 1840s, although it is possible that the rear kitchen represents the original dwelling.

Joseph Suttle (1827–61) acquired the property in 1854. Ordained a Baptist minister in 1849, Suttle pastored Double Springs Baptist Church and later New Bethel Baptist Church, and with Thomas Dixon Sr. and others he founded the Kings Mountain Baptist Association in 1851. Suttle married Elvira Blanton, daughter of Cleveland County's first sheriff, Charles Blanton, in 1846. According to the 1860 census, Suttle owned five slaves and 540 acres (100 improved) on which he grew corn, sweet potatoes, wheat, and oats. After her husband's death Elvira moved into Shelby, and in the late nineteenth and early twentieth centuries the house had a succession of owners. In 1943 the family reacquired ownership when Joseph Linton Suttle Jr., a great-grandson of Joseph Suttle and

Twin Chimneys (JDP)

Gable window; outbuildings (JDP)

president of the Cleveland Savings & Loan Association, bought the property with a partner. J. L. Suttle Jr. and his wife Sara McFarland Suttle restored the house in 1952 and gave it its present name, Twin Chimneys. The property is now owned by a great-great-granddaughter of Joseph Suttle, Carole Suttle Arey, and her husband William Jackson Arey.

The two-story frame house blends Federal and Greek Revival characteristics with later Victorian influence. The three-bay facade features nine-over-six windows and a Greek Revival entry surround with fluted pilasters, molded capitals, sidelights, and a transom. The house wall under the porch has original flush sheathing, and the porch itself has late-nineteenth-century turned posts and sawn brackets and balustrade.

Two stuccoed brick chimneys rise on the north gable end, and a single Flemish-bond brick chimney rises on the south gable end. In each gable are lancet-arched windows, a locally rare Gothic Revival influence. A story-and-a-half frame kitchen with a double-shouldered fieldstone chimney is attached to the rear by a screened breezeway. Originally the kitchen may have been detached; it now connects to the main house by a partially enclosed breezeway. The interior has a modified hall-parlor plan, two rooms in depth. Walls are sheathed with vertical or horizontal boards, and the six-panel doors are set in molded and mitered surrounds. The front hall has paneled wainscoting and a stair with curvilinear tread brackets. The stair's molded handrail, supported by square-section balusters, terminates in a square-section newel with a simple molded cap. The Federal-influenced mantels are composed of pairs of horizontal panels above a mitered frame and are flanked by narrow pilasters supporting a deeply molded shelf. Near the house are a frame smokehouse, possibly as old as the house, and a family cemetery, surrounded by a wrought-iron fence, that contains the graves of Minor Smith, Joseph Suttle, and others.

DANIEL RUPPE HOUSE

1602 Lackey Street
Shelby
Ca. 1830

The Ruppe family settled in the southwest corner of the county around 1830, and Daniel Ruppe (1805–1900) built this log dwelling about the same time. In 1992, after sitting vacant for several decades, the house was purchased by Hal Bryant, an art instructor at Cleveland Community College, who moved it beside his home in Shelby. In the course of rehabilitation the original rear kitchen was determined to be beyond repair and was removed. Bryant used old wood salvaged from deteriorated outbuildings and houses to construct a small frame kitchen addition, and he furnished the house with period pieces. This well-preserved cabin provides a glimpse of early-nineteenth-century life in Cleveland County.

The 18-by-25 foot dwelling has half-dovetail corner notching and stands on stone piers. The modern front porch has a shed roof. The back door is flanked by small windows with iron-hinged shutters, and other windows are typically small. A replica stone and brick chimney with stepped shoulders rises on the west elevation, and a more slender chimney rises to the rear. The interior consists of a single large room with beaded ceiling joists and stairs leading to the loft in the west corner. Pegged roof construction is evident in the loft.

Daniel Ruppe House, left; loft, above (BRE)

PHIFER HOUSE

Broad River Greenway
Boiling Springs vicinity
Mid-19th century

Either Martin Phifer (1794–1854) or John Phifer (1827–1901) is thought to have built this one-story log dwelling. Around 1880 a member of the Phifer family made a frame addition on the south elevation, and about 1900 an ell was added to the rear east elevation. For several generations the Phifers raised cotton and livestock at the original location of the house in the Bethlehem vicinity. By 1970 the house had been abandoned, as had an accompanying smokehouse, barn, and spring.

The Phifer House measures approximately 20 by 24 feet, and the logs are V-notched, a rare form of corner notching in the region. In the late 1990s the house was moved from its original location and reerected at the Broad River Greenway. This painstaking process entailed numbering the logs, dismantling them, and reassembling them utilizing historic construction techniques. Today the cabin is used to interpret farm life in mid-nineteenth-century western North Carolina.

Phifer House (BRE)

JOSHUA BEAM HOUSE

1920 New Prospect Church Road (SR 1908)
Shelby vicinity
1840s

Joshua Beam, son of John Teeter Beam, was born in 1800 in his father's home near Buffalo Creek. Teeter Beam died when Joshua was young, leaving a widow, Joshua, and his younger brother, Aaron. The two sons were the youngest of Teeter Beam's fifteen children. Teeter's widow, Elizabeth Beam, was granted dower rights to 366 acres on both sides of Buffalo Creek, including the homeplace. In 1833 she began releasing her rights to Teeter Beam's heirs, and Joshua acquired a corn mill and sawmill that had belonged to his father.

Joshua Beam married Matilda Mauney (1812–45) in 1830, and four children were born to this union. In the late 1830s Beam formed a merchant trade partnership with Jacob Anthony that operated as Joshua Beam & Company. Business was conducted through the port of Charleston, South Carolina, and Beam began purchasing land there and in Alabama. Beam played a significant role in the drive to create Cleveland County and in 1846–47 served as the county's representative to the state legislature. Beam's second wife was Susan Heavner (d. 1902).

Though he owned a large estate and eighteen slaves, Beam did not depend entirely on cash crop agriculture for his livelihood. From milling he branched into manufacturing, mining—he owned two gold mines—and the iron trade. In the early 1840s Beam erected an iron manufacturing facility near the old home site on Buffalo Creek. In 1850, according to the federal census of that year, the ten workers at this factory were producing 60,000 pounds of hammered iron valued at $2,400. The local iron industry declined during the third quarter of the nineteenth century, and Beam turned his attention to tobacco production, a pursuit he was heavily engaged in at the time of his death in 1869.

Interior. 1980 photo courtesy of the North Carolina Office of Archives and History.

Joshua Beam House. 1980 photo courtesy of the North Carolina Office of Archives and History.

Beam's two-story house is predominantly Greek Revival in style. According to one account it may have been built about 1841. The house has a full fieldstone cellar and a pedimented two-tier portico with an arched opening in the tympanum (the portico was remodeled in the late twentieth century). The present asbestos shingle siding covers weatherboards. The first story of the facade consists of four nine-over-nine sash windows and a central entrance with sidelights and a fifteen-light transom. On the gable ends rise stepped-shoulder brick chimneys laid in common bond. In the pedimented gables, the porch gable, and the house eaves are tightly spaced modillion blocks. Eight-light attic windows flank the chimneys in the gables. A one-story gabled kitchen ell extends off the corner of the house. This kitchen is sheathed with flush boards and features a large fireplace opening in the southeast wall.

The interior has a center-passage plan and transitional Federal/Greek Revival detail. Simple molded baseboards and accompanying chair rails adorn the rooms. Six-panel doors are set in molded Greek Revival surrounds with turned corner blocks. The elaboration of the mantels varies, but common to each are such Greek Revival details as symmetrically molded pilasters and turned corner blocks. The center-passage stair features an open string adorned with curvilinear tread brackets.

ABEL AND MARY EARL HOUSE

2705 Blacksburg Road (NC 198)
Earl
1853

This one-story frame dwelling is probably one of the oldest houses to survive in the Earl vicinity. Abel (1817–89) and Mary (Polly) Sepaugh Earl (d. 1909) had the house built in 1853, as indicated by a bill of materials dated that year. The house has a four-bay facade, a full-facade front porch, interior and exterior end chimneys, and an assortment of double-hung sash and casement windows. Two ells, linked by an enclosed porch, extend to the rear. Near the house stand a well shelter, which has a pyramidal roof on square-section supports, and a garage and shed of frame construction. Abel Earl operated a distillery—presumably on this property—during the Civil War.

Abel and Mary Earl House (BRE)

JOHN M. ROBERTS HOUSE

2205 South Post Road (NC 180)
Patterson Springs
Ca. 1855

John Miller Roberts built this one-story log dwelling about 1855. Roberts grew cotton and served the community of Patterson Springs as a magistrate and merchant. His son Vernon Roberts (1884–1960) was also a merchant and lived here until his death. Currently covered with weatherboard, the house has two exterior end chimneys, a front porch, a small rear ell (probably a kitchen) with its own chimney, and four-over-four and one-over-one windows. Near the house are a well (dug in 1903), a one-car garage, an egg house, and a chickenhouse.

John M. Roberts House (BRE)

THOMAS AND SARAH OATES HOUSE

960 Mary's Grove Church Road (SR 2012)
Kings Mountain vicinity
1856

Thomas Milton Addison Oates (1827–1913) built this house for himself and his wife, Sarah Ann Kiser Oates, whom he married in 1856. Before the Civil War they farmed their property with the help of two or three slaves. During the war, Thomas made gunpowder for the Confederate Army at Fayetteville, and after the war he ran a general store adjacent to his house and a water-powered cotton gin. Oates also served as postmaster for the Fancy Post Office; for a time a post office was run from the house. The Oates property was deeded to Phate and Josephine Lackey in 1912 with the understanding that the younger couple would care for the elderly Thomas Oates.

Originally the Oates House was much smaller, but two bedrooms were added to the west side of the house in the 1880s. The front has two prominent wings; the rear has enclosed and screened porches and two ells. The Oates General Store stands next to the house, and nearby are historic outbuildings, including a garage, a shed, a smokehouse, and a chickenhouse.

Thomas and Sarah Oates House (BRE)

WILLIAM A. MARTIN FARM

3525 Campfield Church Road (SR 1328)
Mooresboro vicinity
Mid-19th century

The land on which this two-story frame house is built has belonged to the Martin family since the colonial period. William A. Martin (1849–1927) was an early owner of the house, a portion of which may have been built as early as the 1840s. Later family members associated with the farm are William's son Byron Martin (1882–1922) and Byron's son John Thomas Martin. The house's restrained Victorian detail includes decorative window lintels, cornice returns, and sawnwork in the gables. A double-leaf front entry, six-over-six windows, and a center chimney are other features. A gabled front wing and a rear kitchen ell and stove tower were probably added about 1900.

Near the house is an extensive complex of domestic and farm outbuildings. Directly behind the kitchen ell is a stone and concrete foundation that once supported a carbide house, the original source of lighting for the house. A stone one-car garage stands beside the house, and a smokehouse and shed are nearby. The washhouse has two cast-iron kettles suspended above a fire pit. Farm buildings include a corncrib, a chickenhouse, a tool shed, a barn, and a tractor shed. Across a farm lane stands a large transverse mule barn.

William A. Martin House, top; rear elevation with stove tower, bottom; washhouse interior, left (BRE)

Featured Properties 75

OLIVER AND ROSANNAH HOLLAND HOUSE (MIRACLE FARM)

2410 College Farm Road (SR 1195)
Boiling Springs vicinity
1850s and later

Oliver Holland built the first story of this house in the 1850s. Holland enlisted in the Confederate Army in 1861 and quickly rose to the rank of captain. After the war Holland returned to his house and added a second story. Holland farmed for a living but was also a magistrate with a reputation as a fair and honest arbitrator in legal matters. Area residents came to his house to get married or settle legal disputes; business was conducted on the front porch. Holland's house has a center-passage plan, two interior chimneys, and a rear kitchen. At least one mantel has a late-nineteenth-century form: pilasters with bulbous caps and a frieze board with a curvilinear lower edge.

Following Holland's death in 1912, the farm passed through a number of owners, and its physical condition declined. Eventually Gardner-Webb University purchased the property with the intention of setting up a self-sufficient farm to be managed and maintained by the students and faculty. All proceeds, monetary and agricultural, were to be channeled back to the university, and the operation of the farm would teach students about crop cultivation, livestock management, and outbuilding construction. The farm would also provide students with opportunities for employment and thereby assist them in paying educational expenses. The work of transforming 182 acres of neglected land into a prosperous modern farm was to be compressed into a single twenty-four-hour period—Miracle Farm Day.

On the appointed day, August 31, 1950, hundreds of volunteers converged on the farm to clear land, plant trees, and construct cinder block poultry houses and barns. Through the efforts of the Shelby Lions Club, a major backer of the campaign, companies from the Carolinas and Tennessee contributed equipment. Three hundred fifty volunteers from the Blacksburg (South Carolina) Veterans Class alone pitched in to help. Equally impressive were the crowds of an estimated ten to fifteen thousand onlookers and a political contingent including Governor Kerr Scott and assorted senators and congressmen. In later years, as Gardner-Webb shifted more to a liberal arts focus, the importance of the College Farm (as it was known) dwindled, and parcels were sold off to timber companies and others. Today only the privately owned Holland House and 3 acres of pasture remain of Miracle Farm, but the excitement of August 1950 is remembered by many older residents.

Oliver and Rosannah Holland House (TJF)

Miracle Farm Day, August 31, 1950, with the Holland House in the distance and a poultry house under construction. Courtesy of the Cleveland County Historical Museum.

Oliver Holland House in a circa 1900 photograph with Oliver Holland seated on the left and Rosannah Holland seated beside him. Courtesy of Gardner-Webb University Archives.

Featured Properties 77

ZION SCHOOL

721 West Zion Church Road (SR 1850)
Metcalfe vicinity
Ca. 1860, 1906

Zion School is one of the oldest surviving schoolhouses in Cleveland County. The simple gabled frame building was enlarged in 1906 by the addition of a hip-roofed section. An interior chimney, porches, and six-over-six windows are other features. Classes began at Zion School shortly before the Civil War but were suspended until after the cessation of hostilities. The school resumed operation in 1872 and remained open until the 1940s. The first through seventh grades were taught here, often by a single teacher. Among the instructors were Jim Elliott (taught in 1898), Nora Elliott (1913), Beulah Falls Harrill (mid-1930s), and Jewel Blanton (1940s). In the 1930s pupils were taught only through the fifth grade and the older students went to Lattimore School. After use as a farmhouse in the latter twentieth century, the school has recently undergone limited rehabilitation by Ronny and Pam Ivester.

Zion School (BRE)

WEARE-GAMBLE HOUSE

315 Stony Point Road (SR 1001)
Kings Mountain vicinity
1868

According to tradition, this one-story frame dwelling contained the White Plains Post Office from about 1868 to about 1893. Boyce Weare probably built the Greek Revival house shortly after the Civil War; the date 1868 etched on the chimney probably represents the date of construction. Weare lost the property as a result of a judgment lien, and in 1892 it was purchased by W. A. Mauney. Mauney lived here ten years before selling the property to Andrew J. Gamble. The Gambles grew cotton which they transported by wagon to Champion's Gin in nearby Oak Grove. The property passed to Andrew Gamble's son Joseph Franklin Gamble and his wife Laura Jane Watterson Gamble. Joseph, in turn, willed the farm to his son Leonard, who lived here with his wife Ruth. Today, Barbara Gamble Hawkins, Andrew Gamble's great granddaughter, lives here with her husband.

The house features a wraparound porch with square posts that shelters an entry with a transom and sidelights. Other features include six-over-six windows, interior and exterior chimneys, and an original ell. A three-sided bay, a carport, and a kitchen were added during a 1992 remodeling. The interior contains original Greek Revival post-and-lintel mantels. Nearby are a ca. 1920 frame tractor shed with accompanying gas pump, a ca. 1925 frame cotton house, a ca. 1950 metal-sided stock barn, and a frame smokehouse, tractor shed, and garage all dating to about 1925.

Weare-Gamble House, bottom; mantel, top (BRE)

ELLIOTT CHAPEL

3001 West Stagecoach Trail (SR 1361)
Polkville vicinity
1871

Elliott Chapel traces its roots to a Methodist camp meeting held here in the early nineteenth century. John Crenshaw Elliott (1787–1827) soon built a log meeting house on the site. In 1854, Elliott's widow, Mary Donoho Elliott, sold a small parcel to the trustees of the Methodist Episcopal Church South, and in 1871 the present church was erected. Although the chapel was officially Methodist, Baptist services were held on alternating Sundays. A ca. 1860 one-room school used to face the chapel but was moved to another location after the opening of Fairview School in 1922. Elliott Chapel remained in regular use until 1926, when a new Methodist church was constructed in Polkville. Subsequently the ownership of the chapel reverted to the Elliott Chapel trustees.

The one-story frame chapel sits on stone piers and has white-painted weatherboard siding, a shingle-pattern pressed metal roof, and cornice returns. On the front is a pair of double-leaf panel doors, and the other elevations have nine-over-nine windows with reproduction louvered shutters crafted by Robert L. Stockton in the 1890s. The interior has a vaulted ceiling with exposed rafters.

Elliott Chapel, left; interior, above (BRE)

BROAD RIVER ACADEMY

Mount Sinai Church Road (SR 1140)
Earl vicinity
1870s

Built in the 1870s on a tract donated by Elias Randall, the Broad River Academy served hundreds of children in the area until the beginning of public school consolidation about 1900. Students who attended Broad River Academy ranged in age from seven to twenty-one. According to an article in the February 5, 1962 issue of the *Shelby Star*, "pupils were divided by grades within the confines of the big room. They sat on slab benches and four desks for writing stood in the front of the room." Some of the educators who taught at the school included C. F. Hopper (taught in 1888); V. G. Rollins (1899–90); Robert Howell (1891–93); and R. J. Balfour (1891–93). Balfour was the school's most prominent educator, having received his teaching certificate from Harvard University. Teacher salary ranged from $30 per month in 1889 to $37.50 per month in 1896.

Measuring approximately 40 by 24 feet, the one-room school has two end chimneys—one in deteriorated condition, one of fieldstone and brick—and two entries. The interior walls are plaster, and the original ceiling is still in place. There are four six-over-six windows: two flanking the fireplaces and two along the rear wall. The historic pressed metal roof has slightly overhanging eaves, and the frame structure rests on fieldstone piers.

Broad River Academy (BRE)

Featured Properties 81

MAUNEY HOUSE

104 North Battleground Avenue
Kings Mountain
1870s

This simple weatherboarded frame building has the double distinction of being Kings Mountain's least-altered early dwelling and one of the county's oldest surviving commercial buildings. The rear ell is the one-story store of William Andrew Mauney, the town's first mayor and an industrialist, and his brother. The store was probably erected about 1872, when the Atlanta & Charlotte Air Line reached town. In 1874 Mauney Brothers moved to another site, and soon thereafter, a story-with-garret structure was built onto the front of the store and the whole made into a dwelling. The house was acquired by Kings Mountain Historic Home Preservation Inc. in 1998 and restored to its original character by preservationist Mary Neisler.

The house has a gable roof sheathed with wood shingles, the original roofing material, and rests on stone foundation piers. A front porch stands on rectangular-section posts cut in profile to resemble tapered columns. The front entry opens into a small triangular-plan vestibule that abuts the rebuilt center brick chimney. Walls and ceilings are sheathed by various materials, including flush boards, board-and-batten, and beaded matchboard. An enclosed stair in the ell rises to the unfinished garret where the dwelling's pegged mortise-and-tenon construction is visible.

Mauney House, bottom; interior, top (JDP)

I. WALTON GARRETT HOUSE

100 North Piedmont Avenue
Kings Mountain
1874

The Garrett brothers of Edgecombe County—I. Walton, Richard, John, and Frank—were prominent Kings Mountain merchants in the late nineteenth century. I. Walton Garrett came to the area in the early 1870s and in 1874 built this two-and-a-half-story frame house at the corner of North Piedmont Avenue and East King Street. The house is essentially Second Empire in style with a mansard roof with multiple dormers and shingle-pattern pressed metal roofing. A wide bracketed cornice, decoratively corbelled brick chimneys, and a wraparound porch with turned posts and balustrade and sawn brackets are other notable exterior features. The interior has a richly ornamented stair and colored glass at the front entrance. The house underwent a remodeling in 1890, when it was acquired by Garrett's grandson, mill owner Charles A. Dilling. The house is said to be the first in town to be wired for electricity (in 1908). Behind stands a ca. 1900 storage building with sliding wooden doors.

I. Walton Garrett House (BRE)

BANKER'S HOUSE (JESSE JENKINS HOUSE)

319 North Lafayette Street
Shelby
Ca. 1875

The Banker's House is a resplendent example of Second Empire domestic design and one of the state's leading works in the popular Gilded Age style. The imposing stuccoed brick house was built for Jesse Jenkins (1832–89), one of the pioneering bankers in the southwestern part of the state during the 1870s, and the first in a long line of bankers to own the house (hence its name). The architect may have been New Jerseyite G. S. H. Appleget, who settled in North Carolina in 1869. This attribution is based on similarities between the Jenkins House and the Heck-Andrews House in Raleigh and the Cabarrus County Courthouse in Concord.

Jesse Jenkins, who married Harriett Brown in 1855, served as a major in the "Cleaveland Guards" during the Civil War and in 1862 was appointed Clerk of the Cleveland County Superior Court, a position he held until 1875. He was also a Shelby commissioner and a state senator from 1874 to 1876. Jenkins experienced financial troubles later in the 1870s, his house was sold at public auction in 1879, and he moved to Texas. The property was acquired by another banker, H. DeKalb Lee, and his wife Sarah, who sold it in 1894 to Pattie Blanton, the wife of Lee's business partner Burwell Blanton (1834–1908). In 1907 the Blantons sold the house to their son Charles Coleman Blanton (ca. 1858–1944), who had joined his father's banking firm B. Blanton & Co. in 1895. Charles in turn sold the house to a nephew, George H. Blanton Jr., also a banker, in 1941.

Banker's House (TJF)

The crowning element of the Banker's House is its three-story center tower, capped by a mansard roof with projecting pediments, cornices, and gabled dormers with segmental-arched windows and scrolled bases. The tower mansard is straight-sided; the mansard roof over the house proper and containing the upper half-story has a concave profile. All roofs are covered with fishscale slate shingles with colored slates forming floral designs on the roof faces. The house mansard also has dormers, with cruciform and fleur-de-lis ornaments and fanciful moldings. The walls of the house and tower rise to elaborate bracketed cornices and have decoratively framed recessed faces. The tall windows are round or segmental-arched. The entry at the base of the tower is contained in an arched surround and is sheltered by a small but richly ornamented porch with chamfered posts and bulbous vasiform balusters. Above, at the base of the third-story tower windows, is a balcony supported by brackets similar to those on the cornices and provided with a balustrade similar to that of the entry porch.

Exterior detail, left; hallway, right. Photos by George Blanton Chapell.

Compared to the exterior, the interior of the house is relatively plain. A cantilevered stair in the main hall has paired turned balusters and tread brackets with vine-and-bud scrolls. A heavy molded handrail terminates at a heavy turned newel. The main parlor features a dark marble (or marbled slate) mantel with an arched opening and a center cartouche. Molded baseboards, heavy cornices, interior window blinds, four-panel doors, and bathrooms added in 1910 are other features. Behind the house stand a wellhouse, a one-story brick building that is believed to have been a kitchen and servants quarters, and a large, two-story stable of frame construction with a clipped cross-gable roof. This stable is actually a replica of the original one, which burned in the early twentieth century. Prior to George Blanton's death in 2001, he and his wife, Nancy, donated the house to Preservation North Carolina for eventual use as the statewide preservation organization's western office, inaugurating a new era for this important landmark.

BURWELL BLANTON FARM

2006 West Dixon Boulevard (US 74)
Shelby
Ca. 1875

Built for Burwell Blanton (1834–1908) and his wife Frances Doggett Blanton, this two-story frame Italianate residence was the focal point of a 271-acre tract in 1880, according to the federal census of that year. The Blantons raised cotton, corn, wheat, oats, sweet potatoes, cattle, swine, poultry, and sheep on the farm. In the 1880s the Blantons moved to Shelby, but they retained ownership of the house, which may have served as the residence of their farm manager. Burwell Blanton quickly involved himself in Shelby business circles. In the mid-1870s he became a partner in the private bank J. Jenkins & Company, which evolved into B. Blanton & Company in 1895. Blanton's bank became the First National Bank of Shelby in 1903. With the assistance of fellow investors A. C. Miller and Rush Oates, Blanton formed the Belmont Cotton Mills in 1887. He also owned a general store and served as a town commissioner and a trustee of the North Carolina College of Agriculture and Mechanic Arts (now North Carolina State University). By the mid–twentieth century Blanton's farm had been converted to dairy production, and today the 759-acre tract is used primarily as pasture for beef cattle. The house, which is still owned by the Blanton family, is used as a rental property.

The two-story frame farmhouse features paired central interior chimneys that rise above a low-pitched hip roof with exposed rafter ends. The three-bay facade features paneled double-leaf central doors flanked by single lights. A one-story porch on square posts shelters the front. A large kitchen ell with a center chimney extends to the rear. The interior follows a center-passage plan.

The oldest outbuilding on the property is probably the log corncrib, which probably dates to the 1880s. Behind the house stands the farm office, strategically located in the center of the property's extensive outbuilding complex. From here, annual production rates were set, tenant farmers were hired and fired, cattle and milk were bought and sold. The small frame building has a door, two windows, and a chimney. East of the farm office are a concrete block bottling house, a frame and concrete block milking house, a well, and a feeding trough. North of the office stand a brick silo, a dairy barn, a chickenhouse, and a granary. West of the office are frame outbuildings that include a chickenhouse, a barn, an animal pen, and a hay feeder. Northwest of the house stand a frame smokehouse and a board-and-batten exterior and a two-story frame barn with shed additions.

Burwell Blanton House (BRE)

HOYLE-STROUP HOUSE

219 North Main Street
Waco
1880s

Daniel Boyd Stroup bought this two-story frame house from the estate of Lightfoot Williams Hoyle Jr. in 1906. Stroup operated a general store in Waco for many years. Following the deaths of Daniel in 1955 and his wife Eura in 1960, their heirs sold the property at public auction. In 1995 a granddaughter of Daniel and Eura's purchased the property, returning it to family ownership.

The one-story west section appears to be the original dwelling and probably dates to the 1880s. It has a porch and original nine-over-six windows. A one-story wing attaches to a two-story section added about 1900. The addition has a symmetrical three-bay facade, a porch with Victorian scrollwork, a double-leaf door with carved panels, and six-over-six windows with louvered shutters on decorative pintels. Extending from the kitchen is a stove tower ventilated by two casement windows and a single four-over-four window. Near the stove tower stands a frame smokehouse.

*Hoyle-Stroup House, below;
rear elevation with stove tower, right (BRE)*

ROSE HILL (HENDRICK-MEACHAM HOUSE)

510 West Grover Street
Shelby
Ca. 1880

Chapel Hendrick is thought to be the original owner of this two-story Victorian house. The property remained in the Hendrick family until the early twentieth century, when O. Max Gardner, O. M. Mull, Charlie Haynes, and Maurice Hendrick (a grandson of Chapel Hendrick) bought it. These four Shelby industrialists retained title to the property until the 1930s, when Mull became sole owner. In 1946 Mull's daughter and son-in-law, Mr. and Mrs. Earl Meacham, moved into the house, which now belongs to their children and is home to the Rose Hill Restaurant.

The three-bay frame house has a bracketed cornice and a front porch with chamfered posts and Victorian scrollwork. The front entry has a double-leaf panel door and windows have six-over-six sash. Rising above the gable roof are two interior chimneys and sawn ornament graces the gable ends. A hip-roofed three-sided bay projects from the west elevation. The large ell has interior and exterior chimneys. The front section of the house has a center passage with a single room on each side; the original decorative mantels are still in place, and the center-passage stair has a decorative newel post. Behind the house stood a log outbuilding, probably originally a corncrib, that was disassembled and moved from its unknown original location in 1949. A chimney and interior mantel were added to the log building at this time.

Rose Hill (BRE)

Mantel (BRE)

Gable, left; log outbuilding, right (BRE)

Featured Properties 89

LATTIMORE SEABOARD AIR LINE RAILROAD DEPOT

205 West Main Street
Lattimore
1882

This one-story frame depot is said to have been prefabricated in 1882 and transported to Lattimore by rail. The depot served its community for many years, until competition from highways rendered it obsolete in the mid–twentieth century. Forrest Crowder bought the depot in the late 1950s, moved it onto his property at the west edge of Lattimore, and lovingly restored it as a museum.

The depot has a board-and-batten exterior and a gable roof with overhanging eaves and exposed rafter ends. The structure rests on brick piers and is rectangular in form, with freight doors on the north and south elevations. The opposing freight doors allowed freight to be moved through the building from trackside to wagons, trucks and other conveyances waiting on the other side. Modern paneling has been added to the interior, but the freight section is intact.

Lattimore Seaboard Air Line Railroad Depot (JDP)

SHELBY SEABOARD AIR LINE RAILROAD DEPOT

536 North Washington Street
Shelby
Late 19th century

This remarkably intact depot is located on what was originally the line of the Carolina Central Railroad, which reached Shelby in 1874. Seaboard acquired the line in the 1880s, and it is now owned by csx. Former station agents included W. W. G. Smart in the 1920s (Smart later managed the adjacent Eagle Roller Mill) and John Clark, who held the position in the 1940s and 1950s. The building served both passengers and freight until 1914, when a separate passenger depot (no longer in existence) was built directly across the tracks. The north and south elevations of the common-bond brick depot feature numerous freight doors and elevated loading platforms. The office is located on the south elevation, easily distinguished by a chimney extending above the roof and a single door and window. Sanborn maps as early as 1909 show this area as the ticket office and passenger section. Exposed rafter ends and brackets grace the eaves.

above: Shelby Seaboard Air Line Railroad Depot (BRE)

left: Depot. Mid-twentieth-century photo courtesy of Jim Willard.

Featured Properties 91

EARL SOUTHERN RAILWAY DEPOT

Bettis Road (SR 2225)
Earl
Mid-1880s

Earl Depot is one of Cleveland County's few remaining depots as well as one of its oldest. Originally located near where a cluster of grain elevators now stands in the center of town, the depot was moved to its present location in the 1960s. This one-story frame structure features overhanging eaves supported by knee braces. The original pressed-metal gable roof remains intact, and six-over-six and four-over-four windows pierce the elevations. A loading dock and ramp constructed out of railroad ties facilitated the transfer of freight to and from the rail cars. Other notable features include large sliding cargo doors on opposite elevations, separate entrances and ticket booths for white and colored passengers, and three flues. Graffiti etched on a wall and dated 1887 provides corroboration for the date of the depot.

Earl Southern Railway Depot, left; ticket window, above (BRE)

OSBORNE-CARPENTER HOUSE

142 Sand Hill Road
Lawndale vicinity
1885

Dr. Joseph Cullen Osborne and his wife Margaret Schenck Osborne, the daughter of mill owner H. F. Schenck, had this two-story Italianate house built. Dr. Osborne practiced dentistry in the Lawndale and Belwood area, and a room in the house was set aside for his office. The property was later acquired by John David Schenck Carpenter, a bookkeeper and assistant treasurer at Cleveland Mills Company in nearby Lawndale, and his wife Zoie Elam Lattimore Carpenter. The weatherboarded frame house has a gable roof with a bracketed cornice and a two-story gabled front wing. The one-story wraparound porch stands on chamfered posts and has sawn brackets and turned balusters. The one-story kitchen ell has a complex form, with a pyramidal-roofed towerlike element and, adjoining it, a brick stove tower with a pyramidal cap

Rear elevation with stove tower and outbuildings (JDP)

(the stove tower is also pictured in the essay section of this book). The property once included a barn and one or more log outbuildings, and the back yard was brick-paved to combat mud and dust. Present outbuildings include a corncrib, wood shed, and a meat house in which the Carpenter family cured hams with salt and brown sugar. The house sits near the site of the old village called Cleveland Mills.

Osborne-Carpenter House (JDP)

Featured Properties 93

CLIFTON AND ALICE CHAMPION HOUSE

111 Champion Street
Mooresboro
1885

Dr. Clifton Otis Champion (1857–1922), a graduate of Atlanta Medical College, married Carrie Alice Crowder (1869–1944) in 1890. A previous owner built this two-story brick house in 1885—the date that appears in the parging on the inside of the gable roof—using handmade bricks said to have been fired on the place. The house is constructed in common bond and features paired interior chimneys. The one-story front porch stands on chamfered posts and has an unusual sawn balustrade. The door and windows of the house and its integral one-story ell have segmental-arched heads. A frame privy and a smokehouse stand nearby. In addition to his medical practice, Dr. Champion was president of the Mooresboro Bank, vice president of the Mooresboro Cotton Oil Mill, and a founder of the Lattimore Telephone Company.

Clifton and Alice Champion House (BRE)

LOGAN-HARRILL HOUSE

Sulphur Springs Road (SR 1100)
Patterson Springs vicinity
Late 19th century

The history of this stylish Italianate residence is rooted in tragedy, as told by Logan family historian Marilyn Logan. John Pinckney Logan, a soldier in the Confederate army, was betrothed to Elizabeth Jane Hogue (1848–1931). Pinckney was mortally wounded in battle at Petersburg, and his dying request was that his brother Benjamin Franklin Logan (1842–90) marry "Jennie" Hogue. Ben Logan, a lieutenant in the CSA and present at Appomattox, returned home and complied with his brother's wish. According to family tradition, Ben and Jennie Logan built their two-story frame house in the early 1870s, possibly in 1872. The house has a front/side-gable roof with a one-story bay window projecting from the off-center front wing. The cornice incorporates sawn brackets in two sizes, and above the roof rise brick chimneys with recessed panels in their shafts. Paired six-over-six windows have decorative surrounds with molded and eared segmental-arched lintels broken at the center by flat sections of molding. The one-story wraparound porch has replacement Craftsman-style supports.

The front entry opens into a center passage that contains a stair with scrollwork and turned balusters. Decorative pilasters and overmantels ornament the mantels. Near the house stand domestic and farm outbuildings, many of which date to the turn of the twentieth century, including a smokehouse, a washhouse, a ca. 1930 two-car garage, a large tractor shed, and two corncribs. Ben Logan served as Cleveland County sheriff while he was a resident in the house. The Logans were strong believers in education and they hired a private tutor, a Miss Eddins, to teach their children at home. Later the Logans moved to Shelby to provide their children greater educational opportunities (Jennie Logan's letters describe her sadness at leaving her country home). The Logan-Harrill House was acquired by dentist John A. Harrill and his wife Hattie, who moved in in 1910, and it remains in Harrill family ownership.

Logan-Harrill House (BRE)

Featured Properties 95

DECATUR AND MITTIE WARLICK HOUSE

911 Warlick Road (SR 1637)
Belwood vicinity
1887

Decatur Warlick (1859–1947) completed this house in 1887, and since then seven generations of the Warlick family have lived here. Decatur and his wife Mittie (1868–1954) farmed the surrounding acreage, concentrating on cotton production and, to a lesser degree, vegetables. This rambling frame two-story L-plan house features a one-story attached porch supported by flared columns. The gables have cornice returns and louvered vents, and the six-over-six windows have molded lintels. Like many houses from this era, the Warlick House has a center-passage plan. The stair has square-section balusters and a beveled newel post and cap. A brick wellhouse attaches to a one-story rear ell. Near the house stand a milkhouse, a smokehouse, a barn, a shed, and a tractor shed.

clockwise from bottom left: Decatur and Mittie Warlick House; smokehouse; mantel; stair detail (all BRE)

JOHN F. BEAM HOUSE

1013 Jim Elliott Road (SR 1804)
Fallston vicinity
Late 1880s

John Frank Beam and his brother Martin Francis Beam moved to the area south of Fallston in the late 1800s and established Beam's Mill on Long Branch. Soon after it opened, the Beam brothers' milling business closed, and in 1891 John moved to Spartanburg, South Carolina. The house now belongs to the Hoyle family.

The two-story frame house features an L-plan form. Its three-bay front is sheltered by a one-story porch supported by turned posts. Central double-leaf paneled doors are flanked on each side by six-over-six windows. A bracketed cornice runs under the eaves, and in the gables are slight returns. The two-story ell has a one-story shed room. The center-passage-plan interior features a finely crafted stair adorned with turned balusters, a turned newel, and scrolled face-string panels, and a paneled wainscot rises with the stair. The parlor features an original post-and-lintel mantel that incorporates a carved spade design. The early-twentieth-century outbuildings include two frame barns dating to about 1910 and 1940 and a ca. 1930 concrete block generator house.

John F. Beam House (BRE)

CLEVELAND MILLS

101 West Main Street (NC 182)
Lawndale
1888 and later

Pioneering Cleveland County textile manufacturer Henry Franklin Schenck began building this large cotton mill complex in the late 1880s; several accounts give 1888 as the construction date of the two-story brick mill building that forms the core of the complex. Originally known as the Cleveland Cotton Mills, it was renamed the Cleveland Mill & Power Company after it erected a hydroelectric plant on the adjacent First Broad River. Rows of board-and-batten and weatherboarded frame mill houses were constructed along Main and Garver streets—the genesis of the community of Lawndale.

In 1898 an insurance company prepared a plan and isometric drawing of the complex that documents its development up to that point. In addition to the main building there were a two-story dye house, a one-story building that later served as a dye house, a boiler house with iron smokestacks, and a water tower. The main building features tall segmental-arched windows (bricked up about 1960) and a shallow-pitched gable roof. Dominating its riverside elevation is a four-story bell tower with a pyramidal roof sheathed with shingle-pattern pressed-metal roofing and capped by a belfry with a finial spike. Single and double windows with projecting brick hood moldings light the upper rooms of the tower. The mill interior features long spinning rooms with rows of chamfered posts, exposed ceiling beams and rafters, and sliding metal fire doors, hallmarks of the slow-burning construction essential for cotton mills. Cleveland County contractor Matthew M. Mauney is believed to have built portions of the complex.

In the twentieth century a long wing was constructed off the north side of the main building and connected to the company store, a fanciful Classical Revival building built about 1900. The handsome new

Cleveland Mills bell tower (JDP)

dye house, a one-story brick building with gable parapets and roof trusses, was incorporated in the process. The wing terminates in ca. 1950 Moderne offices of Roman brick construction with an Indiana limestone, glass, and aluminum entry facade (the offices replaced the company store). In front of the office is the "Hoover rail," a concrete curb at which townfolk gathered during the depression of the 1930s.

Aerial view. Photo courtesy of Tommy Forney.

Other historic features include a ca. 1940 smokestack and a wooden stave water tank that once served the Lawndale railroad at a junction near Dover Mills in west Shelby.

The workforce at Cleveland Mills numbered over five hundred in the mid–twentieth century, and the mill made major expansions during the second half of the century, with precast concrete buildings erected to the north and west of the original complex over the original train yard. At midcentury the mill concentrated on the production of yarns and twines. In 1962 the mill was converted to the production of knit goods and a finishing plant was erected. South Carolina–based Spartan Mills acquired the facility in 1965. The new owners decided to phase out the manufacture of yarn and twine and instead enter the apparel market, so in 1974 the mill began producing "prepared for print" fabrics. By the end of the century, globalization had rendered the parent company uncompetitive; the mill was closed in 2001 but recently reopened.

Mill houses (JDP)

HAWKINS FARM

1311 Burke Road
Boiling Springs vicinity
Late 19th century

Preston Plato Hawkins (b. 1858) and his wife Susan Smith Hawkins were early or original occupants of this two-story Italianate frame house, which began as a one-story two-room dwelling. By the end of the nineteenth century the house featured a bracketed cornice, peaked window lintels, and a front porch with chamfered posts and sawn brackets and balusters. A son, Otho Hawkins, acquired the property, and in

Yates Hawkins and helpers begin construction of the cinder block dairy barn in 1948–49

P. P. Hawkins, his wife Susan (seated), and their daughter Beunah stand in front of the Hawkins House in the early twentieth century. This and other photos courtesy of Rita Harris.

the mid–twentieth century Otho's sons Yates and John operated a dairy farm here.

In 1948–49 Yates and his wife Ruth Weathers Hawkins entered a "Better Acres Contest" locally sponsored by First National Bank in Shelby. To improve the house and farm, the Hawkinses added a bathroom wing to the rear and a Colonial Revival balcony balustrade on the front porch roof, planted foundation shrubs in front of the house, and built a cinder block dairy barn. They won the contest. The house was remodeled again in 1977 by Yates and Ruth's daughter Rita Harris and her husband Kenny, who made a den addition to the rear and built a carport.

The completed dairy barn

Bathroom addition

A bedroom in the Hawkins House, circa 1948–49

Stock barn

Featured Properties 101

DOUBLE SHOALS COTTON MILLS

202 Moss Road
Double Shoals
Late 19th century

From humble beginnings, Double Shoals Cotton Mills rose to prosperity and then, like other early textile mills in the Piedmont, gradually declined into obscurity. It is believed that in 1845 Thomas R. Jackson deeded 268 acres to Albert Homesley, who built a complex including a cotton gin, a cotton factory, and a gristmill on the banks of the First Broad River. Homesley experienced a financial setback as a result of the Civil War and, in 1867, sold the mill to Abernathy Jackson. In 1874 E. A. Morgan purchased the mill from Jackson and, along with his son Fred, proceeded to make improvements, including the construction of the present brick mill building. In the early 1880s, several mill houses were built in Double Shoals to house the workers and the company store was erected next to the mill. Workers purchased all their necessary household goods from the store on credit, and the expenses they incurred were taken out of their paychecks. A 1900 Sanborn map depicts the two-story mill building, which contained 3,500 spindles and was accompanied by brick and frame cotton warehouses, a waste house, and a dam across the Broad River.

The Morgans produced yarn and twine at the mill until 1919, when they sold it to Ralph Royster of Shelby. Shortly thereafter, Royster sold the mill to Lester Hamrick and A. W. McMurry, who managed to hold onto the property until 1932, when a local bank foreclosed on it. Tom Moore and Lloyd Anthony purchased the mill the following year and renamed it the Double Shoals Company, Inc. Moore and Anthony sold the mill and accompanying village to the Schencks of Cleveland and Lily Mills around 1948. In 1950 the Schencks decided to sell the houses, and they gave the tenants the first option to buy their homes for a 10 percent down payment and weekly in-

Double Shoals Cotton Mills (JDP)

stallments taken out of employee paychecks. In 1954, the Schencks sold the mill to Al Slater, who then leased it to the Kings Mountain Neisler Company. The mill, renamed the Lucky Strike Yarn Mill, experienced a change in fortunes in 1973, when it was devastated by fire, and the Neislers and Slaters sold out. It then went through numerous owners, but never again operated as a cotton mill. Until his death in 2003, former mill employee Dwight Perry operated the company store as a museum devoted to the textile industry and local history.

Typical of nineteenth-century mill construction, the main spinning hall at Double Shoals features segmental-arched windows and a shallow-pitched gable roof. The single stair tower has a lancet-arched entry at its base, and wings of utilitarian brick construction extend from the building's ends. The company store has a slightly pitched roof and a two-story porch and small shed addition on the east and west elevations (the 1900 Sanborn map shows a two-story office wing on the north side). Two-over-two segmental-arched windows run the length of the north elevation; those on the south and east (front) elevations have been bricked up. The front features exquisitely crafted brick ornamentation, including a corbeled dogtooth cornice and projecting T-shaped motifs between the second-story windows. Star-shaped tie rod ends pepper the south elevation. Inside, an original walk-in iron safe is ornamented with fluted pilasters and an intricate door surround.

Company store brickwork detail, top; company store, bottom (BRE)

C. J. AND SARAH HAMRICK HOUSE

407 North Main Street
Boiling Springs
Late 19th century

According to one account, a part of this frame house dates to 1856, but most of the visible fabric dates to later in the nineteenth century: the three-sided bay window, fishscale wood shingles in the dormers on the gable roof, and porch detailing are all Victorian. The decorative window surrounds are like those of another Boiling Springs dwelling, the Pinckney Hamrick House. A rear addition features five dormers. The house underwent rehabilitation in the 1990s, and modern wall surfaces, fireplaces, and floors were added to the interior. Charles Jefferson Hamrick (1833–1918) and his wife Sarah Hamrick lived here and ran a general store across Main Street.

Mantel from house (BRE)

C. J. and Sarah Hamrick House (BRE)

SHELBY COTTON MILLS

500 South Morgan Street
Shelby
1899–1900

Established in 1899 by Morgan, Cline & Company, Shelby Mills manufactured textiles into the late twentieth century. Matthew Marcus Mauney, who built mills throughout the region, was the contractor. As originally constructed, the mill featured a two-story brick carding and spinning building with a picker house section and an elevator/stair tower on the east elevation topped by a water tank. By 1909 the building contained 15,000 spindles and 250 looms operated by 250 employees, and additions had been made twice to the north end. The large building features arched door and window openings (many bricked up) and a flat roof. Additions include a machine shop and boiler room (added before 1909) and an early 1920s picker house. At the northeast corner of the lot is a ca. 1920 office of Colonial Revival design under a slate hip roof with dormers. The office has molded concrete window lintels, and the main entrance is defined by a projecting pediment supported by square posts set on brick plinths. Shelby Cotton Mills survives as one of the county's best-preserved historic textile mill buildings. Five mill houses were constructed in 1900; by the early 1950s the number of mill-owned dwellings had surpassed 140. Many of these survive on surrounding streets.

Shelby Cotton Mills, with office in foreground, top; intersection of Smith and Wall streets in mill village, bottom; stair tower, left (all BRE)

VICTOR AND ESTHER MCBRAYER HOUSE

507 North Morgan Street
Shelby
1893

Dr. Victor McBrayer (1853–97), the son of Mooresboro farmer Reuben H. McBrayer, graduated from medical school in New York in 1875 and established his practice in Shelby. He married Esther Suttle (d. 1932) in 1880 and in 1885 purchased two lots in Shelby, where he built this one-story frame house in 1893. The gabled house shows the influence of several late-nineteenth-century styles such as the Italianate, Gothic Revival, and Queen Anne. The front porch stands on chamfered posts adorned with lambstongue moldings on square-section paneled bases. The bases are connected by a molded handrail supported by turned balusters alternating with drop pendants. The tops of the posts have molded caps and heavy curvilinear sawn brackets. In the porch frieze are narrow sawn brackets and curvilinear sawnwork. Window and door openings have segmental-arched heads and are set in wide-shouldered surrounds with molded hoods. The main entrance consists of a double door with round-arched glazed panels.

The gable over the front bay window has board-and-batten sheathing with a scalloped bottom edge, a three-part louvered vent with each louver sawn in a curvilinear fashion, and ornamental cross-bracing with a drop pendant. Gable dormers feature overhanging eaves with returns and sawnwork bargeboards. The dormers have board-and-batten sides and on their fronts are unusual vents composed of scalloped openings creating a fishscale pattern. The north and south gable ends feature floor-length two-over-two sash windows. A gable balcony has a balustrade identical to that of the porch and a decorative roof supported by brackets and trimmed with ornamental sawnwork.

Mantel. 1977 photo by Michael T. Southern courtesy of the North Carolina Office of Archives and History.

The interior has an asymmetrical plan consisting of a wide entrance hall, two parlors, and three rear rooms. The hall is divided by an archway with a multipane colored glass transom and louvered doors. Four-panel doors with wide applied moldings set in simple surrounds, mantels in variations of the post-and-lintel form, and molded baseboards characterize the interior. One mantel incorporates multistaged shelves, an assortment of spindles, a peaked and scrolled cresting, and a mirrored panel in the overmantel. Outbuildings include a frame milk house, a potato house, and a two-room secondary dwelling.

above: Victor and Esther McBrayer House. 1977 photo by Michael T. Southern courtesy of the North Carolina Office of Archives and History.

left: The house as it appeared shortly after completion, with decorative paint scheme. Photo courtesy of Dr. and Mrs. Frank Hannah.

Featured Properties 107

HOTEL CHARLES (BLANTON BUILDING)

106 South Lafayette Street
Shelby
1890s, 1928–29, 1999

The Hotel Charles began as a combination bank, hotel, and commercial building. The original appearance was much different than today's. The three-story brick building featured Classical Revival details such as pediments over the second-story windows, bracketed cornices over the third-story windows, a dentil cornice, and quarry-faced stone storefronts on Lafayette Street with well-defined voussoirs in the arches over doors and windows. The bank was B. Blanton & Company, one of many enterprises of the entrepreneurial Burwell Blanton. Blanton's bank rose from the ashes of J. Jenkins & Co., Bankers, in 1895, and in 1903 it acquired its present name, First National Bank. The bank occupied the corner on Warren Street; the Central Hotel lobby opened under an iron balcony at the north end. The hotel rooms were situated on the second and third floors, and in the early twentieth century a three-story dining room addition was made along Warren Street.

On August 28, 1928, a fire thought to have started in the hotel linen room claimed three lives and caused substantial damage to the building. The building was remodeled in the Mission style and reopened as the Hotel Charles. New features included ornamental iron balconies and a bracketed Spanish tile pent roof below a shaped parapet. The new hotel entry was on

Hotel Charles. Circa 1950 photo courtesy of the Lloyd Hamrick Collection.

Building circa 1900, when it contained the First National Bank and Central Hotel. Courtesy of Betty Rose Heath.

Warren Street, under a canopy and a sign advertising the hotel and its coffee shop. Tall Palladian windows lighted the bank and hotel lobbies. A windowless modernist stone veneer and a clock/thermometer sign were added to the bank facade in the late twentieth century. The building's 1999 renovation by First National Bank, which removed the stone veneer, received the L. Vincent Lowe Business Award from the Historic Preservation Society of North Carolina.

First National Bank in the Charles Building (BRE)

WILLIS HOUSE

5246 Polkville Road (NC 226)
Polkville vicinity
1890, 1936

Joseph Gallashaw Willis (1827–92) commissioned a Mr. Rollins to build this house in 1890 for himself and his wife Mary Wilson (1838–1919). Willis died shortly after construction of the house was completed, and the property passed to his son Thomas Jacob Willis (1874–1955), who later married Addie Alexander (1887–1960). Thomas graduated from high school at Rutherford College in Burke County. He then went to George Peabody College in Nashville and the North Carolina Agricultural and Mechanical College (now NCSU) in Raleigh. After graduation Thomas returned to farm his land. In the late 1930s Thomas and Addie Willis boarded Rutherford Electric Co-Op employees, who were building power lines into the vicinity (the Rural Electrification Administration project brought electricity to the Willis House in 1939).

Originally Victorian in character, the Willis House was transformed into a Foursquare-form dwelling as the result of a major remodeling in 1936. A cross-gable roof was replaced with the present hip roof, and carpenter Tom Alexander remodeled the front porch. The wraparound porch connects to a porch room on the east elevation. A small one-story kitchen ell and six-over-six windows are other features. A woodshed, a smokehouse, two pumphouses, and a washhouse stand to the south of the house. One of the pumphouses was built in 1939 to shelter a well dug the same year. The well provided water for livestock. Across a farm lane from the house are two granaries and a transverse mule barn.

Willis House (BRE)

Mantel; smokehouse (BRE)

110 Architectural Perspectives of Cleveland County

JOHN AND VERTIE LATTIMORE FARM

3957 Five Points Road (SR 1373)
Polkville vicinity
Late 1890s

John Lattimore (1870–1943) married Vertie Mauney in 1895, and the couple built this one-story frame house shortly thereafter. The Lattimores' farm originally consisted of approximately 60 acres devoted to growing cotton, corn, and grain and raising chickens and cows. The Lattimores' ten children helped them run the farm.

The Lattimore House stands on stone piers and is sheathed with unpainted weatherboards. A porch and two gables ornament the front elevation, and a stove tower with four-over-four windows and a pyramidal roof rises on the north elevation. An ell was added about 1905, and two porches project to the rear. The front entry opens into a small hall enclosed with angular walls. Carved post-and-lintel mantels in a variety of forms are found in the parlor, the southwest bedroom, and the two central bedrooms. A rear bedroom dating to about 1905 is located next to a ca. 1950 bathroom. A 1923 ell contains a dining room and connects to the kitchen. The kitchen has not been remodeled, thus offering a rare glimpse of a stove tower in its original state, with an iron and porcelain stove connected to a stovepipe that extends to the roof. Behind the house are several frame outbuildings in relatively good condition. These include a smokehouse, a privy, a chickenhouse, and a woodshed. A brick pumphouse, a cotton house, a corncrib, and a modern barn stand nearby.

John and Vertie Lattimore House mantels, above; corncrib, left (BRE)

below: John and Vertie Lattimore House, stove tower on left (BRE)

LATTIMORE COMMERCIAL DISTRICT

Lattimore sprang up at the junction of the Seaboard and Southern rail lines in western Cleveland County and incorporated in 1899. In 1903 the *Cleveland Star* predicted: "On account of the railroad facilities and the accessible territory that abounds in raw material, Lattimore is destined to become in the near future a manufacturing town." A lumberyard, brick plant, and cotton gin did develop here, providing the industrial base for modest growth. A principal industry was the Cleveland Oil Mill, incorporated in 1899 and conveyed to the Verner Oil Company in 1902.

One of the town's earliest surviving commercial buildings is the 1897 McMurry-Beam Building, a two-story brick building occupied by many tenants over the years. The corner room, entered through an angled corner entry and lighted by a large segmental-arched window, apparently first contained the office of lumberman William T. Calton, but by about 1900 the Farmer's Bank of Rutherfordton had moved in. From 1905 to 1937 the Masons met in an upstairs lodge room, and Dr. R. L. Hunt occupied an upstairs office beginning in 1910. About 1920 Hunt and partner Robert Hewitt opened Hunt & Hewitt General Merchandise in the middle part of the building, which has a storefront with large display windows and transoms. Other occupants included the Lattimore Oil Company (C. Jeff Hamrick, president), and the barbershops of Will Fite and then James Wyatt Martin, who acquired the building.

Dr. L. V. Lee built the present town hall in the early 1920s to house his office, drugstore, and soda fountain. The one-story brick building is enlivened by a cornice with sawtooth corbeling. In 1928 or 1929 J. B. Lattimore built his general store, a two-story brick building with industrial metal windows and facade panels of Flemish-bond brickwork. The two storefronts' display windows, transoms, and recessed entries are sheltered under a porch supported by stout brick pillars. Another early brick commercial building developed around Hone I. Washburn's general store, built in 1899. The Verner Oil Company added on a warehouse in 1907, and the Lattimore Oil Company constructed another warehouse addition in 1933. The Seal Wire Company incorporates a cotton gin and seed house.

Martin Building (BRE)

112 Architectural Perspectives of Cleveland County

Lattimore Town Hall (BRE)

top: *A Lattimore brickyard. Photo courtesy of the Cleveland County Historical Museum.*

bottom: *J. B. Lattimore Store (BRE)*

L. V. AND SUSAN LEE FARM

202 West Lee Street (SR 1161)
Lattimore
1897

The house of Dr. Lawrence Victor Lee (1871–1943) and his wife Susan C. Lattimore Lee (1875–1958) was the first in Lattimore to have electricity, and some of the original electrical fixtures survive. The house adheres to a center-passage plan, with two prominent gables on the facade and a smaller gable symmetrically placed in between on the roof of the attached porch. The gables are richly embellished with spindles, scroll-sawn cutouts, and drop pendants, and two have fishscale wood-shingle sheathing and scalloped louvered vents. A wraparound porch supported by turned posts with scroll-sawn spandrels covers the east, north, and west elevations. Some of the rooms retain chair rails, beaded wainscoting, and beaded ceilings. Furthermore, several of the mantels have original copper firebox covers decorated with pastoral scenes. Near the house stand a frame smokehouse, a sorghum house, a chickenhouse, a hay barn, and a modern garage.

Dr. Lee was a graduate of the Davidson Medical College and the Atlanta Medical College. He practiced in Rutherford County in the mid-1890s and settled in Lattimore in 1897 upon his marriage to Susan Lattimore, a daughter of Lattimore founder Audley M. Lattimore. Dr. Lee was active in statewide medical policy-making organizations, and his wide-ranging business interests included banking, milling, and brick making.

clockwise from bottom left: L. V. and Susan Lee House (TJF); front elevation detail; fireplace detail (both BRE)

JOHN AND BESSIE MAUNEY HOUSE

119 North Piedmont Avenue
Kings Mountain
Ca. 1900

An octagonal turret with a tall pyramidal roof is the defining feature of this Queen Anne house. Built for John David Mauney (1878–1947) about the time of his marriage to Bessie Miller Frantz in 1901, the story-and-a-half frame house is covered by a high hip roof from which projects a corbeled chimney with a channeled shaft. The wraparound porch stands on classical wood columns, spaced singly or in groups, and it has a gable with gridded decoration aligned with the front entry. The Mauneys did not live in the house long; John entered the ministry and served Lutheran congregations throughout the Carolinas and Georgia.

John and Bessie Mauney House. 1999 photo by Megan Eades.

CALTON-MARTIN HOUSE

100 Martin Street
Lattimore
1899–1900

William T. Calton, lumberman and manufacturer, built this unusual Queen Anne house in 1899–1900. The house's location next to the railroad suited it as a boardinghouse where salesmen could spend the night before heading into upper Cleveland County to sell their wares. One room of the house has four doors, each with a lock on it to protect the residents of the house from intrusion by boarders. W. T. Calton manufactured plows and cultivating machinery at Lattimore and was a president of the Verner Oil Company, created in 1902 for trading and manufacturing cottonseed oil, meal, hulls, and linters. Calton's lumberyard was situated across the road from his house. He is said to have been the first resident of Lattimore to own an automobile. His wife may have been a schoolteacher. Julius C. Martin (1870–1953) and his wife Lillie Angeline Walker Martin (d. 1967) lived here beginning in the 1940s. In 1937 a son, James Wyatt Martin (b. 1913), opened the Martin Milling Company in Lattimore, supplier of feed to dairy and cattle farmers throughout the county. Wyatt's widow Donnis Magness Martin now resides in the house.

A striking feature of the exterior are matching glassed-in gazebos at the front corners of the wraparound porch; they apparently served for the overwintering of plants. The porch also boasts intricate spindlework and stout turned posts of unusual design. Gables in the main roof and porch roof are graced with decorative wood shingles and sawn ornament. The rear gabled wing of the house has flared eaves. A later large brick addition encloses a kitchen and dining room. The interior retains many original features, including decorative mantels. Nearby stand a frame smokehouse, a privy, a small cow barn, and a deteriorated wood shop. The architectural twin of this house stood on Warren Street in Shelby but has been demolished.

Calton-Martin House, opposite bottom; porch, left (JDP)

Calton Lumber Yard, Lattimore, opposite top. 1900 photo courtesy of the Cleveland County Historical Museum.

Featured Properties 117

J. W. AND MAUDE BRACKETT FARM

109 Old Belwood Road (SR 1612)
Belwood vicinity
Ca. 1900

Throughout the nineteenth century and into the twentieth, it was not uncommon for a home in a rural area to serve that community as the post office as well. The Brackett House provides a case in point. This one-story farmhouse housed the Belwood community's post office from 1918 to 1932. Postmaster J. W. Brackett (1873–1932) lived here with his wife Maude. J. W. grew cotton in the summer and worked at the Hugh Hoyle harness shop during the winter. His son J. W. Brackett Jr. was born here in 1913 and continues to operate the family farm.

The one-story hip-roofed dwelling has a front porch and one-over-one windows. Basically square in plan, the symmetry of the house is reinforced by evenly spaced chimneys. A kitchen ell with an exterior chimney and a carport addition extends to the rear. The property includes a large collection of outbuildings, many associated with a dairy operation run by J. W. Jr. in the mid–twentieth century. Just west of the house are a 1924 transverse cow barn and a ca. 1940 brick silo. Behind the house is a ca. 1940 concrete block milking parlor that doubled as a milk storage house. In front of the parlor is a tractor shed, and across the farmyard from this shed are a concrete block smokehouse and modern greenhouse. A small garden plot sits adjacent to the greenhouse, and on the other side are a frame tenant house and accompanying barn associated with Robert Gobber, a tenant farmer who lived on the Brackett Farm during much of the 1940s. Like many farms from this era, the complex is separated by the function of the particular outbuildings. A smokehouse is located on one side of the main house while on the opposite side of the farmyard stand the granary, cow barn, silo, milking parlor, and tractor shed. Across a field and away from the main house stand the single tenant house and accompanying barn. During this era, it was not uncommon for tenant farmers to raise a few crops and/or livestock for their own use.

J. W. and Maude Brackett Farm (BRE)

RICHARD M. WHITE HOUSE

2070 Flint Hill Church Road (SR 1148)
Boiling Springs vicinity
Ca. 1900

Richard Meredith White (1870–1958) built this now abandoned Victorian frame house on what was once a prosperous cotton farm. The house originally stood about a hundred yards west of its present location but was moved in the early 1940s to make way for a new road. Decorative features include arched and heavily molded window surrounds, bracketed house and porch cornices, scalloped board-and-batten sheathing in the gables, and a three-sided bay window with original louvered shutters. The north portion of the house dates to 1940–41 and encompasses a well. Outbuildings include a partially metal-sided frame garage, a large shed of frame and metal construction, a 1970s greenhouse, and a frame cow barn with a shed addition.

Richard M. White House, left; gable and bay window detail, above (BRE)

LANCE AND OLLIE HOPPER HOUSE

2616 Blacksburg Road (NC 198)
Earl
Ca. 1900

This fascinating Queen Anne cottage was built for farmer Lance Hopper and his wife Ollie around 1900, possibly by a neighbor named Webber. The defining feature is an octagonal tower, the upper half of which is a roof with concave sides and cap formerly sheathed with wood shingles. Inside the tower's base is an octagonal living room with a front window that can be converted into an entry by sliding the single large sash up into an overhead wall pocket. The window has a stained glass transom and is flanked by stained glass windows. The octagonal geometry translates to a porch that wraps around the tower base and now stands on decorative modern metal supports. Other features include a hip-and-gable roof—a more common feature of the Queen Anne cottages of the era—tall interior chimneys, weatherboard siding, and an octagonal dining room behind the octagonal living room.

Behind the house stands a frame buggy shed later enlarged to serve as a garage, and there is a modern wellhouse nearby. A well on the property once supplied water for the baptistery of New Hope Baptist Church (which then stood next door but now stands across the road) via an above-ground pipe. Another interesting aspect of the property concerns Lance Hopper, who originally intended to make his house two stories in height but broke his leg during construction, had to have the leg amputated, and abandoned his plans for a second story. According to tradition, Hopper had the amputated leg buried under the house in the belief that doing so would prevent the stump from hurting. The Queen family later owned the house, followed about 1950 by Claude Lee and Bessie Sue Lavender, parents of the present owner.

Lance and Ollie Hopper House (BRE)

CLEVELAND COUNTY COURTHOUSE (FORMER)

103 South Lafayette Street
Shelby
1907–8

The former Cleveland County Courthouse, ensconced in its shady square at the heart of Shelby, is the county's best-known building and also one of its finest. The public square was created when Shelby was platted as the county seat in the early 1840s, and in 1845 the first courthouse was built on the site. By the beginning of the twentieth century the county court had outgrown its antebellum lodgings. At their meeting on August 6, 1907, the county commissioners declared the 1845 courthouse "utterly insufficient" due to "the increase in growth in the population and material interests of the County of Cleveland during the last 25 years in which the business of the county has been much enlarged demanding greater facilities."

The county retained the Falls City Construction Company and architect Harry L. Lewman, both of Louisville, Kentucky, to build its grand new Classical Revival courthouse. Lewman was the son of M. T. Lewman, the builder of several Missouri courthouses in the same style. The elder Lewman died in 1907, and H. L. and two brothers formed the Falls City Construction Company to continue their father's business. The company built eight courthouses in Georgia over the course of a few years; the Cleveland County Courthouse appears to be the firm's only North Carolina courthouse commission, and it is more extravagant than most of the Georgia examples. In December 1907 the county paid the Falls City Construction Company $10,000, indicating that work had com-

Former Cleveland County Courthouse and courthouse square. Mid-twentieth-century photo courtesy of the Lloyd Hamrick Collection.

Featured Properties 121

South facade (JDP)

Confederate monument (JDP)

menced. In June 1908 a number of workmen were paid for their work on the building, and the Art Metal Construction Company and Fielden & Allen were paid for the courthouse furniture. Also in June, Commissioners Matthew M. Mauney, who supervised the work, and J. F. Roberts were instructed to make a final settlement with the contractor for the pouring of the cement walkways in the public square.

The Cleveland County Courthouse is square in plan, with light tan limestone walls and a central domed cupola. The dome is divided into eight segments defined by ribbing (and reflecting the octagonal form of the base below) and is topped by a lanternlike element with arched openings. (A copper ball on the top of the lantern is said to have been made from a captured whiskey still.) At the bottom of the cardinal faces of the dome are illuminated clock dials in arched surrounds. At the transition of the dome and base is

122 Architectural Perspectives of Cleveland County

a pronounced cornice, and the base has Ionic corner pilasters and louvered openings in pedimented surrounds. Octagonal domed cupolas were an H. L. Lewman trademark, although similar cupolas were popular with other courthouse designers of the period.

The courthouse proper has identical elevations with center porticoes and projecting corner pavilions with domed roofs. The porticoes stand on Corinthian columns on tall bases, and they have cartouches and other ornamentation in their tympanums. The corner pavilions have banded first stories and smooth second stories with projecting window heads that support large cartouche crestings. Like the main dome, the pavilion domes are octagonal, and a continuous roof balustrade crowns the pavilions and the main body of the building. The one-over-one windows are paired and have transoms, and the recessed entries have double doors with glass panels and transoms. The interior, which has a stairway with metal railings, retains a T-form passage, but when the second-floor courtroom was remodeled in the late twentieth century, a pressed-metal ceiling was removed. The court functions moved out in 1974, and most are presently located at 100 Justice Place. The 1907–8 courthouse is now used as the Cleveland County Historical Museum.

The courthouse square, defined by the historic commercial buildings of Shelby's bustling "uptown," is one of the most evocative civic spaces of its type in the state. The well-kept grounds are shaded by mature deciduous trees and ornamented with memorials, including the 1906 Confederate Memorial, which features the statue of a soldier on a flag-draped granite shaft. To the east side of the courthouse stands a ca. 1920 classical brick springhouse with a pedimented roof, arched openings, and Doric pilasters. Lithia spring waters were once piped here and also sprayed from a fountain in a small circular pool. In later years the springhouse was converted into offices and storage.

Springhouse, built circa 1920, photographed mid–twentieth century. Photo courtesy of the Lloyd Hamrick Collection.

Lithia spring. Early-twentieth-century photo courtesy of the Cleveland County Historical Museum.

WEBBLEY (GOVERNOR O. MAX GARDNER HOUSE)

403 South Washington Street
Shelby
1907 (core, 19th century)

This imposing Classical Revival house incorporates a nineteenth-century dwelling built for attorney Augustus Burton, but the house in its present form is identified with Oliver Maxwell Gardner (1882–1947), governor of North Carolina from 1929 to 1933 and a leading political figure during the first half of the twentieth century. Max Gardner was a key member of the "Shelby Dynasty," a group of influential politicians that included another governor and Gardner's brother-in-law, Clyde R. Hoey. Gardner served North Carolina as a state senator and lieutenant governor, and as governor he helped Cleveland County and the state weather the early years of the Great Depression. Later, President Roosevelt appointed him chairman of the advisory board of the Office of War Mobilization, and he served as undersecretary of the treasury under President Truman. Gardner died in 1947 shortly after his appointment as ambassador to the Court of St. James.

Not surprisingly, Gardner was also influential in Shelby and Cleveland County. After earning degrees in chemistry and law, Gardner entered into partnership with his brother-in-law, attorney J. A. Anthony, in 1907. That same year he married Fay Lamar Webb (ca. 1885–1969), the daughter of Superior Court Judge James L. Webb (d. 1930), a senior member of the Shelby Dynasty. Also in 1907, J. A. Anthony, who had bought Webbley in 1905, enlarged the house to its present grandeur. In 1911 Judge Webb purchased the house, which then acquired the name Webbley, and Judge Webb, his wife Kans (Kansas), the Gardners, and other family members and servants moved in. Max Gardner, who spent time on a farm as a youth, kept cows at the rear of the Webbley property to familiarize his sons with the rural lifestyle. From Webbley Gardner also controlled one of the county's largest cotton-growing operations. After Max Gardner's death in 1947, Fay Gardner returned to Webbley (the Gardners maintained a residence in Washington for much of the 1930s and 1940s), where she died in 1969. Max and Fay's son Ralph Webb Gardner occupied the house until his death in 1982. Webbley has received many distinguished visitors, including Presidents Franklin Roosevelt and Harry Truman, Lady Bird Johnson, and various North Carolina governors. In recent years the house was operated as a bed-and-breakfast inn.

The original house, which forms the back half of the main two-story section of the present house, was an Italianate dwelling with paneled chimney stacks and sawn porch details. As expanded in 1907, the two-story frame house has weatherboard siding and a hip roof with a balustraded deck. The dominant feature is the two-story portico on monumental fluted Ionic columns (were it not for the portico the house could be considered Colonial Revival in style). The portico is flanked by one-story sitting porches on Doric columns. Both the portico and the porches have roof balustrades, and the portico has sawn cornice brackets that extend to the cornice of the main house. Under the portico is a three-sided vestibule with a front entry with fanlight and sidelights. Other exterior features

Servants quarters (JDP)

include a brick foundation and interior chimneys, nine-over-nine and six-over-six windows, a side bay window, a porte cochere, and one-story rear wings.

Inside, the center passage is divided in two by a colonnade with a two-run stair in the rear hall. The stair has slender turned newels, turned balusters, and a molded handrail that descends to a volute. The mantels have been described as Neo-Georgian, Neo-Federal, and Neoclassical in form, and they feature carvings of garlands, swags, and urns. Symmetrically molded door surrounds and corner blocks survive from the original construction. Molded cornices, paneled wainscots, and pocket doors are other highlights of the interior.

Behind the house stands a two-story carriage house remodeled as an office, and a one-story servants quarter with a gable roof. The dwelling was moved to its present spot from elsewhere on the formerly larger Webbley acreage, and it once belonged to a row of similar houses, presumably early tenant houses. The cut nails that attach its weatherboards and other details date it to the nineteenth century. Also behind the house are modern pergolas that evoke earlier ones associated with a former rose garden, and the landscaped grounds reflect the input of Shelby landscape architect Fred B. Blackley. Webbley's rehabilitation in 1989 by present owner Max Gardner III was honored with a Gertrude S. Carraway Award of Merit from Preservation North Carolina. The house is also the county's only National Historic Landmark, a distinction it received in 1997.

Webbley, top; interior, bottom. Photos courtesy of the Gardner family.

HUDSON-HULL HOUSE

710 North Lafayette Street
Shelby
1907 (core, ca. 1880)

According to research by Betty Rose Heath, the core of this two-story frame dwelling was built in the 1870s or early 1880s for Methodist minister Dr. Hillary Hudson (ca. 1823–92). Hudson served Shelby's Central Methodist Church from 1874 to 1876 and again in 1879. Hudson was known as a charismatic speaker and teacher. He was also considered an authority on Methodist doctrine, and two books of his were published in Shelby: *The Methodist Armor* (1882) and *The Shield of the Young Methodist* (1889). He lived in the house with his second wife, Mary T. Lee Hudson.

The house changed hands twice before James Heyward Hull (ca. 1866–1938) purchased the property in April 1907. A native of Catawba County, Hull built a successful business career that spanned several states in the late nineteenth century. Among his varied pursuits was an agency representing the Bowers Snuff & Tobacco Company in the Southeast, an interest in the Cherryville Manufacturing Company in neighboring Lincoln County, and an association with the Shelby firm J. J. McMurry & Company. A month after acquiring the Hudson House, Hull married Loula Abernethy, and soon after that the Hulls commenced an extensive remodeling that added a Classical Revival portico with fluted Corinthian columns, a dentillated cornice, and decorative balustrades at first-story and roof levels. The original floor plan featured a center passage flanked by four large rooms, including a sun parlor or solarium. In 1938 a substantial rear addition was constructed and the house was divided into six apartments. In 1942 the house was again remodeled to restore the downstairs to a single-family dwelling, whereas the upstairs apartments remained in place. A detached garage is accessible via a circular driveway.

Hudson-Hull House (BRE)

CICERO AND HATTIE FALLS HOUSE

401 Carpenters Grove Church Road (SR 1614)
Belwood vicinity
Ca. 1907, 1927

In 1907, shortly after he built it, John Zemri Falls sold this impressive house to his son Cicero Clemmie Falls (1881–1952). Cicero and his wife Hattie Maude Lattimore Falls (1887–1929), who married in 1906, lived in the house for twenty years before undertaking an ambitious remodeling in 1927. Cicero's choice of treatments for his home is consistent with architectural trends of the early twentieth century and reflects his relative affluence. Cicero transformed the dwelling into a Foursquare and added a brick veneer and two porte cocheres. Other exterior features include a front stoop, a low hip roof, and six-over-one windows.

The house has a center-passage plan on both its first and second stories. The first-floor interior features a pressed-metal ceiling, wainscoting, and paneling on the walls of the center passage, a parlor, and the dining room. The mantels are principally of the post-and-lintel form but include a corbeled brick example. On the second floor is a sleeping porch. Behind the house stands a large gambrel-roofed horse barn.

Cicero and Hattie Falls House, left; mantel, above (BRE)

Featured Properties 127

AVRO AND LAURA MCENTYRE HOUSE

2623 Polkville Road (NC 226)
Polkville vicinity
Ca. 1908

Avro McEntyre ran a cotton gin on this property, and he sawed the lumber for his house, which was built with assistance from his father and brothers. A. A. McEntyre later added to the house. The one-and-a-half-story dwelling features a wraparound porch on three elevations. A gabled stove tower projects from the east elevation. A chimney rises on the south elevation, and next to it is an enclosed porch and a screen porch. Nearby stand a granary, a chickenhouse, a garage, and a shed.

Avro and Laura McEntyre House, left; stove tower, above (BRE)

STEPHEN AND OLIVE ROYSTER HOUSE

413 South Washington Street
Shelby
1908–10

This grand Classical Revival residence was designed for prominent physician and businessman Dr. Stephen Sampson Royster (ca. 1867–1948) and his wife Olive Bruce McBrayer Royster (1872–1949) by Charlotte architect J. M. McMichael, who also designed Royster's commercial block at 116 E. Warren. The house is dominated by a portico on monumental fluted Corinthian columns. Dentils and modillions ornament the portico cornice, which extends to the rest of the two-story weatherboarded frame house. The front entry has sidelights and an elliptical fanlight and is repeated above by a second-story entry that opens onto a balcony. The symmetry of the five-bay facade is reinforced by three gabled dormers and by identical Corinthian sitting porches that project from the side elevations. The house is said to have had Shelby's first hot-water heating system and modern bathroom, and the plumbing theme extends to a front-yard fountain. Dr. Royster's sons eventually joined him in business; one, David Wyeth Royster (1893–1973), moved into the Andrews-Royster House next door (417 S. Washington).

Stephen and Olive Royster House. Photo courtesy of the North Carolina Office of Archives and History.

ROYSTER BUILDING

116 East Warren Street
Shelby
1910

Charlotte architect J. M. McMichael designed this interesting commercial block for businessman Dr. Stephen S. Royster. The two-story yellow brick building is classical in inspiration, with a pedimented center element and heavy cornices. A wide frieze with decorative panels runs above the second-story windows; under the center pediment the panels are contained within paired blind arches with a roundel in the spandrel. In the 1940s the east corner storefront was given a Moderne veneer of black Carrara glass and black-painted wood paneling that formerly advertised Loy's Mens Shop (the signage now advertises The Gallery).

Royster Building. 1980s photo courtesy of Betty Rose Heath.

SHELBY CITY HALL (FORMER)

5 East Marion Street
Shelby
1911, 2002

This two-story brick building served as Shelby's city hall and firehouse until the completion of the present municipal building in 1939. The building is distinguished by the three round stained glass attic windows under its dentillated cornice and by segmental-arched window and door openings, including a wide front opening for fire engines (originally horse-drawn). The street-level front was modified to accommodate an A&P grocery store after 1939, when the present city hall was completed. The building was rehabilitated in 2002 by Foothills Builders according to a design by Martin Boal Anthony & Johnson. A restaurant is located on the first floor, and offices are planned for the second.

Former Shelby City Hall. Early-twentieth-century photo courtesy of the Cleveland County Historical Museum.

WILL MCBRAYER FARM

103 McBrayer Lane
Mooresboro
1910

This well-preserved early-twentieth-century agricultural complex was begun by Will McBrayer, who in 1910 built the one-story frame farmhouse that now belongs to the heirs of Will McBrayer's son, John Z. McBrayer. The house stands on a brick foundation and features paired front gables, a large central dormer, and metal roofing. The front wraparound porch stands on turned posts; a screen porch extends to the rear. The center-passage-plan interior features ornate mantels, beaded board walls, and five-panel doors.

Will McBrayer House, bottom; mantel, top (BRE)

Most of the farm buildings date to the same period as the house, about 1910, and they supported dairy farming, cotton production, poultry raising, and cattle breeding. Behind the house is a frame separator house used to separate milk and cream. Near it is a frame smokehouse and a woodhouse with a waist-high hatchway that facilitated the storing and removal of wood. Beyond stands a large frame transverse stock barn that overlooks rolling pastureland. A frame corn-crib with shed wings stands near a frame one-car garage, a story-and-a-half cotton house, a frame seed-house, and a small frame chicken coop used to raise young chickens. Also on the property is a two-bay frame tenant house with a center chimney. According to family tradition, the tenant house was placed at a distance from the farm complex in order to offer its occupants privacy and a sense of autonomy. A wood-shed and privy accompany the tenant house.

Privy interior, left; barn, top (BRE)

PIEDMONT SCHOOL

117 Piedmont Drive
Lawndale
1910 and later

Piedmont School was established about 1896 and was funded in the early years by Major Henry F. Schenck, president of Cleveland Mill & Power Company. The school moved to this site in 1900 and by 1907–8 boasted an enrollment of over three hundred students. In 1910, after fire destroyed the main school building, the decision was made to rebuild. Three large frame buildings were erected: Schenck Hall, an auditorium and music hall, and Waters Library. In the 1920s the institution evolved from a private preparatory academy into a public school, and after the 1926–27 term students were no longer boarded on campus. The school operated as a public high school until 1960–61, when it became an elementary school. Piedmont Elementary School closed at the end of the 1975–76 term. In 1980, the Town of Lawndale bought the school and the remaining buildings from the Cleveland County Board of Education. In May 1990, Waters Library was renovated by architect Lyle Smith and the Sunshine Construction Company.

Waters Library, bottom (BRE); advertising curtain, top (JDP)

134 Architectural Perspectives of Cleveland County

The building was rededicated as the C. D. and Veva C. Yelton Spangler Library.

The defining feature of the Second Empire–influenced library is its mansard roof, which has shingle-pattern pressed-metal roofing and paired dormers on each elevation. Also of interest is the two-tone brickwork on the quoins and under the eaves. The front entry features a magnificent fanlight with a keystone in the arch and two sidelights. The library was named for Confederate Captain A. G. Waters, who was killed at the Battle of Gaines Mill in July 1862. Below the hilltop library is the Piedmont School Agriculture and Home Economics Building, a one-story brick building erected by the National Youth Administration in 1939. The Colonial Revival building features a center pedimented projection with a recessed doorway flanked by three pairs of nine-over-nine windows. The agriculture building was rehabilitated as a community center in 1986–87 with guidance from Shelby architect Lyle Smith. The 1950s shop building now houses the Lawndale Historical Museum, whose collections include a ca. 1950 advertising curtain from the school auditorium. Adding to the historical interest of the campus is a Lawndale Railway boxcar that has been restored by the Lawndale Historical Society.

Piedmont School campus, top (JDP); Agriculture and Home Economics Building, bottom (BRE)

FIRST BAPTIST CHURCH SHELBY

120 North Lafayette Street
Shelby
1910–11, 1928

A public meeting house—a simple white-painted weatherboarded building—was built at this site in 1846. The following year it became the home of Shelby's First Baptist congregation, officially organized in 1847. In 1889 the original meeting house was replaced by a grand Gothic Revival building of brick, but structural deficiencies soon prompted the congregation to consider building a replacement. Charlotte architects Wheeler & Stern were retained to design the present Gothic-inspired building, erected by Lexington contractor W. Lee Harbin in 1910–11. The George Hardy Payne studio of Paterson, New Jersey, made the stained glass windows and J. Gilmer Korner of Kernersville decorated the interiors. By 1928 the fast-growing congregation had outgrown the 1910–11 building, so architect Hugh White designed a large addition, which was built by Charlotte contractor J. A. Gardner & Co. and placed in use in 1929.

The result is one of the county's largest and most architecturally distinguished churches. The 1910–11 yellow brick section features three entry towers with octagonal-section spires, crenelated parapets, and ornate pinnacles. The southwest corner tower, the tallest, is graced by attenuated paired lancet-arched openings containing stained glass and belfry louvers. Between the towers are gabled projections with corbeling, pinnacles, and large stained glass windows with tracery; these projections and the towers have buttressed corners. The

First Baptist Church Shelby (JDP)

door and window openings have lancet arches with corbeled hoodmolds and fleur-de-lis ornaments at their points.

The 1928 extension along North Lafayette blends Gothic elements and modernism in a way that is reminiscent of skyscraper and hydroelectric dam design of the era. The chief feature of this extension, which enlarged the "auditorium" (worship space) of the original church and added educational facilities, was a cubist corner tower that rises to an octagonal louvered cupola. The extension increased the auditorium seating capacity to over a thousand. Added in 1953 were another educational wing and Webb Chapel, which was named in honor of the first pastor, the Reverend James Milton Webb (pastored 1847–49). The Gothic character of the 1910–11 church has been preserved through later additions, but the decorative painting of J. Gilmer Korner, which included frescoes of Christ at the well and trompe l'oeil columns and arabesques, has been lost.

1928 addition (JDP)

WEBBER-AUSTELL FARM

2800 Bettis Road (SR 2225)
Earl
1910s and later

Andrell and Eva Webber bought this frame Craftsman bungalow in the late 1910s and lived in it until they sold it to Bostick Austell in 1923. The house has a Craftsman front porch, an interior chimney, a large ell, and four-over-one and two-over-two windows. Behind the house Austell built an egg production plant with several one- and two-story frame chickenhouses. His business prospered because of his proximity to the railroad, and by the 1940s Austell was one of the largest producers of eggs in Cleveland County. Following Bostick's death, his son Tom Austell took over the business.

The two oldest chickenhouses, two stories in height, were purchased by Bostick in South Carolina and moved here in the 1920s. Two later metal-sided chickenhouses date to the 1950s. In the center of the complex are a ca. 1930 molded concrete block two-story washhouse and, nearby, a ca. 1930 egg packing house constructed of the same material. A small door at grade facilitated the transfer of eggs from the building to trucks. The complex includes a frame pumphouse and a grain storage compound installed by Tom Austell in the 1960s. Through the use of overhead pipes and storage bins, Tom created a highly efficient method of transporting feed to his chickenhouses.

Chickenhouse, below; egg packing house, above (BRE)

EL BETHEL UNITED METHODIST CHURCH

122 El Bethel Road (SR 2250)
Kings Mountain vicinity
1912

The El Bethel congregation was established in 1812 and built this Gothic Revival brick church exactly a century later. Two church buildings preceded it: a log chapel built in 1832, and a frame church in the late 1870s, constructed with lumber sawn by Preston Goforth. The present church has a steeply pitched roof with returns at the gable ends. The bell tower is capped by a metal pyramidal roof and has a corbeled parapet, lancet-arched louvered vents, and corner buttresses that rise above the parapet to form pinnacles. The main entry at the base of the tower is slightly recessed with a lancet-arched stained glass transom that bears the inscription "El Bethel Methodist Church." The main block features lancet-arched stained glass windows; these and the other openings have corbeled arches. A two-story education building and fellowship hall was added in 1960. Early-nineteenth-century gravestones in the adjacent cemetery exhibit exceptional artistry. Notable early graves include those of "Sumul" Collins (d. 1830, age 89), Samuel Collins (d. 1836, age 83), Elijah Spurlin (d. 1845, age 79), and Susanah Spurlin (d. 1845, age 72).

Elijah Spurlin tombstone, top; El Bethel United Methodist Church, bottom (BRE)

Featured Properties 139

FIRST BAPTIST CHURCH KINGS MOUNTAIN (FORMER)

101–103 West Mountain Street
Kings Mountain
1913–15

A portico with fluted Doric columns is the dominant feature of this Classical Revival brick church. Above is a triglyph frieze and a pediment with a plain tympanum, and under the portico is a center entry with a round-arched fanlight and a surround with fluted pilasters and a triglyph frieze. Behind the portico are a parapet and the hip roof of the church itself. The stained glass windows have either square or round-arched heads, and those on the second story cut into a broad white-painted frieze. The cruciform-plan church is raised on a high basement and reached by a flight of concrete steps with decorative metal handrails. To the west side is a one-story stone annex with a gable roof and a gabled projecting bay.

The congregation was organized in 1890, and in 1891–92 the first church was built on this site. The first service was held in the basement of this building while under construction in April 1914, and an education wing was added in 1950. The congregation moved to a new church building at West King and Sims Streets in 1960.

Former First Baptist Church Kings Mountain (JDP)

MOORESBORO COMMERCIAL DISTRICT

Mooresboro was named in 1884 after early resident Lem Moore, and the small western Cleveland County community benefited from the Southern and Seaboard rail lines, which skirted (respectively) the southern and northern edges of the village. Early industries included the tobacco factory of H. C. Burrus and Frank Bland and the pioneering Mooresboro Creamery, founded in 1909. Another industry was the Mooresboro Oil Mill, which consisted of a cotton gin and cottonseed oil production facility.

A prominent surviving historic commercial building is the Mooresboro Masonic Lodge, built in 1891 and vacated in 2001. The two-story brick building features corbeled segmental-arched doors and windows (most infilled with modern siding), a corbeled cornice, and brick quoins. Attached to it is a handsome one-story brick range of three stores, detailed similarly to the two-story section.

Mooresboro buildings (BRE)

G. L. HAMRICK & SON DAIRY FARM

Pleasant Ridge Church Road (SR 1161)
Boiling Springs vicinity
Ca. 1915

George L. Hamrick was one of the county's pioneering dairy farmers. In the early 1920s G. L. and his son Aubrey Yates Hamrick acquired a herd of Jersey cows and began supplying the Shelby area with fresh dairy products. At its height the dairy milked fifty cows. Yates Hamrick closed the operation in 1969 due to pressure from large dairy corporations and a lack of demand for local dairy products. He switched to raising beef cattle, the farm's present emphasis.

G. L. Hamrick's house, which was built for Landrum Hamrick about 1915, is a one-story frame dwelling with restrained Victorian and Craftsman details. The house has weatherboard siding, a hip roof with shingle-pattern pressed-metal sheathing, and a prominent pyramidal-roofed dormer. The house rests on a brick foundation, but there is evidence that stone piers once supported the structure. Some of the windows have been replaced over the years; consequently, there is a variety of sash arrangements, including six-over-one, four-over-four, and six-over-six. Near the house are a brick flowerhouse, a molded concrete block wellhouse, a frame crib, and a gable-fronted frame garage.

Across the road lie the remnants of the once-

G. L. Hamrick & Son Dairy Farm (BRE)

bustling Hamrick dairy farm. A brick pumphouse stands beside the road, and behind it is a gable-roofed frame building that served as the bottling house. Here workers washed and sterilized bottles before filling them with milk and cream. Behind the bottling house is the milking parlor, also a gabled frame structure. Two large barns provided shelter for the cows during the night and during inclement weather.

To the south of G. L. Hamrick's house is the home of his son, Aubrey Yates Hamrick, built in the early 1920s. The gable-fronted dwelling has Craftsman four-over-one and three-over-one windows. Near the house is a concrete block wellhouse, a frame and metal garage, a frame corncrib with a hinged hatchway just below the roofline to facilitate the loading and unloading of corn, and a frame and metal smokehouse. To the north and east of the G. L. Hamrick house stand three frame tenant houses associated with the dairy. The oldest of these, 121 Pleasant Ridge Church Road, was probably built in the late nineteenth century. It is a three-bay, two-room dwelling with a center chimney. The three-bay dwellings at 120 and 123 Pleasant Ridge Church Road are both typical early-twentieth-century examples of gable-fronted tenant houses.

Farmhouse, top; bottling house, bottom (BRE)

EAGLE ROLLER MILL

315 East Avenue
Shelby
1910s

The Eagle Roller Mill, located on the Seaboard line near that railroad's freight and passenger depots, was an important Shelby industry for much of the twentieth century. Two dates have been given for the construction of the facility, 1913 and 1916. George Blanton Sr. was president of the mill in the mid–twentieth century, when forty-seven employees worked here. The mill features a two- and three-story brick building that contained the "rolls" (steel rollers that ground the flour) and purifiers, separators, and other essential machinery; grain was fed to this machinery from a five-story concrete elevator. Exterior features include a gable roof with stepped end parapets, pier-reinforced walls, and six-over-six windows; at midcentury, the walls' painted signage depicted flour sacks. The mill produced flour and also ground cornmeal on a custom basis. Brands included Cleveland Bolted White Cornmeal and Carolina Made Superlative Enriched Flour. In recent years operations have focused on the manufacture of livestock feed. As this book went to press, the Eagle Roller Mill was being demolished.

Eagle Roller Mill (JDP)

PLATE 1: *Banker's House (Jesse Jenkins House), Shelby, circa 1875. Photo courtesy of Mrs. George Blanton, Jr.*

PLATE 2: *Burwell Blanton Farm, Shelby, circa 1875 (TJF)*

PLATE 3: *Calton-Martin House, Lattimore, 1899–1900. Photo by Libby Sarazen.*

PLATE 4: *Victor and Esther McBrayer House, Shelby, 1893 (TJF)*

PLATE 5, LEFT: *William and Nora Leicester House, Mooresboro, early 1930s (TJF)*

PLATE 6, ABOVE: *C. J. and Sarah Hamrick House, dormer detail, Boiling Springs, late 19th century (TJF)*

PLATE 7: *Joshua Beam House, Shelby vicinity, 1840s (TJF)*

PLATE 8: *Webbley (Governor O. Max Gardner House), Shelby, 1907 (19th century core). Photo courtesy of the Gardner family.*

PLATE 9: *Masonic Temple Building, Shelby, 1924–25 (TJF)*

PLATE 10: *Shelby City Hall (former), stained glass window detail, Shelby, 1911, 2002 (TJF)*

PLATE 11, LEFT: *St. Matthew's Lutheran Church, door and stained glass window detail,* Kings Mountain, 1953–54, 2000 (TJF)

PLATE 12, BELOW: *First Baptist Church* Shelby, 1910–11, 1928 (TJF)

PLATE 13: *William A. Mauney House, Kings Mountain, late 19th century (TJF)*

PLATE 14: *Stamey Farm, Fallston, 1929 (house remodeling) (TJF)*

PLATE 15: *Irvin–Hamrick House, Boiling Springs vicinity, circa 1794. Photo courtesy of Robert Jones.*

PLATE 16: *Lattimore House, Polkville vicinity, early 19th century (TJF)*

PLATE 17: *Hoyle-Stroup House stove tower, Waco, 1880s (TJF)*

PLATE 18: *Belvedere Park, Shelby (TJF)*

PLATE 19: *Margrace Mill Village, Kings Mountain, 1910s–1920s (TJF)*

PLATE 20: *Mooresboro Commercial Building, Mooreboro (TJF)*

PLATE 21: *Boggs Cotton Gin, Fallston, 20th century (TJF)*

PLATE 22: *Lawndale First Baptist Church (former), detail, Lawndale, 1948–49 (TJF)*

PLATE 23: *Sunset Cemetery, Shelby (TJF)*

PLATE 24: *Mount Harmony Methodist Church, Polkville vicinity, 1942 (TJF)*

PLATE 25: *King Street Overhead Bridge, Kings Mountain, 1938 (TJF)*

PLATE 26: *Metcalfe Station, Metcalfe, circa 1918 (TJF)*

PLATE 27: *Royster Building, Shelby, 1910 (TJF)*

PLATE 28, ABOVE: *Grover commercial district, Grover (TJF)*

PLATE 29, RIGHT: *Cleveland Mills, Lawndale, 1888 and later (TJF)*

PLATE 30:
Clifton and Alice Champion House, Mooresboro, 1885 (TJF)

PLATE 31: *Ramseur-Sarratt House, Earl vicinity, circa 1800 (TJF)*

PLATE 32: *Osborne-Carpenter House, Lawndale vicinity, 1885* (TJF)

PLATE 33: *Twin Chimneys (Smith-Suttle House), Shelby vicinity, early 19th century* (TJF)

PLATE 34: *Zion School, Metcalfe vicinity, circa 1860, 1906. Photo courtesy of Ronny Ivester.*

PLATE 35: *Waters Library at Piedmont School, Lawndale, 1910 and later (TJF)*

PLATE 36: *Mauney House, Kings Mountain, 1870s (TJF)*

PLATE 37: *El Nido detail, Shelby, 1920–21 (TJF)*

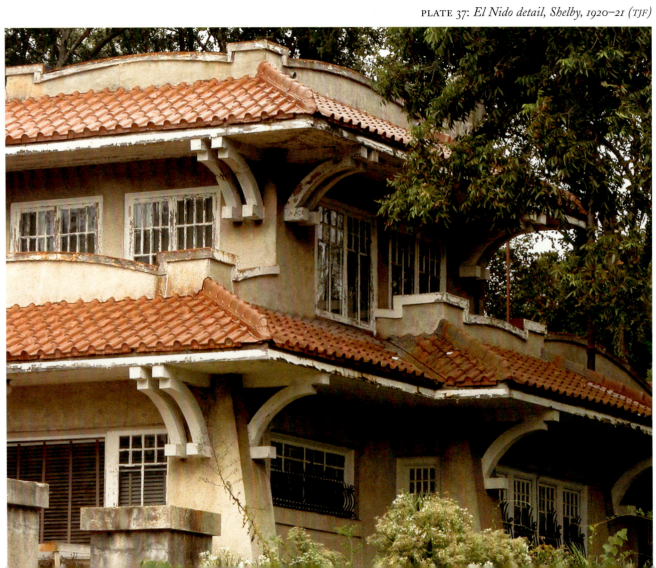

CLIFTON DAVIS FARM

Davis Road (SR 1107)
Earl vicinity
Ca. 1917

Clifton Davis (1883–1969) hired Lawson McSwain to build this house for $300. Davis was a cotton farmer and a member of Sharon Methodist Church. He built all the outbuildings on the farm and helped build Davis Road in the 1920s. The Davis farmhouse has a low hip roof with two interior chimneys. A gable with a louvered vent is centered above the front entry, and the front porch, supported on square columns, has a small gable perpendicular to the entry. The Victorian interior adheres to a center-passage plan and is three rooms deep, with a rear kitchen ell. The center passage is bisected by an archway. The walls are adorned with continuous picture molding, and an original chandelier hangs from the ceiling. The mantels have mirrored overmantels based on the post-and-lintel form.

A picket fence separates the backyard from two frame chickenhouses, a shed, and a game rooster pen. Beyond this stand a privy, a frame garage and corncrib, and two barns. One of these barns formerly served as the McBrayer School, an early-twentieth-century two-teacher facility that about 1946 was moved to its present location from the corner of Davis Road and NC 18. Across Davis Road stands a three-bay frame tenant house that was once associated with the Davis farm.

Clifton Davis House (BRE)

BURRUS MILL

Rockford Road (SR 1194)
Boiling Springs vicinity
1918

Roy Grady Burrus built this combination gristmill and cotton gin along the banks of Grog Creek. The gin catered to local farmers until 1948, when that aspect of the business was discontinued, a casualty of the regional decline in cotton production. The gristmill continued to serve the community until the mid-1950s. Across the road is a millpond that supplied water to the large waterwheel at the rear of the mill. Roy Grady Burrus Jr. recalls that the pond served as a popular gathering place. For many years, students from Gardner-Webb University and local residents would come to swim, bathe, and socialize.

The mill is a rectangular structure with a shed roof, a stone foundation, and two doors and a window in the north elevation. Of particular note are the survival of a well-preserved raceway and the waterwheel, complete with gears, pulleys, and some rubber belts. Stone piers of uncertain former function are placed at regular intervals along the path of the raceway. Between the mill and the present road is the site of the former cotton gin, indicated by a roughly rectangular pile of fieldstones.

Burrus Mill, left; wheel, top left; interior, above (BRE)

METCALFE STATION

2940 Polkville Road (NC 226)
Metcalfe
Ca. 1918

Metcalfe Station was established in 1899 as the midpoint of the Lawndale Railway. Railway roadmaster Quincy Hague Metcalfe (1876–1960) erected this one-story frame building to serve as a combination train station and Texaco service station. The one-room Craftsman-inspired building has an overhanging roof supported by rounded concrete columns made from culvert pipes. Beneath this decorative porch is a single central door flanked on each side by double-hung sash windows.

The Lawndale Railway & Industrial Company used narrow-gauge technology (outmoded by 1899) to connect Cleveland Mill & Power Company at Lawndale to other lines in Shelby. At the mill in Lawndale, a brick engine house torn down in 1961 featured two round-arched openings, 15 feet in height and with heavy wood doors, through which the line's two locomotives entered the building. In 1999, one hundred years after the first train ran on the Lawndale line, Metcalfe Station was acquired by the Lawndale Historical Society from Gene and Irma Metcalfe. The station has been made into a museum for the interpretation of railroad history. A wooden stave water tank now at Cleveland Mills and once associated with the railway at its Lawndale Junction near Shelby will, it is hoped, be moved to Metcalfe.

left: Hague Metcalfe, flanked by Nick Wells on the left and Tommy Hunt on the right, stands on Lawndale Railway & Industrial Company locomotive Number 5. Circa 1930 photo courtesy of Evelyn Metcalfe McCarver.

above: Metcalfe Station (TJF)

DOVER MILL

400 Polkville Road (NC 226)
Shelby vicinity
Ca. 1920 and later

John Randolph Dover, a leader in the emerging textile industry of the region, organized the Ella Manufacturing Co. in 1907. This company was sold in 1921, and in 1923 Dover and associates built the Dover Mill, adding Ora, Dora, and Esther later. Two of John Randolph Dover's sons, John R. Dover Jr. and Charles I. Dover, oversaw the company's expansion, led it through the Great Depression, and fostered its growth to prominence in the textile industry. At one time Dover Textiles was the largest employer in Cleveland County, employing more than 3,000.

The mill's original building features a concrete framework flanked by corner pavilions of brick with arched parapets, diamond-shaped brick and concrete parapet panels, and other Mission/Craftsman-influenced ornament. An expansion from more recent decades features a windowless tan brick block decorated by a gridlike pattern of projecting stretcher bricks. Of the mill village curving along Hawkins Street and Fanning Drive to the west of the mill, all that survives are several frame houses and garages and rows of mature street trees.

Exterior (JDP)

Dover Mill interior. Courtesy of the North Carolina Office of Archives and History.

GOVERNOR CLYDE R. HOEY HOUSE

602 West Marion Street
Shelby
1920

Clyde Roark Hoey (1877–1954) served as governor of North Carolina from 1937 to 1941. Hoey was one of the "Shelby Dynasty" by political inclination and by his marriage to Bess Gardner, the sister of former Governor O. Max Gardner. As governor Hoey presided over the improved economic picture of the late 1930s; his brother-in-law was not so fortunate, having served from 1929 to 1933, during the darkest years of the Great Depression. Hoey has the distinction of being the only North Carolina governor who also served as a U.S. Senator (from 1944 to 1954), a U.S. Representative, and in both houses of the state legislature.

The two-story stuccoed Hoey House shows the influence of several architectural currents of the era, including the Colonial Revival and Mission styles and the Foursquare house form. The front entry and flanking first-story windows have segmental-arched heads, and round arches define the openings of balanced one-story sunroom and sitting porch wings. Pergola-like surrounds front the two side wings and the center entry bay, and a spreading hip roof with hipped dormers caps the house. To the rear are a pergola, fountain, and fish pool. The house was renovated in 1954 by Mr. and Mrs. J. L. Suttle and is owned by their granddaughter, Millie Arey Wood, and her husband, Michael Thomas Wood.

Governor Clyde R. Hoey House (JDP)

EL NIDO

520 West Warren Street
Shelby
1920–21

Artist Maude Sams Gibbs, a native of the western North Carolina mountains, dreamed of living in California with its warm climate and Spanish heritage. Her husband Emmett W.'s medical practice took the couple instead to Cleveland County and eventually to Shelby, where Maude indulged her romantic vision. She received house plans from California architect and friend Aurelia Swanson and in 1920–21 built El Nido ("The Nest" in Spanish), one of the state's premier examples of Mission-style domestic architecture.

The rambling house, built by contractor Augustus Branton, was constructed with brick tile under a coat of stucco finished with pink granite gravel, a treatment known as rock dash. The roof of metal tiles mimics terra-cotta Spanish tiles and has deep eaves supported on heavy curved brackets. Across the front the brackets spring from thick battered (sloped) porch pillars. The house is principally one story high, but a smaller second story containing a master bedroom and Maude's studio is reminiscent of the "airplane bungalows" of the period. Windows with decorative sash, arched parapets, an attached garage reached through an arched porte cochere, and a yard planted with yucca and cactus complete the picture.

The open-plan interior is embellished with Spanish furnishings, painted canvas wall hangings, and a tiled fireplace with ornate shelf brackets. Of the house architectural historian Catherine Bishir writes: "El Nido epitomizes many ideals of its era: the nest as woman's domestic space; the feminine persona as artist in her own right; and the exotic aura of Spain coupled with the compelling American dream of California." Preservation North Carolina has a maintenance agreement with Ray Gibbs, the daughter of Maude Gibbs and the present owner, and has arranged to acquire the house in the future.

El Nido. Photo courtesy of the North Carolina Office of Archives and History.

WILLIAM AND MATTIE LINEBERGER HOUSE

804 Hawthorne Road
Shelby
Ca. 1922

This gracious house was the home of Mattie Flack Lineberger (b. 1886) and her husband William Mundy Lineberger (1886–1936), the developer of Belvedere Park, the subdivision in which the house stands. Lineberger was a businessman, a founder of the Cleveland Bank & Trust Company and the Cleveland Building & Loan Association. He had Belvedere Park laid out in 1921 and chose one of its largest lots as his homesite. His yellow brick house features a U-shaped plan under a hip roof with deep eaves. French doors open onto a balcony over the front porch, which stands on Doric columns and shelters a front entry with sidelights and a transom. A semicircular driveway connects to a basement-level garage. The house remained in Lineberger family ownership until 1960.

William and Mattie Lineberger House (JDP)

JOHN JR. AND EVELYN SCHENCK HOUSE

203 Morton Street
Shelby
1923

Gus Evans built this brick Foursquare-form house for John Franklin Schenck Jr. and his wife Evelyn Pyle Schenck in 1923. Delaware native Evelyn Schenck was a gifted concert violinist and Broadway actress who held performances throughout the country. Her husband John Schenck Jr. was prominent in the county's textile industry. After many successful years at Cleveland Mills in Lawndale, the Schenck family branched into Shelby's textile market in 1903. The Schencks bought a mill from a Mr. Morton and renamed it Lily Mill after John Schenck Sr.'s wife Lily Moore Schenck. The Lily Mill & Power Company operated the mill, and John Jr. and his brother Jean managed it.

The hip roof has a hipped dormer, and the front porch stands on Craftsman brick and wood supports. A hip-roofed porte cochere extends on the west side, and a brick stove tower—one of the last to be built in the county—rises to the rear. The tower has a pyramidal roof and narrow windows. Other elements of the residence include an enclosed porch, four interior chimneys, and nine-over-one windows.

John and Evelyn Schenck House, below; stove tower, above (BRE)

J. G. AND CARRIE HORD HOUSE

100 South Piedmont Avenue
Kings Mountain
Ca. 1923

This two-story Classical Revival house of yellow brick was built for Dr. Jacob George Van Buren Hord (1863–1930) and his second wife, Carrie Belle White Hord (d. 1940). Dr. Hord was active in Kings Mountain business and civic affairs, and he was one of the county's largest landholders in his day. In 1947 the property passed to the Mauney family, who donated it to the City of Kings Mountain. The three center bays of the symmetrical five-bay facade are sheltered by a portico with unadorned monumental columns (presumably replacements of the originals) and a large lunette with keyblock in the tympanum. The front entry has sidelights, an elliptical fanlight, and colonnettes in its surround; above it is a second-story entry that opens onto a narrow balcony. The hip roof is covered with Spanish tiles. A one-story porch on round Doric columns extends on the north side, balanced on the south by a sunroom with rectangular-section Doric pilasters. The nine-over-one first-story windows have jack arches with keystones; the six-over-one second-story windows abut the bottom of a frieze. The interior features paneled wainscots, a butler pantry, and a two-run stair with turned balusters. The house now serves as the Jacob S. Mauney Memorial Library, and it has a modern rear addition known as the Harris Children's Wing.

Harris Children's Wing of the Jacob S. Mauney Memorial Library (JDP)

J. G. and Carrie Hord House (JDP)

DORUS AND SARAH MAUNEY HOUSE

104 East Ridge Avenue
Kings Mountain
Early 20th century

This two-story brick house is one of Kings Mountain's more refined examples of the Colonial Revival style. The broad front facade features a slightly projecting gabled center section with flanking gabled wings. The center section has a front entry with decorative sidelights framed by a surround with a scrolled pediment and central urn. The window above is flanked by shallow elliptical recesses, and above this, in the gable, is a lunette with radial muntins. The large six-over-six windows have projecting keystones, and dentils and small modillions ornament the eaves. Behind the house, and possibly pre-dating it, is a carriage house.

The house was built for Dorris (Dorus) Carl Mauney (1881–1956) and his wife Sarah (Sadie) Elizabeth Fisher Mauney (ca. 1880–1952), who wed in 1904. Dorus Mauney and Larkin A. Kiser organized the Sadie Cotton Mills in 1918, and Mauney was also prominent in the Bonnie Cotton Mills (he served as its president), the Kings Mountain Manufacturing Company, and the Mauney Steel Company. Sadie Mauney was a charter member of the Kings Mountain Womans Club, and with Mrs. C. Q. Rhyne she organized the Thursday Afternoon Book Club, one of the city's oldest social clubs.

Dorus and Sarah Mauney House (JDP)

CENTRAL UNITED METHODIST CHURCH

200 East Marion Street
Shelby
1924

In 1845 Shelby's principal historic Methodist congregation occupied a one-room wooden building on the corner of Warren and South Dekalb. A new church of curious Gothic Revival–Italianate design was erected at Washington and Marion in 1884, opposite the northeast corner of the courthouse square. In 1924 the present Gothic Revival building was built to a design by Charlotte architect J. M. McMichael by Charlotte contractor John P. Little & Son. The building is distinguished by its construction of red, olive, and gray brick with light stone banding and trim. A bell tower with double entries at its base rises at the corner with gabled elements and smaller secondary entry towers to each side. The stained glass windows and transomed entries are contained in openings with shallow lancet arches. The similar belfry openings have perforated cinder block infill. A new education building was dedicated in 1968.

above: Central United Methodist Church (JDP)

left: Church under construction. 1924 photo by Forrest Ellis courtesy of Betty Rose Heath.

MASONIC TEMPLE BUILDING

203 South Washington Street
Shelby
1924–25

Shelby's Masonic Temple Building is western North Carolina's premiere example of Egyptian Revival architecture. Prominently located adjacent to the courthouse square, the four-story buff brick building was the tallest in Shelby at the time of its completion. In form the building is a simple rectangular block. The Egyptian theme is most evident at street level, where wide window openings—some of which formerly contained storefronts—are spanned by concrete lintels with bas-relief carvings of Sun Ra (winged sun disks with serpents). One bay is the main entry, with the lintel supported by stout pillars with lotus capitals.

Visually the first story serves as a base for the upper floors, which are vertically unified by three-story rectangular recesses containing windows and stuccoed spandrels. Rising in the recesses are slender piers with segmented block-on-string capitals. These piers call to mind details in buildings of Frank Lloyd Wright, such as his 1903 Larkin Building and 1906 Unity Church. At the top is a classical cornice with paterae.

The lobby has a tile floor emblazoned with the rule-and-divider symbol of the Masons (the lobby wallpaper uses the same motif) and offers access to Shelby's first electric passenger elevator. The lodge

Masonic Temple Building. All photos from 1981, courtesy of the North Carolina Office of Archives and History.

Lodge meeting room, above; front entry, right

meeting room on the fourth floor features a blue-and-white-checkered tile floor with a gold star at its center. Furnishings in this room and elsewhere in the upper two floors used by the Masons were specially designed for the building and are Mission in character.

The Cleveland Lodge of the Ancient, Free, and Accepted Masons of North Carolina was established in 1858. In the early 1920s the Lodge decided to build a permanent headquarters building that would also contain rental office and retail space (a later tenant was the Dixie-Home Supermarket). Clyde R. Hoey, a future governor of North Carolina (1937–41), served on the building committee. Charlotte architect Willard G. Rogers provided the design, and the Charlotte construction firm J. P. Little & Son erected the building. Other influential Lodge members have included O. Max Gardner (governor 1929–33), Baptist minister Thomas Dixon Sr., and Judge James L. Webb. The Masonic Temple Building was rehabilitated as Mason Square in the early 1980s. Inclusion of residential apartments on the upper two floors stimulated the growth of other residential spaces in Uptown Shelby.

Featured Properties 157

BELK-STEVENS BUILDING

221 South Lafayette Street
Shelby
1920s, late 1990s

A recent rehabilitation has uncovered the original light-colored brick facade of this two-story commercial block, also known as the Belk-Royster Building after the involvement of Dr. Stephen S. Royster in its construction. As depicted in a historic photograph, the building originally featured glass storefronts with stepped-back display windows, recessed entries, prism glass transoms, and striped canvas awnings. The facade above was ornamented with brick panels, stretcher lintels with concrete corner blocks, and a modest cornice. The Belk-Stevens Company department store occupied the building from the early years until 1982, when it moved to the Cleveland Mall. A late 1990s rehabilitation involved the removal of a 1950s metal facade and the insertion of metal-framed display windows and glass doors in the storefronts.

The rehabilitation, directed by Charlotte architects Ron Morgan and Michael O'Brien, received merit awards from the International Downtown Association and the Charlotte Section of the American Institute of Architects. The revitalized building now goes by the name Lafayette Place and includes residential apartments on the second floor.

Building in 2002 (JDP)

Belk-Stevens Building in the 1930s. Courtesy of Uptown Shelby Association.

GEORGE AND LULA SCRUGGS HOUSE (EARL SCRUGGS BIRTHPLACE)

1938 Maple Springs Church Road (SR 1147)
Boiling Springs/Flint Hill vicinity
Early 20th century

Situated amid the rolling pastureland of southwestern Cleveland County, this modest hip-roofed house was built for George Elam Scruggs (1876–1928) and Lula Scruggs. The house retains its original square plan, although two ells were added to the back in 1928. The recessed front porch stands on chamfered posts. Other features include two-over-two windows, interior brick chimneys, and exposed rafter ends. Near the house are a frame shed and a large transverse hay barn.

Earl Scruggs was born into the musically talented Scruggs family in 1924. During his youth, Earl mastered the three-finger banjo picking technique and became an accomplished fingerpicking guitarist. He played with the Morris Brothers and Lost John Miller and his Allied Kentuckians before joining Bill Monroe's Blue Grass Boys in 1945 and contributing to such definitive bluegrass recordings as "Summertime Is Past and Gone" and "Blue Moon of Kentucky." In 1948 Scruggs and fellow band member Lester Flatt formed the Foggy Mountain Boys and enjoyed two decades of popularity playing their brand of bluegrass, which they referred to as "Mountain Music." Best known to general audiences are the theme song and incidental music they recorded for the 1962 television series *The Beverly Hillbillies.* Another memorable Scruggs tune was "Foggy Mountain Breakdown," featured in the 1967 film *Bonnie and Clyde.* Flatt and Scruggs parted ways in 1969, and Scruggs formed the Earl Scruggs Review with his sons Gary and Randy. In 1985, Flatt and Scruggs were inducted into the Country Music Hall of Fame. Earl Scruggs has been described as "one of the most emulated instrumentalists in country music."

George and Lula Scruggs House (BRE)

CLEVELAND COUNTY FAIRGROUNDS

1751 East Marion Street
Shelby
1924 and later

The county fair dates its origins to 1923, when the Shelby Kiwanis Club convinced the Boiling Springs Community Fair Association and the Union Community Fair to merge. The county commissioners secured a 46-acre tract on the county home property east of town, and the Cleveland County Fair celebrated its grand opening on October 14, 1924. Harness horse racing, carnival rides, and agricultural and craft exhibits were among the attractions. The fair owed its early success to the dynamism of local veterinarian Dr. J. S. Dorton, manager from 1924 to 1961, who built the Cleveland County Fair into the state's largest county fair and went on to manage the North Carolina State Fair in Raleigh. African American performers played at the fair, but the black public was barred from admission during the era of segregation. Consequently, African American leaders organized a separate Cleveland County Negro Fair.

A 1920s stone-fronted grandstand with arched openings and a castellated parapet allowed spectators to view the harness races and, later, stock car races and stunt car events. The grandstand burned in 1951, but stonework from the same era dots the grounds. By the late 1940s a large cattle and horse barn had been erected; its octagonal center show ring was capped by a bell-like cupola and curvilinear parapets with projecting Art Deco piers. This building too is gone, re-

above, top: House moved to fairgrounds from Peeler property (JDP)

above, bottom: Present show barn (JDP)

left: Entrance on East Marion Street with the mill wheel in the background (JDP)

placed by a modern show barn with a Wild West false front. One of the few remnants from the early years is a ca. 1924 frame barn with a gabled roof and porch. Older, but not originally associated with the fair, is a log dwelling from the Peeler property near Casar, which features a rare log purlin roof. Near the entrance and the present grandstand is a large steel waterwheel that originally belonged to Peelers Mill in Casar. "Meet me at the waterwheel" is the standard reminder for meeting friends and family.

Racers in front of the 1920s grandstand. Circa 1936 photo courtesy of the North Carolina Office of Archives and History.

Cleveland County Fairgrounds in a circa 1970 aerial photograph. Courtesy of the Cleveland County Historical Museum.

ROARK-GRIER FARM

226 Mullinax Drive (SR 2237)
Grover vicinity
1924

The land that this farm occupies belonged to Lester Herndon in the early twentieth century. Herndon sold 118 acres to James Alex Roark (1882–1933) in the early 1920s, and in 1924 Roark built a one-story frame farmhouse where he resided with his wife Margaret Avalona Earle (1885–1971). The Roarks planted fruit trees and grape vines and erected a mule barn, a dairy barn, a corncrib, a smokehouse, a blacksmith shop, and a potato curing house. The Rev. Thomas L. Grier, who acquired the farm in 1936, raised sweet potatoes, peaches, and apples, produced milk that he sold to Carnation Dairy, and operated a gristmill.

The farmhouse, a Craftsman bungalow, has a recessed porch with exposed rafters and a shed dormer with two-over-two windows. An exterior gable-end chimney is inscribed "19 Roark 28." A semicircular arrangement of frame and concrete block outbuildings extends behind the house. They include a ca. 1930 concrete block machine shop, a frame privy, a ca. 1925 frame corncrib, and a ca. 1925 frame transverse stock barn. The 1930 frame sweet potato house was designed to maintain an inside temperature of at least 40 degrees Fahrenheit year-round. A fire would be maintained within the outbuilding throughout the winter to keep the sweet potatoes from freezing. During the Great Depression the Roarks traveled to mill villages in South and North Carolina selling sweet potatoes for twenty-five cents a peck.

Roark-Grier House, above; transverse stock barn, top right; sweet potato house, bottom right (all BRE)

WHITE HOUSE

310 Camp Highway (US 29)
Grover
1925

The White family built this stylish Craftsman bungalow, which has the date "May 16, 1925" cast in concrete in the porte cochere. The wraparound porch stands on paired square-section posts on brick pedestals and shelters a three-sided bay window. Other features include an enclosed side porch, a back porch, a rear hipped dormer, and a variety of double-hung sash and casement windows. The interior has a Craftsman mantel in the main parlor, panel and pocket doors, and a stair with a square newel and balusters. A brick flowerhouse stands near the house, and beyond it is a cotton barn where the Whites stored cotton bales before taking them to a nearby gin. There are also concrete block and board-and-batten sheds and a frame stock barn.

White House, left; mantel, above top; flowerhouse, above bottom (all BRE)

CASAR COMMERCIAL DISTRICT

The village of Casar—dramatically sited, with views of the South Mountains to the north—served as a trade and commerce center for the sparsely populated north end of the county. This collection of early-twentieth-century commercial buildings is representative of the community's former livelihood. An early store in the village, now gone, was the A. A. Warlick & Co. general store, a large frame building with decorative wood-shingle sheathing in its three-part false front and side shed rooms for bulk storage. Costner's Furniture No. 2 Building, located at 5786 Casar Road, was built by brick mason Otis Wall. The front-gable building was occupied by the Warlick general store for many years and now serves as a furniture shop. Pruett's Grocery, built about 1930, features a center entry flanked by display windows. An angled entry facade gives the Casar Post Office an unusual appearance. The brick building features stepped side parapets and contains a Masonic meeting hall.

left: Casar Cash Grocery. *1940 photo courtesy of the Cleveland County Historical Museum.*

below: Casar Post Office (BRE)

164 Architectural Perspectives of Cleveland County

CASAR HIGH SCHOOL

436 School House Road (SR 1518)
Casar
1925

Casar High School opened in 1925–26, and the first class graduated in 1928. At first only the first through seventh grades were taught by the principal, Tom Green, and teacher Una Dean Allison. Electricity was installed in the school during the original construction, but bathrooms and running water were not added until later.

Casar High School has a corridor plan with classrooms connected by a single hallway. The gabled Colonial Revival building has arched passageways and doorways, multilight transoms, and a symmetrical facade with a recessed main entry flanked by evenly spaced rows of windows. A brick gymnasium with a bowstring roof was added in 1949–50, and a large 1970s brick addition extends to the rear. Behind the school is a field used for recess and extracurricular activities.

Casar High School rear view, above; front view, below (BRE)

Featured Properties 165

BAXTER AND IDA PUTNAM FARM

1712 South Lafayette Street
Shelby
1926

Built by Lee Lowman for Baxter Cleveland Putnam (1885–1955) and Ida Hamrick Putnam (1883–1965), this two-story house stood on a large cotton farm. Baxter, a disabled World War I veteran, arranged with three tenant families to work his farm. He also operated a blacksmith shop where he shoed horses and mended tools. The Putnam House has a wraparound porch supported by brick pillars. Extensions to the house include a sun parlor, a porch room, and a small ell. Notable interior features include wood and brick mantels and panel doors.

Behind the house stands a frame outbuilding that served a number of functions. It contained a two-car garage, a small section where Ida raised chickens, and Baxter's blacksmith shop. A brick flowerhouse that also served as a pumphouse stands near the house, and there are two frame chickenhouses, one gable-fronted, the other with a shed roof. Beyond these structures is the one remaining tenant house.

Baxter and Ida Putnam House, bottom; tenant house, top left; fireplace, top right (all BRE)

BELWOOD SCHOOL TEACHERAGE

145 Carpenters Grove Church Road (SR 1614)
Belwood
Ca. 1926

Originally built as a residence for teachers who taught at the adjacent Belwood School, this brick-veneer bungalow now serves as a town office and senior center for the citizens of Belwood. The facade features a recessed porch supported by brick columns under a central dormer. One-over-one double-hung sash windows pierce each elevation. A small shed is attached to the rear. The Belwood School, built in 1926 by contractor J. H. Brackett, was a fourteen-room facility that served the community until 1960. A gymnasium was added in 1935, additional classrooms were built in the late 1930s, a new gymnasium and agriculture rooms were built in 1950, and a lunchroom was added in the early 1950s. The facility was then made into a junior high school, and the name was changed to North Cleveland. After the 1975–76 school term, the school closed, and students now go to Burns Middle School. Although the 1926 section of the building was demolished in 1979, the later sections are used by the community for meetings and social engagements.

Belwood School Teacherage (BRE)

DOCKERY'S FUNERAL HOME

605 Buffalo Street
Shelby
1920s, 1953

In 1931 Carl James Dockery had just graduated from embalming school in Nashville, Tennessee, and was on his way to look for business opportunities in Charlotte when he stopped in Shelby. The African American community needed an undertaker, and Dockery and his wife Alma Dwin Dockery were asked to stay. Dockery's Funeral Home opened at the corner of Buffalo and Frederick Streets in November 1931. "This was the heart of the Depression," Dockery later recalled. "I thought I had made a mistake in judgment—no one had the money to pay for services." By way of a solution, Dockery organized Dockery's Mutual Burial Association, an insurance plan that assured members a proper burial. Membership grew to 16,000 individuals by the early 1940s.

The second funeral home was a converted frame dwelling that stood behind the present building. Dockery acquired Ellison Cromer's dry-cleaning establishment at 605 Buffalo, a brick building with a stepped front parapet, for his third location, and he later attached the second building to the rear gable end of the third building. Carl Dockery was originally

Clock (JDP)

trained as a brick mason—his father and grandfather had been prominent brick makers and contractors in eastern Tennessee—and in 1953 he added a new segmental-arched brick parapet to the front of the funeral home with help from his father, Charlie Dockery.

The clock on the corner of Dockery's Funeral Home is its best-known feature. In the 1953 parapet is a granite date block and a triangular louvered vent, and on the south side are a 1953 glass block window and a porch with a decorative brick pillar. The front office has a 1953 terrazzo floor with the name "Dockery" in gold letters. A white enamel embalming table, once used by county coroner Robert Lutz, is still in use in the back. Carl Dockery's son Carl Jr. gradually took the helm of the business, and father and son planned a new facility about 1980, but instead Dockery's Funeral Home continues in its original location.

Dockery's Funeral Home (JDP)

COMPACT SCHOOL

152 Dixon School Road (SR 2283)
Kings Mountain vicinity
Late 1920s

Compact School has its origins in 1872, when twelve men joined together to establish a school for their children. Peter Forney donated land for the school, and Hill Culp was hired as the teacher. The twelve founding fathers formed a compact (hence the school's name) to contribute two and a half bushels of wheat or two dollars and fifty cents a month for Mr. Culp's salary. In 1924–25 Compact School received support from the Rosenwald Fund to build a three-teacher school building. Compact received state accreditation in 1940, when L. L. Adams was principal. The school closed about 1965, and from 1966 through 1969 it served as the Early Childhood Education Center. Today the facility is the home of Barrett's Salvage and Floor Covering. The original nineteenth-century buildings are now gone, but the remaining early- and mid-twentieth-century structures testify to the im-

portant role this facility played in the education of the local black population.

The earliest surviving building associated with this property is the agricultural building, which probably dates to the late 1920s. The large corridor-plan school is the second oldest building on the property and dates to 1955. The gymnasium was completed in 1958, the workshop/office in 1959–60. A dining area connects the educational area to the gymnasium. All of the buildings have stretcher-bond brick exteriors.

left: Compact School students. Circa 1940 photo courtesy of the Cleveland County Historical Museum.

above: 1958 gymnasium (BRE)

Featured Properties 169

GARDNER-WEBB UNIVERSITY

110 South Main Street
Boiling Springs
1920s and later

Gardner-Webb University was founded in 1905 as the private Boiling Springs High School with support from the Kings Mountain Baptist Association and Sandy Run Baptist Association. The high school opened in 1907 with 135 students, a number that grew to 335 by 1920. An early alumnus was Wilbur Joseph Cash (1900–1941), who went on to write a famous critique of southern society, *The Mind of the South* (1941). Increased enrollment created a need for expanded facilities, and in 1919 fund-raising began for an all-purpose building that would double as a memorial to World War I servicemen. The E. B. Hamrick Hall, completed in 1925 and named after a local businessman and benefactor, is a two- and three-story brick building that was substantially renovated in 1943 after a 1937 fire. The architect for the renovation was John McCulloch of McCulloch-English Associates of Charlotte, and the contractor was David White of A. White & Sons Construction of Shelby. The building's dominant feature is a portico-like front formed by monumental Ionic pilasters supporting a pediment with a dentil cornice and the building's name in the frieze. Between the pilasters are three French doors with tall rectangular transoms and, above them, windows with round-arched fanlights. This front section, reached by a flight of steps, projects from the front elevation of the hip-roofed building, which has a longer rear projection that gives the building an overall cruciform plan. Student Junius McAllister served as foreman for the renovation. Hamrick Hall suffered a small fire in the upper story in 1990, and it was remodeled in recent years.

Competition from the public schools prompted the reorganization of the high school as a junior college in 1928, and the depression of the 1930s nearly closed the fledgling institution. The school rebounded in the 1940s and was renamed Gardner-Webb in 1942 and accredited by the Southern Association of Colleges and Schools in 1948. Student enrollment rose from 164 in 1943 to 420 in 1946, and the college inaugurated an ambitious construction program. The Shelby-based Webber & Sons Construction worked on the campus during this period. One product of the postwar expansion is the 1947 President's House, a two-story Colonial Revival residence of brick with Doric columns and a cast-iron balustrade on the front porch, a circular front window, and brick wings, including an attached garage on

E. B. Hamrick Hall. 1980 photo by Michael T. Southern courtesy of the North Carolina Office of Archives and History.

the west elevation. The building now houses the campus radio station, WGWG.

The postwar expansion was expressed by brick construction in the prevailing Colonial Revival style. The Boiling Springs Springhouse dates from this period. The spring itself, which formerly spurted out of the ground, gave its name to the community and the school. The water flow is less vigorous today owing to an unsuccessful 1940s attempt to increase the flow by blasting the spring with dynamite. Older residents of the area know the spring by another name, Church Spring, for its association with an early church known as Woods Meeting House that stood nearby.

In recent years Gardner-Webb absorbed the public

Aerial view of Gardner-Webb University, top; Boiling Springs Springhouse, bottom. Both courtesy of Gardner-Webb University Archives.

Featured Properties 171

Boiling Springs High School (former) (BRE)

Boiling Springs School into its campus. The original building in the complex, a four-room elementary school with large classroom windows and a hip roof, dates to 1923. In 1938 a Colonial Revival high school was constructed. This larger hip-roofed building has a pedimented front with quoins and a circular medallion. In later years the school served only grades one through six, and in 1993 it closed. The complex now provides office and storage space to the university (Gardner-Webb added graduate programs in 1993) and to the town of Boiling Springs.

CHARLES AND EFFIE HARRY HOUSE

106 Spruce Street
Grover
1926–27

Charles Franklin Harry Sr. (1885–1952) and his wife Effie Jeanette Holmes Harry (d. 1958) had this Colonial Revival Foursquare-form house built of red and olive-colored brick in 1926–27. The front entry is sheltered by a pedimented stoop with a vaulted ceiling, and it has a Colonial Revival surround with sidelights and an elliptical fanlight. A porte cochere on the east elevation is balanced by a porch on the west elevation. A rear walkway leads to Minette Mills, founded by Harry in 1919. The stylish interior includes ample closets and bathrooms.

Charles and Effie Harry House, below; Minette Mills water tower, right (BRE)

Featured Properties 173

KINGS MOUNTAIN COMMERCIAL DISTRICT

Kings Mountain's commercial core is located on both sides of the Southern Railway line as it passes through the center of town. The Kings Mountain community has its origins in the village of White Plains, which was located two miles to the west. Kings Mountain was incorporated in 1874 and owes its existence to the railroad. A fire ravaged the downtown area in 1890, so most of the buildings date to the early twentieth century. The two-story Plonk Building features a recessed entrance in a Carrara glass storefront. Several other two-story buildings feature recessed entrances. Metal and Permastone facades were added to a number of buildings in the second half of the twentieth century.

top: Corner of Mountain and Railroad streets about 1900. Courtesy of the North Carolina Office of Archives and History.

middle: Battleground Avenue in 1953. Courtesy of the North Carolina Office of Archives and History.

bottom: Battleground Avenue, Kings Mountain (JDP)

SHILOH PRESBYTERIAN CHURCH

307 Cleveland Avenue (NC 226)
Grover
1926–30

The Shiloh Presbyterian congregation may have formed as early as the late eighteenth century. A log church was constructed in the 1820s, and a successor in the early 1880s was built by contractor David F. C. Harry, who also supplied the seats. The present Classical Revival building, dedicated in 1930, is the congregation's fifth. The church has a portico on monumental Doric columns and a low-pitched pediment with a brick tympanum. Boldly projecting cornices with modillion-like elements define the edges of the pediment and wrap around to the sides of the nave. Large round-arched stained glass windows with stone or cast stone keystones and imposts are on the side elevations. Textured red brick laid in stretcher bond, a double-leaf entry with a transom and pedimented surround, and a two-story rear education wing are other exterior features. The sanctuary was renovated in 1968. A cornerstone gives the dates "1780–1925."

Shiloh Presbyterian Church (JDP)

GEORGE AND MARY JANE SPERLING FARM

1219 Fallston Road
Shelby
1927

The impressive Classical Revival home of George Elzie Sperling (1871–1953) and his wife Mary Jane Justice Sperling (1878–1977) was built on the site of an earlier Sperling residence. George Sperling, a graduate of Teacher Training School, taught school for seven years in Cleveland County. He married Mary Jane in 1899, and the couple initially lived in the one-story frame house that stood across Fallston Road from this house. Not satisfied with the teaching life, Sperling concentrated on farming and other business ventures. His cotton farm eventually included a general store, cotton gin, gristmill, blacksmith shop, and sawmill. Sperling amassed a fortune by investing in the cotton futures market after World War I and in the NuWay Spinning Company, located in Cherryville. A civic-minded individual, Sperling was also a member of Ross Grove Baptist Church and one of the founders and directors of the Cleveland County Fair.

The two-story brick house, built by contractor Augustus Branton, has a five-bay facade with a portico on fluted Ionic columns. The front entry has a fanlight and sidelights. A widow's walk with a concrete railing tops the roof, and a single-car garage extends off the north elevation. In keeping with symmetrical appearance, a sunporch extends off the south elevation. Interior features include paneled mantels, crown moldings accented with dentilwork, built-in cabinets, and a servant's staircase. The basement contained servants quarters.

Much of the 1920s farm complex remains in excellent condition. Behind the house are a molded concrete block generator house, a frame smokehouse with vertical slatted vents, and a two-story frame granary. South of the granary are a concrete block tackhouse and accompanying horse trough. The Sperlings usually kept two to three horses as well as mules. Other buildings include a frame wood house, a frame hog pen with a concrete floor, a frame crib, and an impressive transverse mule barn.

left: George and Mary Jane Sperling House (TJF)

above: Outbuildings (left to right): granary, smokehouse, and generator house. Photo by Sybil A. Bowers.

EDWARDS HOUSE AND CLINIC

6439 Fallston Road (NC 18)
Belwood vicinity
1927

Dr. Forrest Edwards (1885–1964) was one of the area's few licensed general practitioners in the early twentieth century; consequently his circuit embraced Lincoln, Catawba, Burke, and Cleveland Counties. He also operated a maternity clinic next to his house where many older Belwood residents were born. The doctor's wife, Hattie Ola Bingham Edwards (1890–1973), aided her husband in the clinic and raised a family at the house.

The rough-cut stone-veneer Edwards House dates to 1927, the same year the front four rooms of the adjacent clinic were built. Both the house and clinic have low-hipped terra-cotta tile roofs. The house has a prominent stone arch that defines the main entrance. The small shed dormer on the roof has casement windows, and a small three-sided bay window with six-over-six sash extends from the north elevation. The clinic features a central recessed front door flanked by windows and a large rear addition of stone construction. Behind are the remnants of a stone garage and a gabled storage building that doubled as a maid's residence. As with many of the area's stone-faced houses, the rock used in the construction of the Edwards House came from Acre Rock. The large stone outcrop was located approximately half a mile away and was quarried extensively in the early and middle decades of the twentieth century. Albert Bleynat, an accomplished stonemason from Valdese, executed the home's stonework.

Edwards House, left (TJF); porte cochere, above (BRE)

STAMEY BROTHERS STORE

4726 Fallston Road (NC 18)
Fallston
1927

Founded in 1890 by Tom and Clarence Stamey, Stamey's Store was a thriving enterprise that served the residents of upper Cleveland County for over one hundred years before it finally closed in 1994. Thirty-seven years after the Stameys opened this business with $5,000 in capital, they decided to build the present building. Constructed in 1927, this two-part brick commercial building features plate glass storefront windows in aluminum frames and two recessed entries. Above this are the inscription "Stamey Stores Inc." and three sets of four-over-two windows on the second story. The Stamey Stores slogan was "Everything from the cradle to the grave." Before 1947 this was the literal truth, as the Stameys operated a mortuary on the top floor. The store stocked items as diverse as garden seeds and cosmetics. Competition from supermarkets and discount stores eventually forced Stamey's out of business.

right: Stamey Brothers Store (BRE)

above: A period advertisement

STAMEY FARM

815 East Stagecoach Trail (NC 182)
Fallston
1929 (house remodeling)

Thomas Stamey, one of the founders of Stamey's Store, had this house built. His children remodeled the house in the Colonial Revival style in 1929, shortly after Thomas's death. The two-story frame house is graced by a two-story portico on Doric columns with a Chinese Chippendale balustrade. Six double-leaf doors open onto the portico. To the rear are several additions. Inside, the formal living room boasts fluted pilasters on the walls. The stairway features scrolled tread brackets and turned balusters, and the library has built-in shelves. Original mantels follow the post-and-lintel format. A two-car garage stands at the end of the house, and a frame transverse barn and a small corncrib and shed are located behind. East of the house is a wellhouse attached to another frame outbuilding that may have served as servants quarters.

Stamey House, top right; barn, middle right; wellhouse and possible servants quarters, lower right

Stair hall, above (all BRE)

Featured Properties 179

JOHN MCBRAYER BARN

238 McBrayer Homestead Road (SR 1162)
Boiling Springs vicinity
1928

Local contractor A. A. Ramsey built this barn for John Albert McBrayer (1876–1941) in 1928. McBrayer was a farmer and successful mule trader who acquired mules in Tennessee and drove them over the mountains to Cleveland County, where he sold them to area cotton farmers. The frame transverse barn's gambrel roof has exposed rafter ends, and its windows open into the mule stalls within. Inside, an ingenious mule-powered pulley system facilitated the storing and removal of hay from the loft above the stalls. Nearby are a frame farm office and a creekside springhouse, both dating to 1928.

John McBrayer Barn, below; barn and farm office, above (BRE)

BETHLEHEM BAPTIST CHURCH

476 El Bethel Road (SR 2250)
Kings Mountain vicinity
1928–29

Organized in 1842, Bethlehem Baptist Church has served its congregation for over 150 years. The first church building was a small log chapel located approximately one mile southeast of the present site. In 1871 the congregation completed a new building between the cemetery and the present location at a cost of $300. In the late 1920s the congregation raised funds for a new church by selling cotton, chickens, quilts, and aprons. Construction of the present Colonial Revival brick church began in 1928 and was completed in 1929 (possibly with work continuing into the early 1930s). A major renovation took place in 1960.

The facade is dominated by a full-height portico with a wide cornice above four brick columns. The double-leaf paneled door is flanked by fluted engaged columns and surmounted by a denticulated pediment. Another Colonial Revival element is the half-elliptical window centered in the facade's gable end. The sanctuary boasts handsome stained glass windows and paneling.

Bethlehem Baptist Church (BRE)

VAUXHALL

1215 East Marion Street
Shelby
Late 1920s

Built for John Dixon Lineberger Jr. and Nannie Belle Sherrill Lineberger between 1925 and 1929, Vauxhall is a classic example of Tudor Revival architecture. To capitalize further upon the English theme, the Linebergers named their stately manor Vauxhall after the famous Vauxhall Gardens in London. John Dixon Lineberger Jr. was a part owner of Lineberger Brothers, a profitable commercial venture. In addition, he owned large real estate holdings throughout Shelby. Lineberger was also directly associated with the S & W Cafeteria chain, which his wife's family was instrumental in establishing.

Although much of the original structure has been altered through numerous additions, the facade remains largely intact. Tudor Revival features evident on the facade include half-timbering over the pedimented entry, a single dormer on the side-gable roof, groupings of casement lights, and battlements. The east and west bays feature pointed arches, and the central door is also adorned with a pointed arch. Half-timbering is evident on the three remaining elevations. Vauxhall features three chimneys, consisting of a single exterior end chimney on the east elevation and two exterior rear chimneys. A large incompatible one-story modern block and brick addition extends to the rear of the house, and another addition is being attached to this intrusive element. The first floor features a series of rooms concentrated around a central hall. A stairway adorned with metal rails leads to the second floor, which has been remodeled several times over the years. Original features that survive on the first floor include passages adorned with pointed arches, paneled mantels, and paneled doors. In later years Vauxhall served the community in many capacities, including use as the Elks Club. Currently it is serving as a restaurant.

Vauxhall (BRE)

FRANK AND BONNIE SUMMERS HOUSE

1220 North Piedmont Avenue
Kings Mountain
1928

Frank Rickert Summers (1893–1958) and his wife Bonnie E. Mauney Summers (1897–1976) had this two-story brick Tudor Revival house built on land that formerly belonged to W. A. Mauney. Bonnie designed the house, and it was built to her specifications. In addition to her talent as a designer, Bonnie was a local historian and the author of *Kings Mountain: Her Background and Beginning, 1780–1920*. Frank, a native of Statesville and a World War I veteran, owned and operated Summers Drug Store on Battleground Avenue. He also served as president of First National Bank at the corner of Mountain Street and Battleground Avenue.

With its false half-timbering, multiple steeply pitched gables, and prominent fieldstone chimney, the Summers House is one of the finest examples of Tudor Revival architecture in Cleveland County. As was common for the style, the chimney is positioned near the front entry, sheltered under a flared extension of the main roof. There are a number of decorative touches, including a wood porch railing with trefoil cutouts, wooden corbel brackets, and a clipped gable.

A long hallway on the first floor leads to a living room, dining room, and kitchen. Original hardwood floors, heavy oak doors, casement windows, and a stone mantel with Tudor-arched opening are among the decorative features on the interior. An unaltered stairway leads to the second floor, which contains three bedrooms and a bath. A smaller staircase ascends to the attic's two large storage rooms. Although slightly modified, the basement of the Summers house still has a maid's bedroom, a ca. 1940 playroom, a two-car garage, and an old coal furnace ensconced in the boiler room.

Frank and Bonnie Summers House (BRE)

CARL AND ELVA THOMPSON HOUSE

106 Cherryville Road
Shelby
1929

Built for Carl (1882–1952) and Elva Thompson (1888–1973) by contractor R. L. Lowman, this two-story Colonial Revival house has many refinements. Carl Thompson owned Thompson Lumber Company in Shelby, and he provided Lowman with superior materials for the construction of the house. Thompson hired a landscape architect to lay out a formal garden and to construct a teahouse at the edge of the parcel. This garden now consists of a brick-paved walk that meanders around various plant and flower beds. At one time, there was a lake just northeast of the garden, but this has been filled. Thompson situated his house so that family and friends could sit out on the front porch (not visible from Cherryville Road) in the late afternoon and not have to contend with the sun's rays. Northeast of the house is a ca. 1950 frame smokehouse.

The principal facade, which faces east, features a two-story porch supported by fluted Corinthian columns. Continuous dentilwork runs under the eaves of the gable roof, which supports three dormers. The south elevation features an enclosed porch room topped with a balustrade and balanced on the north elevation by a kitchen. The west elevation, the one visible from the road, has a gable with lunette opening and a porte cochere on fluted columns. The house now serves as the Cecil M. Burton Funeral Home, and the present owners have added a curved enclosed hyphen to connect the original house to a funeral chapel.

Carl and Elva Thompson House and Cecil M. Burton Funeral Home chapel (JDP)

SHELBY WATERWORKS

801 West Grover Street
Shelby
1929, 1953

This large complex occupies both sides of Grover Street on the high ground above the First Broad River. The 1929 waterworks stands on the north side of the street: a brick and concrete building with a geometric glazed terra-cotta cornice and industrial-type metal windows. Concrete steps flanked by paneled concrete piers that formerly supported light fixtures descend to the building's classical concrete entry. The 1953 and later waterworks stands across the street. The modernistic brick building has a two-story center block distinguished by a tall entry recess with curved pebbledash concrete walls and glass and aluminum windows and doors. One-story wings with ribbon windows extend to the sides, and glazed floor tiles and tile block give the interior a shiny hygienic quality. The Charlotte engineering and architectural firm of J. N. Pease designed the original 1953 section and the 1959 east wing, which are similar to water plants Pease designed for communities across the state. The machinery was manufactured by the Roberts Filter Manufacturing Company of Darby, Pennsylvania. A bulbous water tank with a globe finial looms over the complex.

above: 1929 building (JDP)

left: 1953 building. Courtesy of the City of Shelby.

SHELBY SOUTHERN RAILWAY FREIGHT DEPOT

310 Market Street
Shelby
1929

This Colonial Revival freight depot of stretcher-bond brick construction has a parapeted gable roof with metal roof tiles and brickwork of variegated color. The main entrance has a transom and sidelights and is flanked by paired nine-over-one windows. Other exterior features include a circular louvered vent, roll-up freight doors, and a loading dock. The interior boasts an exposed steel-truss roof, original light fixtures, and wood floors. The building is currently occupied by the Shelby Farm and Garden Supply Store. The passenger depot and water tanks (which no longer stand) were located just north of the freight depot.

above: Former Shelby Southern Railway Depot about 1900. Courtesy of the North Carolina Office of Archives and History.

below: Shelby Southern Railway Freight Depot (BRE)

ROBERT AND ALMA HUNT HOUSE

340 West Lee Street (SR 1161)
Lattimore
1932

Dr. Robert Lee Hunt (1885–1957), a 1910 graduate of Atlanta Dental College, served Lattimore as a dentist until he decided to pursue other endeavors. He began trading livestock, buying horses from Tennessee, pigs from Georgia, and cattle from throughout the Southeast. Hunt shipped the animals by rail to Lattimore and sold them to farmers throughout upper Cleveland County. Hunt was also active in Lattimore business and civic affairs, serving two terms as mayor, and he was apparently involved in building spec houses in the town. Hunt married Alma Harrill (b. 1888) in 1911.

By 1932 Hunt was successful enough in his new calling to hire carpenter Grady Brooks to build him a two-story frame Foursquare-form house. Brooks was well regarded as a carpenter in the area; another example of his work is nearby Lattimore Baptist Church, built in 1949. The Hunt house features a low hip roof, eight-over-one windows, and two interior chimneys. Despite its Foursquare form, the house has a center passage flanked by four rooms. A small enclosed porch with an added attached garage extends to the rear. Nearby stands the original garage, which has a pyramidal roof.

Robert and Alma Hunt House and interior (BRE)

J. W. AND MITTIE BORDERS HOUSE

2008 Stony Point Road (SR 1001)
Waco vicinity
1932

J. W. Borders (1907–93), his four brothers (Miles, Calb, Mills, and Filet), and G. B. and Bable Borders all contributed their time and energy to the construction of this house in 1932. J. W., who farmed cotton and taught school in Cleveland, Gaston, and Rutherford Counties, lived here with his wife Mittie, a first-grade teacher at Washington School.

The one-story frame Craftsman bungalow features a stone front porch and stone interior and exterior end chimneys. One chimney is engraved with the date "1932" within a surround of pebbles forming the letter B. Ornate brackets support the overhanging eaves. Groups of six-over-one and eight-over-one double-hung sash windows ornament the elevations. The interior features two unaltered mantels that share fluted pilasters, dentilwork, and a centerpiece featuring a star and crescent motif. This craftsmanship is attributed to Filet Borders, who designed the house and carved the mantels. A concrete block and frame corncrib and a concrete block garage/shed stand near the house.

J. W. and Mittie Borders House, bottom; mantel detail, top (BRE)

DIXON SCHOOL

603 Dixon School Road (SR 2286)
Kings Mountain vicinity
1933

W. Gordon Hughes built the Dixon School in 1933 with the aid of volunteer labor. The one-story stretcher-bond brick building served the community as a seven-year elementary school until the 1951–52 school year, when it closed and the students were transferred to Grover School. Marion Jackson bought the school at public auction in 1952 and converted it into a residence. After Jackson remodeled the interior, he sold the building to Delbert and Lilly Jackson. The Jacksons lived here until 1993, when Dixon Presbyterian Church, located across the road, bought the former school and rehabilitated it as a fellowship hall.

A small stoop with a pyramidal roof is centered on the facade, and another stoop shelters an entry on the northeast elevation. The building has a low hip roof, interior chimneys, and two banks of relatively unaltered five six-over-six windows. A portion of an original sign reading "Dixon" survives. Originally the school had a center-corridor plan with a classroom on each side and a large auditorium with a stage. The stage survives and has recently been used for church Christmas plays.

Dixon School (BRE)

CENTRAL HIGH SCHOOL

105 East Ridge Avenue
Kings Mountain
1933, 1938

Kings Mountain Military School, also known as Captain Bell's Boys School, was established in 1876 and originally occupied a two-story frame building with an appropriately militaristic tower. Captain Bell also operated schools in Shelby and in Rutherford County. Bell's Kings Mountain school evolved into a public high school, and in 1910 new facilities were constructed. The 1910 building featured a portico on monumental Ionic columns, a modillion cornice, and a monitor roof with crestings along its edge. It burned in November 1932 and was replaced by the present two-story brick school. The Colonial Revival school features projecting center and end pavilions. The pedimented center pavilion has an oval window in the tympanum and an entry under a large round-arched fanlight. The end pavilions have windowless front elevations adorned with soldier-course brick bands and light-colored quoins. Numerous windows, their sash altered about 1950, light the classrooms. An auditorium was added in 1938. The school is now used for school district offices and the gymnasium and auditorium remain in use by the community.

left: Central High School (JDP)

below: 1910 school. Courtesy of the Cleveland County Historical Museum.

LATTIMORE SCHOOL

101 Stockton Street
Lattimore
1930s

The first Lattimore School was built in 1895. The one-story frame building was raised to two stories in 1905 and a louvered belfry added to the roof. An attic vent in the front gable had decorative louvers, a local Cleveland County architectural detail. This school was replaced by the present Colonial Revival building, built with Works Progress Administration funding. The school features a symmetrical facade with a projecting center bay with four pilasters, a recessed entrance, and a dentil cornice. The building has a low hip roof and a corridor plan. Lattimore School closed in the 1980s as a result of consolidation and sat vacant for a number of years. It is now owned by Ambassador Baptist College, which moved to Lattimore from Shelby.

top: A three-story school facility now gone. 1930s photo courtesy of the Burnette Hunt Collection.

middle: Lattimore School (BRE)

bottom: First Lattimore School. 1923 photo courtesy of the Burnette Hunt Collection.

CASAR BAPTIST CHURCH

1519 Casar-Lawndale Road (SR 1004)
Casar
1934

The charter members of Casar Baptist Church, organized in 1894, were D. S. Downs, J. H. Magness, Ellen Newton, J. A. Newton, and Reverend Abram Hollifield. At first this small congregation worshiped at Joe Parker's Store until the first church building was erected in 1896. Membership grew, and in 1903 the church was accepted into the Kings Mountain Baptist Association.

The present church building dates to 1934, and its fellowship wing dates to 1955. With the exception of minor renovations to the facade and the addition of a spire, both executed in 1965, the small brick-veneer church has undergone few changes. The entry in the gable front and the stained glass windows of the front and sides are round-arched. From each side projects a small hip-roofed wing. The rear is two stories in height and has windows with decorative brick surrounds. Behind the church is a large cemetery with several notable early-twentieth-century monuments. A historic photo suggests the church as built in 1934 differed in appearance from its present conventional Colonial Revival character. The photo shows a low-pitched hip roof, a front porch on brick pillars in place of the present front section, and a louvered cupola.

above: Casar Baptist Church as built in 1934. Courtesy of the Cleveland County Historical Museum.

left: Modern view (BRE)

CLOVER HILL UNITED METHODIST CHURCH

1225 Oak Grove–Clover Hill Church Road (SR 1509)
Polkville vicinity
1935

Clover Hill Methodist Church's cornerstone reads "Clover Hill M.E. Church South Organized 1834 Rebuilt 1854, 1876, 1895, 1935." The present church, built with stone quarried at Acre Rock, is virtually identical in form to the remodeled St. Peter's Methodist Church near Belwood. The imposing facade features two corner towers of unequal height that flank a broad segmental archway. The arch has modern glass infill, but the original entrance is visible just beyond the glass. A prominent stained glass widow is centered on the gable end, and single stained glass windows pierce each tower. Arched stained glass windows run down the sides. To the rear is a three-story administration and education wing under a low hip roof. A single interior chimney extends above the roofline at the junction of the sanctuary and three-story section. A large cemetery is located just south of the church.

Clover Hill United Methodist Church (BRE)

EBENEZER BAPTIST CHURCH (FORMER)

1621 County Line Road (NC 216)
Kings Mountain vicinity
1935–38

This rough-cut stone church building served the Ebenezer congregation until 1987, when a new brick church was built next to the 1930s building. Currently the older building is used for education and youth activities. Reverend Cornelius F. Gingles was the first pastor from 1939 until his death in 1945. Later ministers included Dwight Costner, W. M. Murray, R. D. Lucas, and the present pastor, Reverend D. C. Wilson, who has been at Ebenezer since 1971.

The church has buttresses on the north and south elevations, with two-over-two windows between them. A front portico stands on square stone columns and shelters a double-leaf entry. Centered in the gable end is a circular louvered vent, and there are rectangular louvered vents in the spire. The west elevation has a 1970 brick addition.

Ebenezer Baptist Church (former) (BRE)

ST. MARY'S CATHOLIC CHURCH (FORMER)

406 Beaumonde Avenue
Shelby
1937

Belmont Abbey established a Catholic mission in Shelby in 1884, and mass was celebrated in private homes until 1937, when this Gothic-influenced stone church was erected. The building has a gable-fronted nave form; the projecting vestibule has a front entry in a splayed lancet embrasure. A short belfry tower with narrow louvered openings and a decorative parapet rises from the juncture with a small side wing at the rear. Stone buttresses support the walls, slate shingles cover the roof, and exposed beams span the interior. The building was later used as a residence and has most recently served as the home office for Blue Ridge Environmental Specialists.

St. Mary's Catholic Church (former) (BRE)

SHELBY HIGH SCHOOL (FORMER)

400 West Marion Street
Shelby
1937

V. W. Breeze melded classicism and modernism in his design for Shelby's former high school. The long two-story brick building has a central entry pavilion defined by channeled piers. Fluted and channeled concrete copings cap the facade and piers, and a concrete panel above the recessed entry is inscribed with the stylized initials SHS. A front terrace has ornamental metal railings. True to its type, the school features banks of large classroom windows in the brick upper stories and a concrete basement level. Annexes have been added to the side and rear of the building, which now serves as the Shelby Middle School.

Shelby High School (former) (JDP)

Graduates stand in front of the pre-1937 high school. 1934 photo courtesy of Uptown Shelby Association.

ROGERS THEATRE

213–221 East Marion Street
Shelby
1936, early 1940s

The Rogers Theatre is one of the county's premier examples of the Art Deco style. Designed by Wilson architect Charles C. Benton, the building was named for its original owner, Robert Hamer Rogers, who came to Shelby from Durham in 1931, and it opened in 1936 with a showing of *Love on the Run,* starring Joan Crawford and Clark Gable. The gray limestone facade features channeled piers with black Carrara glass in the channels, and the same material is used in ziggurat-form motifs over the side entries. Stylized egg-and-dart cornices run at the top and under the second-story windows, and a lotiform band runs across the window heads. Panels with floral and wave designs and wave-and-bubble grilles provide other decorative touches, as do square panels in the parapet—the center one with the mask of comedy. The marquee is original, but the signage mast above, which reads "theatre" and was once outlined with wave-form neon, is an early addition. As with other cinemas of the era, a separate entrance led to a balcony for black patrons.

Inside, the lobby has been modernized, but remnants of a marble floor survive, and historic photographs show decorative painting on the plaster walls. A partitioned-off section of the balcony fronted by a large picture window served as the "crying babies room." In addition to movies, the theater showcased traveling stage shows, and the Southeast Saturday Night FM Network radio show was performed here and broadcast nationwide from a transmitter on Mount Mitchell. In the early 1940s a commercial addition was made on the east side. The addition is similar in character to the original section, although Art Deco flourishes are limited to a sunburst band that runs above the storefronts. The addition once contained the Rogers Ford dealership: a showroom was located on the street level, and a drive-through bay led to a ramp and a rear basement-level repair garage.

The Rogers Theatre was vacated in the 1980s, but in recent years the Rogers Theatre Consortium was formed to bring it back to life. The Uptown Shelby Association (USA) helped secure a grant from the National Trust for Historic Preservation to fund a study of the building's interior. The Trust has also designated the Rogers Theatre an American Treasure, and in 2001 it placed the building on its list of America's 11 Most Endangered Properties. Hopefully an extensive rehabilitation now in planning will return this grand movie house to a central place in the cultural life of Shelby.

opposite: Rogers Motors interior. Mid-twentieth-century photo courtesy of the Lloyd Hamrick Collection.

above: Rogers Theatre and addition. Mid-twentieth-century photo by Willis courtesy of the Cleveland County Historical Museum.

left: Candy counter. Mid-twentieth-century photo courtesy of the Lloyd Hamrick Collection.

Featured Properties 199

STATE THEATRE

318 South Washington Street
Shelby
1939

"As Beautiful as it is Luxurious," assured the promotional pamphlet that announced the opening of the State on October 27, 1939. The theater originally featured a stepped Art Deco parapet with simple vertical scorings and a prow-shaped marquee. Porthole doors opened into a stylish lobby with curved partitions, chrome trim, and frond-pattern carpeting. The proscenium arch around the screen featured a colorfully painted scrolling wave border. Hearing-impaired patrons were welcomed to the theater, which provided an "Acousticon head phone" for their use, but Shelby's black population was barred from the establishment. The theater was later stripped of its detail and operated as the Flick; it now serves as an antiques market.

Proscenium arch. Circa 1939 photo courtesy of the Lloyd Hamrick Collection.

State Theatre. 1939 photo by Floyd M. Willis courtesy of the Cleveland County Historical Museum.

SHELBY CITY HALL (PRESENT)

300 South Washington Street
Shelby
1939

Architects Fred Van Wageningen and L. Pegram Holland of the firm of V. W. Breeze evoked the dignity of Georgian civic architecture in their design for Shelby's city hall. The two-story center section of the brick building housed the city offices and is set at an angle to the corner of East Graham and South Washington Streets. Hyphens connect to a one-story south wing, which originally contained the public library, and a similar west wing that contained the fire and police departments. The centerpiece of the composition is the principal entry, surmounted by a scrolled pediment with a center urn. Above, centered on the ridge of the gable roof, is an octagonal cupola with arched openings and a domed roof. Secondary features include eight-over-eight windows —those on the first story have keystones centered in jack arches—brick quoining, a modillion cornice, and false-chimney parapets on the side wings. Fred Van Wageningen's name appears as delineator on a watercolor rendering of the building at the Cleveland County Historical Museum, and the Works Progress Administration provided some of the funds for the building's construction. In the late 1990s the building underwent an energy-efficient rehabilitation supervised by the Shelby firm Holland Hamrick & Patterson, the successor to V. F. Breeze's firm. The city hall stands on the site of the former Shelby Female Academy.

Shelby City Hall (present) entry (JDP)

KINGS MOUNTAIN POST OFFICE (FORMER)

100 East Mountain Street
Kings Mountain
1939

The cornerstone of Kings Mountain's Colonial Revival post office credits its design to Treasury Department supervising architect Louis A. Simon and lists Neal A. Melick as the supervising engineer. Decorative elements include a cupola; a low hip roof; a pronounced cornice; six-over-six, four-over-four, and eight-over-twelve windows with arched lintels; and a water table. A rear wing has a flat roof and original loading dock doors. The lobby has marble wainscoting, stained wooden doors, and built-in mailboxes. A dramatic Works Progress Administration mural depicting the Battle of Kings Mountain once ornamented the lobby but has since been moved to the Kings Mountain City Hall. The interior of the postmaster's office has wainscoting and a personal bathroom. A ladder climbs from the bathroom to a small room that allowed undetected observation of the employees by postal inspectors. Next to the postmaster's office is a 1940 Schwab Safe Company vault ornamented with a depiction of the federal spread eagle. Historic brass and metal light fixtures hang from the ceiling. During the Cold War, the basement was intended to serve as a Civilian Defense bomb shelter in the event of nuclear attack. After closing in recent years, the building was considered as the location for the city police department. Instead, the Kings Mountain Post Office has been rehabilitated to serve as offices, storage, and exhibit space for the Kings Mountain Historical Society. Recently the John Barber House, a log cabin believed to date to about 1810, was moved to the post office site and re-erected as part of the Kings Mountain Historical Museum's interpretive program. A corner from the ca. 1800 Robert and Nancy Patterson House, a log house that formerly stood on Dixon School Road near Kings Mountain, was used in the restoration of the Barber House.

above: Former Kings Mountain Post Office (JDP)

below: John Barber House in the process of restoration behind the museum (TJF)

WACO WOMEN'S CLUB (WACO COMMUNITY BUILDING)

200 South Main Street
Waco
1939–40

Built by the New Deal National Youth Administration, this one-story stone building served as a meeting place for Waco townswomen. It also served briefly as a cafeteria for nearby Waco High School in the 1940s, and it is now Waco's community center. A projecting pediment shelters the front door, and a shed extension on the west elevation contains the kitchen. Other exterior features include six-over-six windows and an exterior end chimney. The interior, though altered, retains its original layout: a common room, two bathrooms, and a food preparation room. Original features include metal light fixtures and panel doors.

Waco Women's Club, left; mantel, above (BRE)

COCA-COLA DISTRIBUTING PLANT

925 East Marion Street
Shelby
Ca. 1940

This two-part brick commercial building is laid with Flemish bond brickwork and features several artistic motifs. Among these is a concrete lintel panel decorated with a bas-relief Coke bottle and "Coca-Cola" in the company's trademark cursive script. The lobby retains an original office door, partition glass, and a recessed alcove. Originally built as a bottling plant, the flat-roofed building later served as a distributing plant.

Coca-Cola Distributing Plant, below; inscription detail, above (BRE)

SHELBY ARMORY (FORMER)

308 Gardner Street
Shelby
1941

Built with funds and labor supplied by the Work Progress Administration—the famous New Deal public works program that brought relief to unemployed construction workers—in conjunction with local city and county government, the Shelby Armory is a good example of depression-era architecture. The armory consists of a two-story center block surrounded on three sides by a one-story section, both sections of brick. A cavernous recessed entrance is framed by fluted pilasters and features a flagstone floor and heavy wooden doors on ornate iron hinges. In the cornice above is the inscription "Armory," with flanking federal seals. Commemorative plaques name city officials involved in the project and identify the contribution of the WPA. The interior features a large space with a steel-truss roof and an elevated stage. The renovated building serves the Cleveland County government in various capacities.

Interior (BRE)

Shelby Armory (former), bottom; front entry, top (BRE)

ST. PETER'S UNITED METHODIST CHURCH

108 St. Peters Church Road
Belwood
1941 (core, 1904)

Founded in 1843, St. Peter's United Methodist Church was rebuilt in 1878 and then again in 1904. According to the cornerstone, the present building was given a stone exterior in 1941. Like many churches in the area, the construction and subsequent remodeling of St. Peter's resulted from a collaborative contribution of resources. Instrumental in the 1941 remodeling were Dr. Forrest Edwards and Albert Bleynat. Edwards owned the Acre Rock quarry in the Toluca vicinity, about a mile and a half north of the church, and donated the stone needed for the building. The stonework was executed by the accomplished Bleynat, a Valdese stonemason who had done similar work on Edwards's own house. The church is distinguished by two front towers with simplified crenelation that bracket a broad segmental-arched entry recess. The taller of the two towers contains a belfry, and the stained glass windows on the front and sides of the church have round-arched heads. Behind the church is a small 1949 education building known as The Hut, constructed of stone with a stone chimney.

St. Peter's United Methodist Church, bottom; interior, top (BRE)

206 Architectural Perspectives of Cleveland County

MOUNT HARMONY METHODIST CHURCH

229 Mount Harmony Church Road (SR 1379)
Polkville vicinity
1942

Founded in 1791, Mount Harmony Methodist Church is one of the oldest established congregations in Cleveland County. Charles Lattimore donated 2.5 acres for the original church and cemetery. The fate of the first two churches is unknown, but the third church, built in 1923, burned down on Easter Sunday 1942. The decision was soon made to rebuild. The preacher at this time was W. L. Scott, who also served Casar, Clover Hill, Polkville, Lee's Chapel, and Rehobeth Methodist churches. Joe Elliott poured the foundation for the new church, Tommy Willis donated lumber, and Morgan London provided the brick. Declining membership led to a cessation of regular services in 1991; since then an annual service is held the third Sunday in May. As new residents move into upper Cleveland County, it is hoped that regular services can once again be held here.

The main entrance is defined by a shallow vestibule projection containing paneled double-leaf doors. Centered above is a square brickwork panel with a checkered motif. A cornerstone bears the inscription "Mount Harmony Methodist Church 1st Church, 1791; 2nd, [unknown date]; 3rd, 1923; 4th, 1942." Square-headed memorial stained glass windows run the length of the north and south elevations, and small wings extend from the back corners, each with a single door. The unaltered and spartan interior features exposed ceiling timbers. Classrooms occupy the rear of the building. The cemetery contains graves from the mid–nineteenth century and later. It is believed that slaves who attended church here are buried a few yards north of the northwest corner of the church. Several sunken unmarked graves in this section may support this claim.

Tombstone of Mary H. Wells in the cemetery (BRE)

Mount Harmony Methodist Church, top; interior, bottom (BRE)

Featured Properties 207

WILSON CORNWELL COTTON GIN

2802 Polkville Road (NC 226)
Metcalfe vicinity
1943

The Wilson Cornwell Cotton Gin is one of the few buildings of its type to survive in Cleveland County. The impressive building features brick walls approximately 2 feet thick and a gable roof with three large dormers. The machinery was removed after the gin closed in 1993, but some original exterior features still exist. These include scales and a winch used to weigh bales of cotton, large wooden sliding doors, and a vacuum chute used to suck up raw cotton from a truck parked under it. Wilson Cornwell started his business in July 1943 with the help of fellow stockholders Jack Wilson and Lee Cornwell. Clyde Scism bought half of the gin in 1970, then bought the remainder the following year. A decline in cotton production prompted the closing of the gin in 1993. As this book went to press, this cotton gin was being demolished.

Wilson Cornwell Cotton Gin, below;
machinery, right (BRE)

BOGGS COTTON GIN

807 East Stagecoach Trail (NC 182)
Fallston
20th century

Boggs Cotton Gin is one of Cleveland County's last operating cotton gins. (The only other gin operating here in the late 1990s was that of Max Hamrick, near Swainsville.) A gin has stood at the location since 1930, but the present building was moved to the site from an unknown location in 1962. It produces approximately 1,500 bales a year, according to owner Max Boggs. The building is covered with corrugated metal and has shed additions on all sides. The interior has two rooms; the larger room contains several ginning machines, and the smaller one houses belts, pulleys, and gears.

The cotton ginning process is a relatively simple procedure that has changed little since Eli Whitney introduced the gin in the early nineteenth century. The basic process involves separating the lint from the seed, thereby providing the farmer with a marketable seedless bale of cotton. Ginning is usually carried out during the months of October and November.

Boggs Cotton Gin, right; interior, below (BRE)

RUFUS AND KATHLEEN PLONK FARM

500 Rollingbrook Road (SR 2008)
Kings Mountain vicinity
20th century

Rufus Lawrence Plonk (1887–1971), a 1910 graduate of Lenoir College, married schoolteacher Mary Kathleen McGill (1896–1992) in 1918. As the Plonk family grew, additions were made to the farm's one-story three-room frame house. Two rooms were added in 1940, and after World War II a rear porch was enclosed for use as living space. Rufus Plonk originally focused on cotton growing, but in the 1940s he switched his emphasis to dairy production and began to develop what is today one of the county's most impressive twentieth-century dairy farm complexes.

A key building in the complex is the concrete block Grade A milk facility, built in 1948. The Plonks delivered their first shipment of Grade A milk to Sunrise Dairy in Gastonia in September 1948, and production continued to 1990 under Rufus's son Bill Plonk. West of the Grade A facility is a concrete block and metal holding lot. The Plonks milked approximately half of their 325 cows at a time, thus requiring extensive facilities. Three long rows of stalls provided shelter for the cows during cold or inclement weather. Among the stalls is a feed auger connected to two large metal silos dating to 1965 and 1969. The Plonks made silage out of grain, barley, wheat, cornstalks, or sorghum. The silos are currently unused, since the farm now raises beef cattle, which are grazers. One of the earliest dairy-related buildings on the farm is a large transverse milking barn built about 1925.

A host of other agricultural and domestic outbuildings stand on the farm. The frame smokehouse has an overhanging roof. Near it stands a frame granary, and directly across the road are a frame woodshed and car shed with two antiquated gas pumps in front. A frame corncrib, a grain distribution house, elevated grain pipes, a large metal chickenhouse and a smaller chicken coop, and two small concrete silos also stand on the property.

Rufus and Kathleen Plonk House, left; silos, right (BRE)

DUKE POWER CLIFFSIDE STEAM STATION AND CLUBHOUSE

3066 McCraw Road (SR 1002)
Boiling Springs vicinity
1940s

The Cliffside Steam Station, built in four phases between 1941 and 1948, is associated with Duke Power's initial expansion into western North Carolina in the mid–twentieth century. The brick and steel building retains most of its original exterior features, including long rows of louvered windows, a flat roof, and a rectangular overall form. The open-plan interior features a historic elevator and original boilers and storage facilities. In the 1970s, Duke Power added a five-story pollution control unit to the west elevation. The only other addition is a small medical building attached to the west elevation. Conveniently located on a Seaboard spur line, the steam station is now surrounded by modern industrial buildings. The facility continues to play an important role in Duke Power's regional operations.

Nearby at 3056 McCraw Road stands a one-story frame clubhouse built between 1948 and 1950. The Duke Power Clubhouse served as a gathering place for hundreds of employees, many of whom lived in a mill village (now gone) that sprawled to the southwest of the structure. The gable-fronted clubhouse features a recessed porch that wraps around the east and west elevations. Nine-over-nine, nine-over-six, and six-over-six windows pierce the elevations, and an enclosed porch covered with latticework extends to the rear. Original streetlights illuminate the grounds.

The interior features a main room with original hardwood flooring and a gambrel-type ceiling with original light fixtures. All of the paneled doors and most of the hardware is original. Off the main room are the ladies' lounge, furnished with couches and a bathroom, and the men's bathroom, and to the rear is a kitchen with original lights. The kitchen leads to a porch and an outdoor barbecue pit.

top to bottom: Duke Power Cliffside Steam Station; interior; clubhouse (all BRE)

SHELBY CITY PARK

Dorton Drive at 901 West Sumter Street
Shelby
1948 and later

Dr. Stephen S. Royster donated 100 acres to the City of Shelby for use as a city park, and in 1948 construction began on a large community center with brick walls, a bowstring roof, and a 1,200-seat auditorium. From its early years, the park has had a quasi-amusement park character. In 1951 the city installed a ca. 1920 carousel manufactured by the Herschell-Spillman Company of North Tonawanda, New York. The gaily painted horses and sleighs were protected from the elements by a canvas tented roof with roll-down sides. An Art Deco rounding board was probably a carnival retrofit from a few years before the city's acquisition; the present rounding board has painted scenes and is more early-twentieth-century in appearance. In 1998 the Anne Dover Bailey Carousel Pavilion was constructed to house the carousel; the pavilion features historic exhibits and a wood-piped Artizan A-2 Military Band Organ that plays waltzes, marches, and foxtrots from paper rolls. Another attraction from the 1950s is the Rotary Special, a miniature train of authentic diesel streamliner design. A train station was built in 2001 to a design by Holland Hamrick & Patterson Architects of Shelby, who also designed the carousel pavilion. Other amenities include a swimming pool, a nine-hole golf course, tennis courts, and a sitting garden with a trail.

left: Shelby City Park Carousel. Photo by Randy McNeilly.

above: Auditorium (JDP)

JOY THEATRE

202 South Railroad Avenue
Kings Mountain
1948–49

The Joy Theatre opened its doors to the Kings Mountain public on June 1, 1949, with a showing of Betty Grable's *The Beautiful Blonde from Bashful Bend.* The Moderne-style cinema was built for brothers Charles and David Cash, originally of Gaffney, South Carolina, who operated a succession of cinemas in Kings Mountain before starting the Joy. Architect M. R. Marsh drew up plans for the theater in 1947, but a change of site delayed construction. A number of area contractors were involved in the Joy, including the Charles S. Besser Company of Charlotte, which installed the all-important Westinghouse air-conditioning unit. Fire prevention was an important consideration, and the building is fabricated almost entirely from concrete, brick, and tile block.

The exterior features a stucco facade, originally white in color, delicately fluted and scribed with a gridlike pattern. As built, a futuristic neon signage mast towered above a curved marquee. The marquee survives, but an appropriate modern neon sign replaces the original signage mast. Inside are tile lobby walls, originally pink in color, doors with round ocean-liner glass panels, and seats with fluted arm rests. The seats were originally upholstered with maroon cowhide and had tan sides. As built, the theater held 772 seats, of which 234 were located in the balcony. Of the balcony seats 112 were set aside, according to a period newspaper account, for "colored persons, who will have their own entrance way at the north side." For mothers of young children there were soundproofed "crying rooms" with picture windows looking onto the screen. The theater closed in the late twentieth century, but in 2001 it reopened as the Joy Performance Center. Holland Hamrick & Patterson Architects of Shelby supervised the rehabilitation.

Joy Theatre; seats in the auditorium (JDP)

Featured Properties 213

LATTIMORE BAPTIST CHURCH

303 Peachtree Street (SR 1162)
Lattimore
1949

This Gothic-influenced church, built by contractor Grady Brooks, has a pleasant pastoral setting on the southern edge of Lattimore. The brick building has a recessed lancet-arched entry with limestone moldings and two-leaf doors hung on decorative strap hinges, small paired casement windows in lancet-arched openings, and brick buttresses with stone weatherings. The rear of the church is of standard institutional construction. Exposed heavy-timbered rafters and iron hinged wooden doors adorn the interior. The church building that preceded this one had an unusual form, with a domed octagonal cupola and lancet-arched openings. A cemetery extends to the south; several obelisks for the Jones and Stroud families dot the grounds, and a Doric colonnade monument marks a DeBerry family burial.

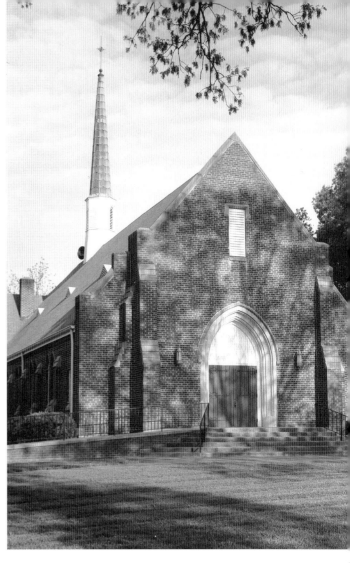

Earlier church. Courtesy of the Cleveland County Historical Museum.

Lattimore Baptist Church, top; cemetery, bottom (JDP)

BRIDGES BARBECUE LODGE

2000 East Dixon Boulevard (US 74)
Shelby
1952

Red and Lyttle Bridges opened Bridges Barbecue in 1946, and the eatery moved to its present location on Highway 74 in the early 1950s. The land that the lodge occupies once belonged to Red Bridges's father, who farmed cotton in this part of the county. Red and Lyttle hired the Shelby architectural firm of Van Wageningen & Cochran to design their modernist restaurant, which was built by contractor Virgil McIntyre and completed in 1952. Bridges Barbecue opened for business at the new location and has since served North Carolinians, national celebrities, and at least one person from each of the fifty states. The restaurant's fame continues to grow, and it was recently featured in a Texas Pete Hot Sauce commercial. The eatery also made it into the December 1994 issue of *Gourmet* magazine.

The one-story frame and brick restaurant features an original sign on the highway and a pig on the roof, both illuminated with neon. The glassed-in main entrance projects slightly; above it is a neon sign reading "barBcue." The west, north, and south elevations have board-and-batten siding, and the east elevation has a brick exterior. Casement windows run the length of the west elevation, and a chimney dominates the east wing, where the cooking is done. Along with the decorative signs, dancing pigs adorn the facade. Hickory logs are piled in back next to the original cinder block cookhouse, now used for storage.

The restaurant interior has changed little since the building's construction; the booths, tables, and chairs exemplify the streamlined design of the era. Light fixtures with perforated wood valences reminiscent of the designs of Frank Lloyd Wright adorn the ceiling. At the end of a hallway that connects the kitchen, refrigerators, and main office are the fireplace and cooking pits.

Bridges Barbecue Lodge, bottom (BRE); former uptown location, top. Photo courtesy of the Lloyd Hamrick Collection.

ST. MATTHEW'S LUTHERAN CHURCH

201 North Piedmont Avenue
Kings Mountain
1953–54, 2000

St. Matthew's has had more than its share of calamity since its establishment in the 1870s. The original church was Gothic Revival in character, with a center tower, quoins, and lancet-arched openings. This building appears to have been the one that burned in 1921, although a portion of the pre-1921 church complex survives. The present church, erected and dedicated in 1953–54, also burned, on Christmas morning 1999. Despite extensive damage, the congregation chose to rebuild within the walls of the 1953 building, thus preserving one of the county's leading examples of academic Gothic Revival architecture. The Flemish-bond brick building was designed in the parish

St. Matthew's Lutheran Church, below (BRE); tower window, above (JDP)

church genre first popularized by the Episcopal denomination in the nineteenth century. A stubby corner tower with crenelation and ornate pinnacles rises to an octagonal metal-sheathed spire. The tower and nave have angled corner buttresses and lancet-arched stained glass windows with tracery. The parapet gable front of the nave features double-leaf wood doors with elaborate medieval strap hinges set within a much larger entry surround of carved stone with tracery, trefoil panels, and heraldic shields.

Earlier, possibly original church. Circa 1900 photo courtesy of Philip Baker and the Cleveland County Historical Museum.

PPG INDUSTRIES

940 Washburn Switch Road (SR 1382)
Lattimore vicinity
1958–59 and later

When it was placed on line in April 1959, Cleveland County's PPG plant was the nation's largest facility for the production of fiberglass reinforcements. Pittsburgh Plate Glass (its name was changed to PPG in 1968) located in the county to take advantage of water and natural gas provided by the City of Shelby. At its peak PPG employed about 1,800 workers in the production of fiberglass for tub and shower enclosures and molded automobile parts. The sprawling one-story plant, begun in February 1958, features hoodlike rooftop heat vents known as Thomson louvers. The site is served by branches of the Seaboard and Atlantic Coast Line, over which pure silica sand from mines in Georgia, Kentucky, and Tennessee are shipped to the facility.

PPG *Industries. 1959 photo courtesy of* PPG.

CLEVELAND COUNTY COURTHOUSE (PRESENT)

100 Justice Place
Shelby
1974, 1992

At the core of this building is the county Justice Complex, built in 1974. As originally constructed, the Justice Complex was not intended for use as a courthouse, but it served as one beginning in 1975. The building was greatly expanded in 1992 according to a design by O. Stanhope Anthony of the Shelby architectural firm Martin Boal Anthony & Johnson, with Beam Construction Company as general contractor. With its central copper-finish dome and porticoed front, the Postmodern-style building evokes the civic architecture of the 1907–8 courthouse, which stands several blocks away. Walls of tan brick, decorative quarry-faced cinder block, and synthetic stucco; spreading metal-sheathed hip roofs; and a main entry under a pediment supported by cylindrical stuccoed columns complete the exterior. In the lobby is a mural of carved brick depicting the 1907–8 courthouse and symbols of county progress such as factories, the railroad, and cotton bolls. The mural concept was developed by art instructor Doug Pruett and art students and faculty at county high schools, and the carving was done by a South Carolina artist named Zourras. At the southwest corner of the building stands the aluminum sculpture *Spirit of Justice*, crafted by artist Dexter N. Benedick in 1975.

Cleveland County Courthouse (present) (JDP)

State Theatre lobby, Shelby. 1939 photo courtesy of the Cleveland County Historical Museum.

SELECTED INVENTORY

SAMUEL YOUNG HOUSE

5 Raft Place (SR 1228)
Boiling Springs vicinity
1818

A fieldstone from the chimney bears the date 1818, making the Young house one of the county's oldest. The house originally stood about half a mile west of the present location along the banks of Grog Creek, but in 1976 Mitchell Guffey purchased it and moved it to its present site. The story-and-a-half house has half-dovetail corner notching and a three-bay window-door-window front elevation. Mitchell Guffey remodeled the house at its new location, modifying the two-room interior and adding an exterior brick end chimney, a front porch, doors and windows, and an ell.

Poston House (BRE)

Samuel Young House (BRE)

POSTON HOUSE

1500 Polkville Road (NC 226)
Shelby vicinity
Early 19th century

The construction of this log house is attributed to Samuel Poston (1765–1819), who married Rachel King (d. 1853) in 1790. The story-and-a-half dwelling has remained in family hands for several generations and has been restored by Madge Harris, a Poston descendant. The house has half-dovetail corner notching and a front porch (not original) with square posts. A fieldstone chimney rises on the south elevation, and the rear features a modern board-and-batten shed addition that contains the kitchen. Inside, a large fireplace with a stone firebox dominates the main room. Next to the fireplace, a set of narrow stairs leads to the loft, where log rafters joined with wood pegs are visible.

OLIVER AND VIRGINIA
ELLIOTT FARM

Elliott Circle Drive (SR 1385)
Polkville vicinity
1840, 1902

Oliver Beam Elliott (1853–1932) was born in Cleveland County but left the area in 1873 in search of employment. His travels took him first to South Carolina, then to Georgia, and finally to Texas, where he worked as a carpenter and foreman of a bridge crew that was engaged in building the Great Gulf, Colorado, and Santa Fe Railroad. Oliver Elliott returned to Cleveland County in 1889 and helped his brother, Thomas Elliott, run a harness shop. Oliver married Virginia Ann Stockton (1875–1951) in 1891. After living with various family members, the Elliotts built their own home in 1902.

The one-story frame Victorian dwelling has a front porch supported by chamfered posts. Three chimneys rise above the gable roof. The windows have a variety of sash configurations, including one-over-one, four-over-four, and six-over-six. At the rear of the house is an attached frame well shelter. Inside, the unaltered front parlor has unfinished walls and an original post-and-lintel mantel. Near the house stand two frame garages, a

Brackett House (BRE)

details such as window surrounds with blank corner blocks and a wide frieze support an antebellum date. A front porch on tapered square-section wood columns with fillets at their tops shelters the front entry, which has sidelights and a transom. A hip roof, large six-over-six windows, interior brick chimneys, and an early or original two-story ell are other features of one of Shelby's oldest houses.

wellhouse with a pyramidal roof, and a privy. Farm buildings include a barn, a granary, and a chickenhouse. Also on the farm is the two-story weatherboarded log house built by Oliver's father, John Paxton Elliott (1817–73), in 1840.

BRACKETT HOUSE

739 Moriah Church Road (SR 1530)
Casar vicinity
1841

The Bracketts were early settlers in the Casar area, where they raised corn and cotton. Their house, attributed to builder George Parker, is a two-story hall-parlor-plan dwelling with replacement Craftsman three-over-one windows. An impressive stone and brick chimney has the date *1841* etched into its face. The second story features three evenly spaced six-over-six windows. A one-story kitchen ell with a stone chimney extends to the rear. Adjoining the house is a frame smokehouse.

REUBEN GREENE HOUSE

246 North Main Street
Boiling Springs
Mid–19th century

Reuben Greene built this log dwelling in the mid–nineteenth century directly across the street from its present location. Much of the house is now covered with weatherboards, but half-dovetail notching is visible at some corners. The house rests on concrete blocks and is covered with a metal roof. Its rectangular plan measures approximately 18 feet by 22 feet. The house was apparently moved to its present site in the 1950s or 1960s.

J. K. WELLS HOUSE

514 West Marion Street
Shelby
1852

A plaque identifies 1852 as the date of construction for this two-story frame house. Simple Greek Revival

Reuben Greene House corner notching (BRE)

J. K. Wells House (JDP)

Selected Inventory 223

Fulenwider-Ebeltoft House. Courtesy of North Carolina Office of Archives and History.

FULENWIDER-EBELTOFT HOUSE

323 South Washington Street
Shelby
1850

Swiss-born Eli Fulenwider built this two-story frame house, one of the few surviving antebellum buildings in Shelby. Fulenwider was involved in the local iron industry. Later owners included T. E. Ebeltoft, a Baptist minister, confectioner, and bookstore owner, and Judge James L. Webb. Webb's daughter Fay and her husband, future Governor O. Max Gardner, lived here before moving down the street to Webbley in 1911. The weatherboarded house is distinguished by its front entry with sidelights and decorative transom, double interior chimneys with pronounced corbeled caps, and a later one-story front porch with classical columns and a roof balustrade. The house is now used as office space for Software Training Service.

HOYLE-WARLICK HOUSE

111 Rockdale Road (SR 1609)
Belwood vicinity
Ca. 1860

Early occupants of this two-story frame dwelling were William and Theresa Self Hoyle. The property passed to Theodore Warlick in 1924, and it remained in the Warlick family until 1981. A one-story wraparound porch, now partially enclosed, was added in 1926 during an extensive remodeling. The cross-gable house has asbestos-shingle siding, a large rear addition, and an original stone fireplace. A frame transverse stock barn stands nearby.

JOHN AND MARY CLINE HOUSE

1805 McBrayer Springs Road (SR 1831)
Shelby vicinity
Ca. 1860

This L-plan frame house, built by John Franklin Cline for his wife Mary Elizabeth Hoyle Cline, has a wraparound porch and several additions. A stove tower projects from the west elevation, and there is an interior corbeled brick chimney.

E. B. HAMRICK HOUSE

101 West Homestead Avenue
Boiling Springs
Ca. 1865, ca. 1875, 1940s

Elijah Bly Hamrick was a prominent Boiling Springs businessman during the early twentieth century. He was associated with the store and related businesses that belonged to his father, C. J. Hamrick, and was active in the establishment of Boiling Springs High School, the forerunner of Gardner-Webb University. In 1909 he served as the school's first bursar, and he donated some of the land for the school. The institution decided to recognize his contributions to its growth by naming E. B. Hamrick Hall in his honor. The original part of Hamrick's house is thought to date to about 1865. It attained its present form about 1875, and modifications were made in the 1940s. The two-story weatherboarded frame house features a two-story ell, interior chimneys, and six-over-six windows. Twentieth-century modifications include a projecting picture window and a front porch on ornamental metal supports.

DURBRO POST OFFICE

104 Ida Circle (SR 2208)
Patterson Springs vicinity
19th century

Identified on the 1886 Kyzer map of Cleveland County as the "Durbro Post Office," this small building was the center of one of south-central Cleveland County's oldest settlements. An early postmaster at Durbro was L. M. H. Roberts. The former post office is a one-story frame building with an exterior end chimney and shed porch additions. It now serves as a farm storage shed. Durbro, like other small crossroads communities, faded away as population shifted to Kings Mountain and Shelby in the late nineteenth and early twentieth centuries.

THOMAS HAMRICK HOUSE

3518 Cliffside Road (SR 1186)
Boiling Springs vicinity
19th century

Mud and fieldstone chimneys, a wraparound Victorian porch, and nine-over-six windows with ornamental surrounds indicate that this house was constructed in the nineteenth century. Farmer Thomas Hamrick is thought to be the home's original owner. After his death the property was acquired by Haynes Mills (later Cliffside Mills and now Cone Mills), which bought the tract with the intention of building the Nicholsonville Cotton Mill on it. The projected mill took its name from Nicholsonville, a village that disappeared in the early twentieth century. Bonds for the mill fell through, and Haynes rented the house to a succession of tenant farmers in the early and mid–twentieth century. P. G. Jolley bought the house for his parents in the 1960s. At present the house is unoccupied, but area farmers use the outbuildings for storage. The property's domestic and farm outbuildings, which are representative of the turn of the twentieth century and are well preserved, include a frame smokehouse, a chickenhouse, a frame transverse stock barn with two small shed additions, a corncrib, and a privy.

DAVID AND MARTHA MCBRAYER HOUSE

237 McBrayer Homestead Road (SR 1162)
Boiling Springs vicinity
Ca. 1870

After the Civil War, Private David McBrayer (1844–1935), who served in the CSA, Ninth Regiment, Company I, Cleveland County, returned to his ancestral land a few miles north of Boiling Springs. There he resumed cotton farming and was successful enough to build a substantial two-story Victorian house shortly before his marriage to Martha Ann Blanton (1852–1936) in 1871. Now unoccupied, the house is still owned by family members, who hope to restore it to its original grandeur. The frame house has an L plan; the enclosed porch on the second story served as a sleeping porch in later years. Decorative treatments include cornice returns in the gables, scrollwork and chamfered posts on the porch, an ornate bracketed cornice, and shingle-pattern pressed-metal roofing. Judging from window treatments and decorative brickwork, the rear ell probably dates to the early twentieth century.

David and Martha McBrayer House, top; cornice detail, bottom (BRE)

WILEY HAMRICK HOUSE

320 North Main Street
Boiling Springs
Ca. 1870

Built shortly after the Civil War, this one-story frame dwelling has a one-room-deep center-passage plan. In the 1880s cotton farmer Wiley Hamrick added two rooms to the rear. Victorian exterior details include decorative roof brackets, beautifully detailed bargeboards, board-and-batten treatments in the gables, Gothic Revival–influenced lintels, and, on the front porch, chamfered posts and scrollwork. The only remaining out-

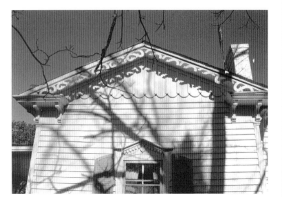

Wiley Hamrick House, right; gable detail, below (BRE)

Green-Hoey House, right; privy, above (BRE)

buildings are a deteriorated shed at the rear of the property and a frame smokehouse.

GREEN-HOEY HOUSE

149 Bryon Place (SR 2209)
Grover vicinity
Ca. 1875

George Green built this one-story three-bay frame dwelling about 1875 and lived here for many years before moving into Grover. He sold the property to Clyde Hoey, who bought it for his brother, Will. Will Hoey lived here until 1937, when he sold the property to Charlie and Sudie Mae Fortenberry. Charlie farmed the property and worked at Minette Mills in Grover for twenty-six years. The Fortenberrys raised six children in the house, which remains in the family. The house has several interior and exterior chimneys, six-over-six windows, and a center entry with a double-leaf panel door. The center-passage-plan interior has plaster-and-lath walls and ceilings and carved post-and-lintel mantels. Outbuildings include a smokehouse, a privy, and a tractor shed.

226 Architectural Perspectives of Cleveland County

GAITHER PHILBECK FARM

1702 New House Road (SR 1351)
Lattimore vicinity
Ca. 1875

Gaither Philbeck is the earliest known owner of this farm, which was later owned by Lyn Grayson. The Cogdells lived here in the early twentieth century. The two-story frame farmhouse probably dates to about 1875. Period decorative features include slight returns in the gables and Gothic Revival–influenced lintels above the four-over-four windows. Other features include a foundation of stone piers, paired interior chimneys, and a full-length front porch. A one-story rear ell has two-over-two, four-over-four, and nine-over-six windows. Beyond the house is a frame and metal barn. East of the barn is a frame smokehouse with an extended roof that shelters a well with a stone foundation. North of the smokehouse is a frame transverse stock barn that has loft doors over the opening to the central passage.

ELIJAH W. HAMRICK HOUSE

302 North Main Street
Boiling Springs
1880s

Elijah Wright Hamrick probably built this Italianate house in the 1880s. Details include board-and-batten sheathing in the gables, decorative window lintels, and paired cornice brackets that are identical to those of another Boiling Springs Hamrick family house, the ca. 1870 Wiley Hamrick House. The similarity suggests that the two houses were built by the same craftsman. Other features include a one-room-deep center-passage plan, two ells, and four chimneys.

WILLIAM O. WARE HOUSE

206 West Gold Street
Kings Mountain
Ca. 1882

William Oates Ware built a saw- and gristmill known as Merchant Mills on West Gold Street in 1882, and he is believed to have built this two-story Victorian house across the street the same year. The frame house features a two-story porch with sawn ornament and decorative chimney stacks. The mill was one of Kings Mountain's first industries. William O. Ware's son William Alexander Ware joined the business in 1898, the year a cotton gin was added to the complex. W. A. Ware's son Moffat joined the business in 1918. The mill was demolished before 1980.

LEE'S CHAPEL

108 Lees Chapel Drive
Polkville vicinity
Ca. 1883

This simple Methodist church of weatherboarded frame construction is situated on a beautiful knoll just east of the Rutherford County line. The facade features a porch on brick columns that shelters a single door.

Lee's Chapel (BRE)

Gaither Philbeck Farm (BRE)

Selected Inventory 227

The interior remains largely intact, with wood pews, polished hardwood floors, and a piano. The pulpit stands on a dais with an altar rail supported by square spindles. Behind the pulpit hangs a simple wooden cross. Behind the church, pathways wind through the woods to two frame privies, and a small graveyard is situated to the southeast. Because of declining membership, the church was decommissioned in 1980, but the building is lovingly maintained by former members.

BENJAMIN FALLS HOUSE

325 New Bethel Church Road
(SR 1665)
Lawndale vicinity
1883

Shortly after graduating from Tennessee's Vanderbilt University Medical School in 1883, Dr. Benjamin Falls set up practice in the Cleveland Mills vicinity of northern Cleveland County. Falls treated patients in an office located on the first floor of his two-story L-plan Victorian house, built in 1883. Like many rural physicians, Falls designed his office in such a way as to separate his practice from his household. He also boarded teachers employed at Piedmont School. In 1903 Falls sold the house to Decatur Elmore, who sold it to Schenck Carpenter in 1913. Situated on a hilltop and shaded by mature trees, the Falls House retains much of its original historic character. Turned posts support a one-story porch adorned with Victorian scroll-sawn brackets. The two-over-two and six-over-six windows have simple molded lintels. A broad one-story ell extends to the rear. Outbuildings include a ca. 1883 smokehouse and a ca. 1950 frame transverse barn.

ARTHUR H. HERNDON HOUSE

1310 Bethlehem Church Road
(SR 2245)
Kings Mountain vicinity
1885

Shortly after Arthur Henderson Herndon (1849–1902) married Martha Poston (1853–1926), the couple moved into this two-story frame house. A finely crafted porch graces the three-bay front. The porch has slender posts in twos and threes joined with delicate cross-bracing and with intricate sawn brackets, pendant ornament, and balustrades. Rising above the low hip roof are a pair of interior chimneys with stuccoed lancet panels on their faces.

MOORE-HAMRICK HOUSE

930 West Warren Street
Shelby
Ca. 1885

Leander Hamrick (1854–1934) bought this two-story frame Victorian house from a Mr. Moore in 1896 and lived here with his wife Sarah (1862–1955). In addition to farming cotton, Hamrick served as a director of three Shelby building and loan associations. Following Leander's death in 1934, his son Hubbard (1902–88) and Hubbard's wife Frances (1904–85) took over the management of the farm. Hubbard continued growing cotton until the 1950s, when demand fell off. He then focused on real estate and sold off parts of the farm for residential development. The house has a cross-gable roof, interior chimneys, and a wrap-around porch adorned with turned posts, spindle and scrollwork, and

Arthur H. Herndon House (BRE)

decorative brackets. The six-over-six windows have pedimented window hoods, and the second-story windows are further enhanced with decorative brackets on each side of the window hoods. Two historic outbuildings survive: a frame kitchen and a poultry-house in which turkeys, ducks, and chickens were raised.

AUDLEY AND MARY JANE LATTIMORE HOUSE

109 Main Street
Lattimore
Ca. 1885

Audley Martin Lattimore (1845–1931), who is credited with founding Lattimore and served as its first mayor, built this house shortly after coming to the area in the early 1880s. Here he lived with his wife Mary Jane Hamrick Lattimore (1849–1914). His one-story frame dwelling has a center-passage plan, fieldstone chimneys, and a front porch with turned posts and restrained Victorian detail. The present owners, Audley's great-grandson Tom Lattimore and his wife Ann, use the surrounding pastures and outbuilding for raising sheep.

NEWTON HOUSE

5431 Casar Road (NC 10)
Casar vicinity
Ca. 1885

The Newton family lived in this simple one-story frame house, which afterward served as a rental house. The weatherboarded house has a wraparound porch on square posts, gables with scalloped vents, and a foundation of stone piers. A notable feature is a relatively large stove tower with two four-light casement windows and a pyramidal roof from which projects a brick flue (the stove tower is also pictured in the essay section of this book). The west elevation has two ells connected by a porch.

PINCKNEY HAMRICK FARM

321 South Main Street
Boiling Springs
Late 19th century

The Pinckney Hamrick House exhibits some of the most exuberant Victorian detailing in the southwestern part of Cleveland County. The frame house has a bracketed cornice with a wide frieze, molded architraves, louvered vents, and a porch with scrollwork and chamfered posts. Little is known about the Reverend Pinckney Hamrick other than that he was active in the Boiling Springs area at the turn of the twentieth century. The impressive farm complex northwest of the house includes a number of interesting buildings. The earliest of these are a frame five-stall horse barn set on stone piers and a shed-roofed frame hog pen on a stone foundation, both dating to the 1920s. The large frame and metal chickenhouse dates to the mid-1940s. In 1944 later owner Albert Glenn constructed a privy from concrete blocks that he cast on the farm, and ten years later Glenn erected a transverse barn. The support posts used in the construction of this barn were salvaged from the old Boiling Springs to Lattimore Telephone Exchange, and the steel roof trusses came from the original Gardner-Webb University gymnasium. Farms with this variety of historic buildings are becoming increasingly rare in the growing Boiling Springs area.

Newton House (BRE)

Allen and Leola Bettis House (BRE)

William A. Mauney House (JDP)

ALLEN AND LEOLA BETTIS HOUSE

3022 Star Hill Road (SR 2225)
Earl vicinity
Late 19th century

When Allen Erastus Bettis (1854–1928) and his family fled to this site from Tennessee during the Civil War, the only belongings they had were those they could carry with them over the Appalachian Mountains. Upon settling on this tract about a mile south of Earl, Bettis began farming cotton and wheat and built this three-bay frame I-house, which he is said to have presented to his wife Leola Austell Bettis (b. 1861). The dwelling has a wraparound Craftsman porch with a small second tier (leftover from an earlier porch) with Victorian sawn and spindle brackets, turned balusters, and half-timber-like ornament in the gable. Two central interior corbeled chimneys are situated along the ridge, and there is a large one-story ell extending off the main block. In 1915 Pete McSwain, a local carpenter, added a dining room to the house. A ca. 1920 frame garage and tenant house stand to the rear.

JACOB AND MARGARET MAUNEY HOUSE

107 North Piedmont Avenue
Kings Mountain
Late 19th century

This two-story frame house was built for Jacob Simri Mauney (1846–1936) and his wife Margaret Juletta (Julia) Rudisill Mauney (1850–1930). An early Kings Mountain merchant, banker, and industrialist, Mauney was the general manager and later president of his brother W. A. Mauney's Kings Mountain Manufacturing Company. The Jacob S. Mauney Memorial Library was named for him in 1947. The Mauney House was altered in the early twentieth century and features a hip roof with gables and Classical Revival details.

WILLIAM A. MAUNEY HOUSE

106 North Battleground Avenue
Kings Mountain
Late 19th century

William Andrew Mauney (1841–1928), Kings Mountain's first mayor, postmaster, and newspaper editor, built this two-story Victorian house next to his original store at 104 N. Battleground. The weatherboarded frame house features a hip roof with multiple gables and two corbeled brick chimney caps, and a wraparound one-story veranda with turned posts and balusters and sawn brackets. A bracketed cornice shows the influence of the Italianate style, and a shed-roofed flowerhouse stands in the side yard. Mauney's store, said to have been built in 1878 as Kings Mountain's first brick commercial building, was remodeled as Keeter's Department Store in the mid–twentieth century. In the late 1880s Mauney founded the Kings Mountain Manufacturing Company.

Elijah and Margaret Bowen House (BRE)

Stockton-Scism House (BRE)

Roberts-Cash House (BRE)

In the early twentieth century he served as a state congressman and senator representing Cleveland County.

ROBERTS-CASH HOUSE

2626 Oak Grove Road (SR 2033)
Shelby vicinity
Late 19th century

This board-and-batten gable-front-and-wing dwelling once served as a tenant house on the Roberts farm. Freemon Cash bought the property in the early 1940s and lived here until he built another house in 1953. Cash then used this house as a tenant house until 1963–64. The house stands on stone piers and has a fieldstone chimney, a front porch, two front doors, and six-over-six windows. A ca. 1940 frame barn stands nearby.

STOCKTON-SCISM HOUSE

3269 Ramseur Church Road (SR 1811)
Double Shoals vicinity
Late 19th century

Although the exact construction date of this frame house is unknown, in 1898 area residents met in the front two rooms to organize Double Shoals Baptist Church. At the time George Robert Stockton owned the property. In the late 1910s Stockton sold the house to cotton farmer W. C. Scism (1862–1951). Scism and his wife Amanda probably made the present Craftsman-style alterations to the house shortly thereafter. W. C. and Amanda's daughter Mindy operated Scism's Store at the corner of Ramseur Church Road and Double Shoals Road. The house has a wraparound porch with Craftsman brick and wood supports, four-over-one windows, interior chimneys, and several ells and wings. A frame transverse barn stands nearby.

ELIJAH AND MARGARET BOWEN HOUSE

3207 Shelby Road (SR 1813)
Double Shoals vicinity
Late 19th century

Elijah and Margaret Bowen inhabited this one-story frame Victorian L-plan dwelling during the late nineteenth century. The house has a wraparound porch with chamfered posts and a decorative railing. Centered in the gable ends above the north and south bays are diamond-shaped louvered vents. A large portion of the house is adorned with a bracketed cornice. Behind the house are a frame transverse barn, a tractor shed, and a smokehouse. The Bowens grew cotton in the

George and Josephine Simmons Farm (BRE)

surrounding fields, and when their son Forrest decided to marry, they gave him land across the road to build his own house.

WHISNANT HOUSE

Polkville Road (NC 226)
Polkville vicinity
Late 19th century

John O. Whisnant or his son Abraham Whisnant had this frame Victorian house built. The house has a hybrid appearance, with a decorative one-story front wing grafted onto the front of a plain two-story dwelling. The front wing features a gable with sawtooth wood shingles and a wraparound porch. Other features include a small rear wing, an exterior gable-end brick chimney, and several nine-over-six windows. Nearby stand a smokehouse and corncrib of frame construction; apparently gone is the shop of Abraham Whisnant, who was a blacksmith.

GEORGE AND JOSEPHINE SIMMONS FARM

3120 Polkville Road (NC 226)
Polkville vicinity
1888

George Hampton "Hapt" Simmons (d. 1932) built the two-story frame house on this farm in 1888 and lived here with his wife Josephine Perlina Martin Simmons (d. 1946) and their eleven children. Simmons was postmaster for the Pearl Post Office, located within the house, which received mail on Thursdays from Blacksburg, South Carolina. Simmons also farmed and operated a cotton gin, corn mill, and shingle mill on the property. A son, Wilbur, operated a dairy at the farm, and following George's death in 1932, Wilbur and his wife, Margaret Louise Mauney Simmons (d. 1957), moved into the house to care for Josephine, who died in 1946. The Simmons family sold the property to the Burnham family in 1988. In 1989 a fire gutted the second story, which was subsequently rebuilt.

The gabled house has a one-story wraparound porch on Craftsman wood and brick supports (either the supports or the porch in its entirety were added in the 1920s or 1930s). A second-story portico has turned posts. A two-story ell with an exterior chimney is located on the east elevation, and a one-story ell extends from the west elevation. East of the house is a row of early-twentieth-century frame outbuildings, including a smokehouse, a flowerhouse, and a granary. Other outbuildings include a tractor shed and barn, a second smokehouse, a milking barn, two log barns, and a small frame tackhouse used to store horse equipment. The milking barn's concrete floor has built-in trenches to facilitate the removal of waste.

BEASON HOUSE

910 Goodes Grove Church Road (SR 1191)
Mooresboro vicinity
1890

Little is known about this house except for its historic association with the Beason family, longtime residents of the Cliffside area. Built in 1890, it is an excellent example of a center-passage I-house. The three-bay two-story frame house has a one-story Victorian porch with square posts and scrollwork that shelters an entry with a double-leaf paneled door. Slight returns serve to accentuate the ends of the gable roof, and a decorative bracketed cornice runs along the eaves. A one-story ell extends off the west elevation. Chimneys with corbeled caps rise from the interior.

PEOPLES BANK

201 Putnam Street
Waco
Ca. 1890

Peoples Bank, Waco's first financial institution, prospered until the Great Depression, when it closed. The building later served as the Waco Post Office and more recently as a video rental outlet. The one-story building is constructed of brick laid in American bond with a corbeled cornice on the front and stepped parapets on the sides. A segmental-arched door and window are located on the front, and to the rear is a central door. The interior contains a large lobby, an office, and a walk-in safe.

GAMIE LEE HOUSE

502 South Main Street
Boiling Springs
1890s

This large two-story frame house is located on the edge of Boiling Springs on the site of the former Metal Post Office. Exterior features include a gable roof with a front pediment, a pair of interior chimneys, and a one-story ell. The house has a double front door and six-over-six and three-over-one windows. Although the interior has been made into rental units, the house retains its original center-passage plan.

J. F. MOORE HOUSE

1336 College Avenue (NC 150)
Boiling Springs vicinity
1896

Cotton farmer J. F. Moore built this frame Victorian house for his large family. A wraparound porch extends around three-fourths of the exterior. The house's most interesting feature is the celestial theme of the decoration in its multiple gables, including representations of full and crescent moons

Beason House (BRE)

Peoples Bank (JDP)

Selected Inventory 233

and a five-pointed star. Unfortunately, the name of the person who crafted these mysterious motifs has been lost to history.

LAWSON AND PONOLA KENDRICK FARM

2056 Pleasant Hill Church Road (SR 1103)
Patterson Springs vicinity
1897–98

Prominent area cotton farmer Lawson Irvin Kendrick (1862–1942) and his wife Zuar Ponola Camp Kendrick (1868–1949) built this one-story frame dwelling. The five-bay facade has a projecting center gable and three entries. The full-length porch has square columns and spindle ornament. Other features include cornice returns, interior chimneys, and an ell with an enclosed porch and an exterior chimney. Around the house stand several outbuildings, including a stretcher-bond brick pumphouse, a story-and-a-half cotton house and granary, a frame stock barn, a frame corncrib, and a frame meathouse, where meat was salt cured. In the early twentieth century the farm also included a log stock barn and cotton house and a blacksmith shop. Late in life "Loss" and Ponola moved to a house in Shelby.

GEORGE AND JULIA CORNWELL FARM

3335 Robert Cornwell Road (SR 1812)
Double Shoals vicinity
1898

This two-story frame I-house has a Craftsman-style brick porch that replaced an earlier wooden porch in the 1920s. The facade features three bays with a porte cochere extending off the north elevation. Two central interior chimneys extend above the side-gable roof. Projecting from a large ell is a stove tower with small vents near its top. One surviving Victorian porch has chamfered posts, turned spindles, and scroll-sawn spandrels. A log smokehouse and a frame granary stand to the west of the house. Other outbuildings include a frame barn, a second smokehouse (frame), a combination barn and corncrib, and several sheds. George L. Cornwell (1870–1961) married Julia Gold (1872–1964) in 1891. He served as a county commissioner from 1936 to 1940.

HENRY AND SUSAN WARLICK HOUSE

951 Oak Grove–Clover Hill Church Road (SR 1509)
Lawndale vicinity
1898

Henry and Susan Warlick were early owners of this impressive two-story frame Italianate house. Gables project

J. F. Moore House (BRE)

Henry and Susan Warlick House (BRE)

George and Julia Cornwell House (BRE)

from the hip roof, and corbeled chimneys rise above it. A prominent feature is a two-tier porch on the west elevation with an exquisitely carved balustrade on the upper tier. A wraparound porch has a small gable in line with the front door. A stove tower has casement windows and a pyramidal roof from which protrudes a brick flue. The most significant architectural feature on the north elevation is a three-sided bay window on the first floor. Directly above this is a square bay. The corresponding gable has Victorian adornment on each of its three ends.

J. B. Blanton House porch detail, top; stove tower, bottom (BRE)

J. B. BLANTON HOUSE

323 West Main Street
Mooresboro
1899

This frame I-house has a center-passage plan with a pair of chimneys that rise from the interior. The one-story front porch features chamfered posts and a decorative balustrade with spade and heart motifs. Attached to the side of one rear ell is a stove tower with three-light casement windows and a pyramidal roof. A second ell, two stories in height, has a shed addition, an exterior chimney, and an upper-level sleeping porch. The house was remodeled in 1999. Nearby stands a frame outbuilding that serves as a combination smokehouse, corncrib, and storage shed.

JAMES AND CLORA CARPENTER FARM

102 Starhill Drive
Waco vicinity
1899

James Buchanan Carpenter (1858–1936) built this house in 1899 and moved into it the same year with his wife Clora Louvenia Carpenter (1865–1938). Like their contemporaries, the Carpenters relied heavily on cotton for their livelihood. Their son, Will W. Carpenter (1894–1978), acquired the farm in 1938 after his mother's death and erected four chickenhouses. The one-story frame dwelling, an L-plan structure with an ell, has two interior chimneys and a wraparound porch. With the exception of a single frame chickenhouse located across the farm road and directly in front of the house, the outbuildings—all frame and most dating to about 1938—are scattered southwest of the dwelling. These include a granary, a corncrib, a one-story chickenhouse, and a remarkably intact two-story chickenhouse with an interior chimney. Other outbuildings include a large transverse stock barn with shed additions and a ca. 1900 smokehouse.

SOUTHERN COTTON OIL MILL

520 South Morgan Street
Shelby
1900 and later

Capt. J. Frank Jenkins, J. J. McMurray, and J. P. Dellinger established this mill in 1900 in order to convert cottonseed—a waste product of cotton ginning—into cooking oil. The newly constructed brick mill, which was also known as the Shelby Cotton Seed Oil Mill, was purchased in 1901 by the Southern Cotton Oil Company. By 1905 the complex included the main building, a ginnery, a seed house, and a hull and meal house, the latter two buildings connected to the mill by conveyors. Twenty-five hands were employed by the plant, which operated six months out of the year. In 1907 a fertilizer plant was added. In 1916 the mill crushed approximately 5,000 tons of seed and shipped the extracted oil to a refinery in Savannah, where it was converted into Snow Drift Lard, Wesson's cooking oil, and salad oils. Numerous cotton oil mills operated in the region during the early twentieth century—Kings Mountain and Mooresboro also had such mills—but declining cotton production after 1930 forced many to close, and in 1960 the

Glenn-Stamey House (BRE)

Shelby plant was said to be the last one operating in western North Carolina. In the early 1980s the complex included a metal-sided cottonseed house; a brick press house with a roof monitor and a pre-1921 concrete block addition; and a two-story metal-sided fertilizer and meal warehouse with a front railroad shed. The complex is now used for warehousing.

RALPH HOLLAND HOUSE

McBrayer Homestead Road (SR 1161)
Boiling Springs vicinity
Ca. 1900

This house, built in the late nineteenth or early twentieth century, has a recessed porch supported by square posts on brick piers. The low hip roof has a central hipped dormer with louvered openings and shed dormers on the north and south sides. The land surrounding the house was once a part of a much larger Pruett family estate, but the house is best known for its association with Ralph Holland, a minister and farmer.

Joseph and Cynthia Bingham House (BRE)

JOSEPH AND CYNTHIA BINGHAM HOUSE

St. Peter's Church Road (SR 1606)
Belwood vicinity
Ca. 1900

Joseph Pinkney Bingham (1864–1945) and his wife Cynthia Jane Brackett Bingham (1868–1965) lived in this frame house for many years and raised a family here. Bingham grew cotton and operated a sawmill on the property. He supplied local residents with dressed lumber and cut the lumber used in the construction of his home. A later owner of the property was Joe Hege. A double-tier portico with balustrade dominates the facade of the two-story house, and two chimneys rise from the interior. A one-story porch appears to have been incorporated into the portico. Double-leaf doors pierce the center bay on both the first and second story, and these are flanked on each side by single four-over-four double-hung sash windows. A large ca. 1930 brick and frame addition extends to the rear. Situated behind the house are several frame outbuildings, including a smokehouse, granary, and chickenhouse. A ca. 1900 frame transverse horse barn stands nearby.

GLENN-STAMEY HOUSE

105 Merton Road (SR 1651)
Belwood vicinity
Ca. 1900

Built by the Glenn family about the turn of the twentieth century, this frame house was purchased by Frank and Annie Alexander Stamey in 1922. The Stameys planned to raze the house, but the hard times of the 1930s convinced them to remodel instead. They used stones from surrounding fields to face the house, extended a north side porch, and excavated a basement. Front and side entries are contained in arched openings, paired six-over-six windows light the interior, a porch extends across the front, and the saltbox roof is interrupted by two interior chimneys.

Bill and Melinda Boggs House, left; flowerhouse, above (BRE)

John Moss Store (BRE)

BILL AND MELINDA BOGGS FARM

106 Carpenters Grove Church Road
Belwood
Ca. 1900

Bill and Melinda Boggs were the original occupants of this one-and-a-half-story frame house. Later Bill's nephew, John Boggs (1874–1960), and John's wife Ella Spurling Boggs (1885–1969) lived here. Following John and Ella's deaths, Lloyd and Vangie Mull Boggs resided in the house until 1991. Today, the house stands vacant among brick and frame outbuildings that once formed a thriving agricultural complex. The house features a cross-gable roof with a prominent central dormer between two smaller gables. There are clipped gables on the north and south ends, pressed-metal roofing, a bracketed cornice, and the corbeled caps of two brick chimneys. A one-story wraparound porch supported on square-section Doric columns is enhanced by a small centered gable. Molded surrounds with peaked lintels frame the first-story windows. Extending to the rear is an ell covered in asbestos siding. Nearby stand a brick flowerhouse with eight-light casement windows and several frame outbuildings, including a smokehouse, a washhouse, a corncrib, a shed, and two tractor sheds.

JOHN MOSS STORE

117 Putnam Street
Waco
Ca. 1900

This gable-roofed frame store has a front porch that shelters a double-leaf paneled door and flanking windows. To the rear is a double-leaf freight door with diagonal battens. Next to the store is a frame and metal cookhouse used to prepare meats and vegetables for sale.

DICK AND PATIENCE SPANGLER FARM

2250 North Lafayette Street (SR 1005)
Double Shoals vicinity
Ca. 1900, 1915–16

Abson Dixon "Dick" Spangler (1867–1946) built this two-story frame house no later than 1901, possibly in the late 1890s. He lived here with his wife Nannie Patience "Patie" Green Spangler (1867–1925) and their twelve children. The Spanglers raised cotton, vegetables, and livestock. With the growth of the Spangler family, Dick recognized the need for a larger house, and in 1915–16 he added a second story. Eventually his son E. Yates Spangler (1901–93) and Yates's wife Daisy Beam Spangler (1907–85) inherited the property and continued the cultivation of cotton. Yates Spangler also sold real estate. The T-plan house features a one-story porch with square posts. A rear ell has a stove tower with a pyramidal roof. Other features include a large dormer and one-over-one windows. A smokehouse stands beside the dwelling, and across the road are several early-twentieth-century frame outbuildings, including a garage and workshop, a transverse barn, a corncrib, and a shed. In the center of this agricultural complex stands a wellhouse. The house remains in the family.

WASHBURN BLOCK

101–117 North Lafayette Street
Shelby
Ca. 1900, 1920s

The Washburn Block illustrates several decades in the architectural evolution of Shelby's downtown. Early elements of the block are the 1905 Washburn Hardware Building and the Hamrick Jewelers Building (firm established in 1898 by T. W. Hamrick), which feature metal cornices, decorative window surrounds, and recessed entries. At the corner with West Marion Street is the former Cleveland Bank & Trust Company, with a stuccoed facade and modillion-like cornice dating to a 1922 remodeling. The 1920 Wilson Building features a Carrara glass storefront from the 1930s or 1940s.

PUTNAM-ADAMS HOUSE

2309 Pleasant Hill Church Road (SR 1103)
Patterson Springs vicinity
1901

The Putnams were cotton farmers who in 1901 hired W. B. Lowery to build this one-story Victorian dwelling. The picturesque house was sold to the Adams family about 1920. The house has an L plan with a gable roof. The front entry contains a double-leaf

Dick and Patie Spangler House (BRE)

Washburn Block. Circa 1950 photo courtesy of the Lloyd Hamrick Collection.

Stice Shoals Power Plant (BRE)

Putnam-Adams House gable vent (BRE)

Dobbin and Jane Hicks House (BRE)

Putnam-Adams House (BRE)

door and is sheltered by a gabled stoop on chamfered posts with scrollwork tops. Other features include interior and exterior chimneys and louvered gable vents. A concrete block washhouse stands nearby.

STICE SHOALS DAM AND POWER PLANT

570 Stice Shoal Road (SR 1215)
Shelby vicinity
1904–5

Built by the Lily Mill & Power Company, this hydroelectric dam on the First Broad River provided power for the Lily Mill. Surplus electricity was sold to the city of Shelby for a number of years. During the early to mid–twentieth century, John Elliott operated the dam and lived in an adjacent house with his wife Mildred. The early-twentieth-century brick powerhouse at Stice Shoals has a corbeled cornice, and its turbines receive water through a large pipe. Original gears, metal walkways, causeways, and a long riverside wall for erosion control are other features.

DOBBIN AND JANE HICKS HOUSE

101 Queens Circle (SR 1618)
Belwood vicinity
1905

Dobbin Hicks (1867–1928) built this modest Victorian house in 1905 for his wife Jane (1873–1929) and their family, which eventually numbered ten children. The one-story frame house has a gable roof with two front gables that flank a smaller center gable. The wraparound Victorian porch has turned and bracketed posts. Other features include a bracketed

Selected Inventory 239

cornice, two interior chimneys (one with a corbeled cap), and a small ell. A frame smokehouse stands near the ell, and a frame transverse stock barn is nearby. On their farm the Hicks family grew cotton and corn.

BIG HILL METHODIST CHURCH

6639 Casar Road (NC 10)
Casar vicinity
Ca. 1905

This gable-fronted frame church is typical of the simple rural churches built throughout the region in the late nineteenth and early twentieth centuries. It stands on stone piers now infilled with concrete block and has weatherboard siding and metal roofing. Two paneled doors open on the front, and above them is a rectangular louvered vent. Four six-over-six windows run down each side, a polygonal apse extends to the rear, and a brick stove flue rises on the east elevation. The austere interior has board-sheathed walls and ceiling, slat-back benches, and a pulpit with Gothic pointed panels. Nearby lies the cemetery, which contains graves dating to the late nineteenth and early twentieth centuries. Regular services were discontinued at Big Hill Methodist Church in 1959, but members of the community continue to use the historic building for revivals and other events.

TATE HOUSE

205 North Main Street
Grover
Ca. 1905

Mannasseh Masshaw Tate (1843–1904) and his wife Annie Bridges Tate (1865–1921) spent most of their lives in South Carolina. After Mannasseh's death in 1904, Annie and her son Roland Clifton Tate (b. 1891) moved to Grover, where they had this one-story Victorian frame house built. R. C. Tate operated People's Drug Store in Grover from 1919 to 1952. He married Fannie Ellis Tate in 1921. The hip-and-gable Tate House features an unusual front porch, which has a prominent gable ornamented with quatrefoil cutout vergeboards and a stanchion with a turned pendant. The gable rises above a tall paneled frieze supported by chamfered posts with sawn brackets that create an arched effect.

MOSS-HOPPER HOUSE

2730 Bettis Road (SR 2225)
Earl
1905–6

Merimon T. Moss (1877–1918) built this Victorian house for himself and his wife Alice Runyan Moss. Merimon drove a taxi in Blacksburg, South Carolina, and Alice worked in a South Carolina boardinghouse owned and operated by Duke Power Company. Merimon died during the 1918 influenza epidemic; Alice continued to live here until the Hopper family purchased the property in 1950. Buri Hopper operated an automobile repair garage behind the house. The hip-

Big Hill Methodist Church (BRE)

Tate House (BRE)

roofed house features two front gables with cornice returns and two-over-two windows. Turned posts and a turned balustrade adorn the one-story wrap-around porch. Two small gables with half-timber-like detail embellish the front corners of the porch. Three interior chimneys, one exterior chimney, and a rear ell with an enclosed porch are other features. Buri Hopper's ca. 1950 molded concrete block and frame garage and an accompanying shed still stand.

J. B. AND SUNIE LATTIMORE FARM

317 Peachtree Street (SR 1162)
Lattimore
1908

John Broadus Lattimore (1877–1969) built this one-story frame Victorian house for his wife Sunie Jones Lattimore (1885–1971) in 1908. Lattimore wore many hats. He was Lattimore's second mayor and its Seaboard depot agent, he built the J. B. Lattimore Store Building, he operated the Bostic Brick Company in Bostic, and he farmed cotton. His house has a low hip roof with a large dormer and a front porch that originally wrapped around to the south elevation. A large brick ell projects to the rear. The property's extensive household and farm outbuilding complex includes an unusual hay crib with a shed roof on brick supports. A farm office, a garage, a smokehouse, and three chickenhouses (all frame), a flowerhouse, a privy, a tractor shed, and hay barns round out the group.

COLEMAN BLANTON FARM

1615 Chatfield Road (SR 1343)
Shelby vicinity
Ca. 1909

Also known as Brushy Creek Dairy Farm, this establishment was one of the first large commercial dairies in the county and the first to offer home delivery service. Coleman Blanton opened Shelby's first bottling works and was also a founder of the Cleveland County Fair. He owned a sawmill, a Delco generating plant, a block house, and a water pumping tower.

The approximately 73-acre farm is located northwest of Shelby and comprises an excellent assortment of agricultural buildings associated with dairy farming, including a dairy barn, bottling house, smokehouse, granary, coal house, block house, and tractor shed, all of which were constructed between 1909 and 1950. The dairy barn is particularly noteworthy for its concrete block construction, which adhered to new state hygiene laws that required concrete floors. Similarly, the impact of new building techniques recommended by the agricultural extension service can be seen in the block house (used for manufacturing concrete block), the coal house, and the bottling house (all built with concrete block). The farm complex also includes frame structures such as the novelty-sided granary, tractor shed, and smokehouse.

At the center of the farm, surrounded by a pecan grove, is the ca.

Moss–Hopper House (BRE)

J. B. and Sunie Lattimore House (BRE)

William and Corrie Bettis House (BRE)

Smokehouse (top) and outbuilding on the Clarence and Ellen Plonk Farm (BRE)

1909 Queen Anne farmhouse. This one-story frame dwelling features a standing-seam tin gable-on-hip roof and wraparound porch with turned balustrade. Other decorative elements consist of an original widow's walk at the top of the roof, box eaves, corner pilasters, Eastlake-style doors, and pointed arch vents with scalloped louvers. The rear ell of the irregular-plan house features a stove tower or "German chimney." Interior features include beaded board wainscoting in the hall and dining room, plaster walls, paneled wood doors, and hardwood floors. The house retains its original four mantels with decorative side columns and overmantels.

BOILING SPRINGS POST OFFICE (FORMER)

109 South Main Street
Boiling Springs
1910

This one-story brick building served as Boiling Spring's post office in the 1930s. It also had an association with the Beason family and contained a general store and a barbershop at different times. For many years—until a renovation in 2000, when a stucco finish was added to the exterior—the building was vacant. It is now occupied by a gift shop.

WILLIAM AND CORRIE BETTIS HOUSE

2710 Bettis Road (SR 2225)
Earl vicinity
1910–11

William French Bettis (1879–1960), a cotton farmer and investor in the Sarratt Cotton Gin, built this austere two-story frame house. A small one-story porch supported by turned posts defines the main entrance. The one-story ell has an enclosed porch and a kitchen with a stove tower. Two interior chimneys are situated in the two-story portion of the house. A ca. 1930 molded concrete block garage stands to the rear. Will was the son of Allen E. Bettis; his wife was Corrie Towery Bettis (1886–1978).

CLARENCE AND ELLEN PLONK FARM

219 Saint Lukes Church Road
(SR 2008)
Kings Mountain vicinity
1911

The two-story main house in this extensive farm complex was built by John Goforth for Clarence Sloan Plonk (1883–1966) and his wife Ellen Patterson Plonk (1886–1986) in 1911.

Voidrey and Dorsey Wright House (BRE)

The wood used in the construction of the house came from trees that had been cleared from the property to create pasture and cotton fields. The Plonks focused on cotton production until the late 1940s, when the boll weevil forced them to diversify into wheat, barley, and egg production. Today, much reduced in acreage, the farm raises wheat, oats, and beef cattle.

A narrow drive meanders through fields to the house, a frame dwelling with a low hip roof and a hipped dormer. A wraparound porch supports a pediment that lines up with the front entrance. Other features include exterior and interior chimneys, one-over-one windows, and several historic additions. The interior contains a stair with a sawn newel post, post-and-lintel mantels, and a farm office in the northeast corner of the first floor that is reached through its own entry. Here Clarence Plonk engaged in another line of business: mule trading.

Many of the ca. 1911 outbuildings are still in use today, including the smokehouse, where hams are hung up to salt cure following the annual fall slaughter. Directly behind the house is the wellhouse; beyond it are a ca. 1950 hog vat, a woodshed, and a flowerhouse. North of the wellhouse are a car shed, a large mule barn, a gear room (where harnesses for the farm's twenty mules were stored), and a corncrib. West of the smokehouse stand a chickenhouse, a two-story granary, and a blacksmith's shop. The granary has a loft door and a small platform extending just beyond the door that facilitated the loading and unloading of grain. Other farm buildings include a cotton house, a second granary, and a transverse mule barn.

A farm lane crosses a creek and leads to the Gordon-Wilson House, a ca. 1915 tenant house of gable-fronted form with a front porch, a five-room plan, and a mantel with dentil ornament. At different times the Gordon and Wilson families lived here. East of the Gordon-Wilson House are a cow barn and small field that were intended for the tenant farmer's private use. South of the Gordon-Wilson House is another tenant house that was occupied for many years by Jessie and Tildon Jackson and their children. This one-story frame has a front porch and an interior chimney.

VOIDREY AND DORSEY WRIGHT FARM

2233 New Prospect Church Road (SR 1908)
Waco vicinity
1912

Voidrey Wright and his brother John built the story-and-a-half frame dwelling on this farm. Here Voidrey and his wife Dorsey Hoyle Wright grew cotton, corn, wheat, barley, and oats. In order to increase their profits, the Wrights also engaged in the egg production business. Voidrey and Dorsey kept as many as a hundred chickens at a given time, and they sold their eggs to "Hatcher" Jones of Jones Hatchery in Shelby. Today the farm produces beans, peas, corn, and peanuts.

The Wright House has a front porch on chamfered posts. The clipped gable roof has shingle-pattern pressed-metal sheathing and supports a hipped dormer. The one-story rear kitchen ell has an enclosed porch and an interior chimney. Other features include two interior chimneys, two-over-two and four-over-four windows, several casement windows, and a rear ell. South of the house stand a molded concrete block garage, a frame milkhouse, and a well. Beyond the kitchen ell lies the main concentration of frame outbuildings, including a corncrib, a chickenhouse, a gear house, a smokehouse, a transverse mule barn, a wheat granary, and a privy.

FORREST AND CARRIE BOWEN HOUSE

3230 Shelby Road (SR 1813)
Double Shoals vicinity
Ca. 1912

Forrest Bowen (1868–1966) married Carrie Williamson (1891–1962) on May 16, 1912. Shortly afterward the couple moved into this newly completed one-and-a-half-story frame house, built with the assistance of Lawndale carpenter John Eaker. Forrest Bowen, who was gifted with an entrepreneurial spirit, recognized the potential of the automobile at an early date and opened the first dealership in Forest City. Several years later the Bowens moved to Sanford, Florida, where they operated a large dairy farm. Eventually they moved back to their picturesque Double Shoals area residence.

The house has a wraparound porch, a bay window, louvered gable vents, and a large central dormer with windows and a louvered vent. The cross-gable roof is covered with pressed metal. Over the north elevation is a clipped gable ornamented with a modified Palladian window. A similar clipped gable with a Palladian window treatment dominates the south elevation. The east elevation has a one-story rear ell with a porch and a prominent stove tower. Like the county's other flues, this one features casement windows on two sides, louvered vents near the top, a pyramidal roof, and a small chimney.

top to bottom: Will Carpenter Farm smokehouse; washhouse; outbuilding (all BRE)

WILL CARPENTER FARM

Cherryville Road (NC 150)
Waco vicinity
Ca. 1915

Will Carpenter was the original owner of this one-and-a-half-story dwelling. The low hipped roof has decorative gables, and there are multiple chimneys, a porch, and an addition. Directly behind the house stands an unusual stretcher-bond brick washhouse with a gable-on-hip roof and

Forrest and Carrie Bowen House stove tower (BRE)

exposed rafter ends. Adjacent to the washhouse is a molded concrete block smokehouse, and beyond are sheds, a chickenhouse, a corncrib, and a transverse mule barn, all of frame construction.

GOLD'S STORE

4015 Polkville Road (NC 226)
Polkville vicinity
Ca. 1915

Located on Highway 226 between Polkville and Shelby, Gold's General Store supplied farmers, travelers, and merchants with a range of merchandise. The frame rectangular building features a stepped parapet that par-

Gold's Store interior, above; exterior, right top (BRE)

Biddie Jones Stroud House, above; corncrib and wagon shelter, right middle (BRE)

Pisgah Lodge 9080, above (JDP)

tially obscures a gambrel roof. The storefront retains original double-leaf doors flanked by double-hung sash windows. Other features include an exterior end chimney and loading doors.

PISGAH LODGE 9080

Wilson Street
Shelby
1910s

Fraternal organizations historically played an important role in African American communities; black counterparts of the white Masons, Elks, and Odd Fellows were especially popular in the late nineteenth and early twentieth centuries. The Pisgah Lodge appears to be one of the county's oldest surviving black lodge buildings. Its concrete cornerstone gives a partial 1910s date of organization and identifies the two-story building as a branch of the G.U.O. of O.F. The lodge is constructed of rock-faced concrete block, a material that was popular for its affordability and durability. Other features of the abandoned building include a gable roof, two-over-two windows, and wood panel doors.

BIDDIE JONES STROUD FARM

318 Peachtree Street (SR 1162)
Lattimore
Ca. 1915

Biddie Jones Stroud (1846–1919), who had this house built, was the widow of cotton farmer William Stroud (1820–1900). The gable-front-

and-wing one-story frame dwelling features beaded weatherboard siding and a front porch with turned posts and scrollwork. Both of the two ells have interior chimneys. A pyramidal-roofed wellhouse in the back yard has Victorian attributes. Beyond it are a frame smokehouse and a frame transverse stock barn attached to a smaller half-dovetail log transverse stock barn. An original metal fence survives in the front yard.

PARK GRACE SCHOOL

115 Parkgrace Road
Kings Mountain
Early 20th century

Park Grace School is a classic example of the Colonial Revival style as applied to school construction. The T-plan building of common-bond brick construction has pedimented dormers. The front entry is highlighted by four Doric columns that support heavy gable returns. The entry itself has a double-leaf door with a transom and flanking windows. An exterior rear chimney and banks of classroom windows complete the picture. Park Grace School and others in Cleveland County Township 4 (Beth Ware, Compact, and Grover) consolidated with Kings Mountain in 1961, and Park Grace was used for first through seventh grades. In 1969 the school closed, and the Kings Mountain maintenance department used the space for offices and equipment storage until 1992, when Park Grace was sold to a Kings Mountain–based welding operation.

ESSIE AND EVERETT GOODE HOUSE

210 West College Avenue
Boiling Springs
1905

When his children married, prominent farmer Noah Hamrick gave them acreage and helped them build houses on their new farms. In the early decades of the twentieth century, Hamrick's daughter Essie married Everett Goode and her father assisted the newlyweds in the construction of this story-and-a-half frame Victorian dwelling. The house features a gable roof with front and rear dormers; the front gables have decorative wood-shingle sheathing. The porch wraps around three sides, and the kitchen ell has a shed room (probably a pantry) and a screen porch. The center-passage-plan interior is two rooms deep.

JONAS A. LOVELACE HOUSE

411 Pleasant Ridge Church Road
(SR 1161)
Boiling Springs vicinity
Early 20th century

Cotton farmer Jonas Alvin Lovelace constructed this modest Victorian-style dwelling in the early 1900s. The center-passage-plan house has a large kitchen ell, a front gable with fishscale wood-shingle sheathing, and a wrap-around porch on chamfered posts. Only minor changes have been made to the interior, which retains original mantels in variations of the post-and-lintel form. A smokehouse with shed additions stands near the house, and a tenant house is located across a field. The traces of cotton rows are still evident in the fields behind the house.

Park Grace School (BRE)

Essie and Everett Goode House (BRE)

Charles and Ida Neisler House (BRE)

Capernaum Arbor (BRE)

CAPERNAUM ARBOR

Capernium Road (SR 2075)
Waco vicinity
1919

Capernaum Arbor marks the site of Capernaum Baptist Church, which was constituted in 1842. The church flourished in the nineteenth century, its membership growing from 35 in 1842 to 170 in 1882, and may even have supported a school in the 1850s. The congregation moved to Waco and became Waco Baptist Church; the church building at Capernaum was used as an African American school and later demolished. The sanctity of the site is remembered at an annual memorial service held in the arbor the first Sunday in August. The arbor is representative of the arbor and tabernacle type—a large open-air structure supported by stout timber posts with brackets—and it replaced an impermanent brush arbor that stood at the same location. A metal-sheathed hip roof shelters a concrete floor, picnic tables, and slatted benches. Near the tabernacle is a commemorative marker (with the church name misspelled "Capernium") and a cemetery with granite headstones and several marble obelisks. Washington Missionary Church stands a short distance away.

CHARLES AND IDA NEISLER HOUSE

510 North Piedmont Avenue
Kings Mountain
Early 20th century

Charles Eugene Neisler (1868–1931) came to Kings Mountain to serve as supervisor of the Kings Mountain Manufacturing Company in 1893. The Neisler family is one of the anchor textile families of Kings Mountain, and Charles was instrumental in founding several textile plants, including the Margrace, Pauline, and Patricia mills. Charles and his wife Ida Pauline Mauney had eight children. Their two-story frame Classical Revival dwelling has a shingle-pattern pressed-metal hip roof; above the roof rise two interior brick chimneys. On the second story, the central bay of the three-bay facade projects slightly and contains a Palladian window. A dentil cornice adorns the one-story porch, which stands on Ionic columns. The front door features beveled leaded glass multilight sidelights and a fanlight. Ionic pilasters flank the door.

GLENN MCDANIEL HOUSE

1629 Bethlehem Road (SR 2245)
Kings Mountain vicinity
Early 20th century

Glenn McDaniel built this house and lived here with his wife Francis and their children. In the mid–twentieth century, the United States Gypsum Company bought the house from McDaniel and converted it into its main office. Constructed of fieldstone, the dwelling has six-over-six, four-over-four, and one-over-one windows and small front and back porches.

C. J. HAMRICK STORE

402 North Main Street
Boiling Springs
Early 20th century

Two stores stood on this site prior to the present building. The first, a frame building, was probably built about 1875. It burned, and its replacement was razed. The present building features a flat roof with a tiled coping, common-bond brick walls, and evenly spaced doors and windows. According to longtime Boiling Springs residents, the store sold a wide range of merchandise and ordered what was not in stock. Charles Jefferson Hamrick (1833–1918) and his sons operated the first John Deere dealership in this part of the county, thus contributing to the transition to mechanized cotton farming. Elijah Bly Hamrick ran the store after his father's death and built the present building. The Hamricks also operated a cotton gin behind the store and a sawmill on an adjoining lot.

OLIVER HAMRICK HOUSE

417 North Main Street
Boiling Springs
Early 20th century

Oliver Hamrick had this house built between 1900 and 1915. The one-story frame Queen Anne dwelling has a wraparound porch and a gable roof with a decorative front gable. The gable ends have board-and-batten sheathing, three chimneys rise from the interior, and the windows have two-over-two sash. A small pyrami-

Glenn McDaniel House (BRE)

C. J. Hamrick Store (BRE)

Oliver Hamrick House (BRE)

Bridges House (BRE)

Shelby Cafe Block. Circa 1950 photo courtesy of the Lloyd Hamrick Collection.

Carver S. Bridges acquired the farm and constructed four large chickenhouses for his egg business. One of Carver's most important customers was the local Number 3 Egg Producers, a company that is still in operation today. Like other farmers in the area, Carver also sold his farm-fresh eggs to nearby grocery stores. The poultry operation includes a small front-gable frame egg processing house, and there are also a concrete block wellhouse and a frame corncrib/garage. The main house has a high hip roof and two interior chimneys. Its facade features a bay window with four-over-one sash and a one-story wraparound porch supported by square-section wood columns.

SHELBY CAFE BLOCK

220–228 South Lafayette Street
Shelby
Early 20th century

The highlight of this row of one-story brick commercial buildings is the Shelby Cafe (220 S. Lafayette), which features a streamlined black Carrara glass facade and neon signage from the 1940s. The tall rectangular structure in the middle of this highly modified block is what remains of the Princess Theatre, Shelby's first cinema. The Princess was later operated as the Carolina Theatre.

dal-roofed structure is attached to the rear of the dwelling and probably once served as the kitchen. Outbuildings include a smokehouse with a shed addition, a frame chickenhouse, and a stock barn that later served as a garage.

BRIDGES FARM

1306 Mount Sinai Church Road
(SR 1140)
Earl vicinity
Early 20th century

Joseph C. Bridges was the original owner of the main house on this property. Following his death in the 1940s,

Selected Inventory 249

Shelby Post Office (former) (JDP)

Ed and Edith Olive House (BRE)

SHELBY POST OFFICE (FORMER)

111 South Washington Street
Shelby
1916

The names of Treasury Department acting supervising architect James A. Wetmore and architect Lee Young appear on the cornerstone of this Classical Revival brick post office. Doric pilasters march across the building's facade in evocation of a portico, capped by a stone cornice. Period lamps on decorative metal shafts flank the front steps. The two-story building now houses the Cleveland County Arts Council. Behind this building, at 211 E. Warren, stands the former Post Office Annex, a two-story 1920s building that contained the office of "Shelby Dynasty" Judge Edwin Yates Webb.

ED AND EDITH OLIVE HOUSE

2730 Johnson Street
Earl
1916

Ed and Edith Olive bought this frame Craftsman bungalow shortly after it was completed in 1916. Ed served as Earl's Southern Railway depot agent for several years. Unfortunately, the Olives were forced out of their home during the Great Depression due to the failure of cotton futures investments. Thomas Moss bought the house, and it remains in the Moss family. The most prominent feature of the one-and-a-half-story dwelling is the central three-bay gabled dormer. Other typical Craftsman features include a porte cochere, three-over-one windows, and a projecting side bay. Squat frame columns on brick plinths carry the arched spans of the front porch. A frame garage stands beside the dwelling.

NEW PROSPECT BAPTIST CHURCH

1960 New Prospect Church Road (SR 1908)
Shelby vicinity
Early and mid–20th century

In 1801, John Teeter Beam (1732–1807) built a Lutheran church on this site. Because of the scarcity of churches in the area, other denominations worshiped here as well. Around 1820 the church evolved into a Baptist congregation, and in 1827 the Broad River Baptist Association officially recognized New Prospect as a member. The church's first full-time pastor was Reverend Thomas Dixon (1820–1909). Reverend Dixon's son was Reverend Thomas Dixon Jr., author of *The Clansman* and *The Leopard's Spots*. The stretcher-bond brick-veneer church has a front-gable orientation with cornice returns and lancet-arched stained glass windows. A two- and three-story classroom and administrative wing dominates the rear. The majority of the openings found in this section are fifteen-light casement windows. Rev. Thomas Dixon Sr. and John Teeter Beam are buried in the adjoining cemetery. Early interments include infant Jacob Carpenter (1819–19) and Martha Carpenter (d. 1826 age 36).

MARGRACE MILL VILLAGE

Margrace Avenue and adjacent streets
Kings Mountain
1910s–1920s

Margrace Mill Village is Cleveland County's best-preserved mill village. The compact neighborhood consists of forty-seven three- and four-room mill houses built between 1914 and 1925. These small houses feature central chimneys, half-length recessed porches, and stone foundation piers with concrete block infill. The mill village includes a ca. 1920 stone-veneer clubhouse at 500 Margrace Avenue. Charles E. Neisler Sr. had the houses built for employees of his Margrace Mill, located directly across Margrace Avenue. Neisler came to Kings Mountain about 1890 to supervise the Kings Mountain Manufacturing Company for his future father-in-law, W. A. Mauney. The Mauneys and Neislers employed thousands of people in the manufacture of textiles in the early and mid–twentieth century. Neisler named Margrace Mill after his daughters Margaret and Grace.

MARION AND DOVIE JOLLEY HOUSE

126 Flint Hill Church Road (SR 1148)
Boiling Springs
1920

Marion Augustus Jolley (1888–1969) built this frame Craftsman bungalow and lived here with his wife Dovie Hopper Jolley and their family. Like most of his neighbors, Jolley farmed cotton, but he also served as chief deputy sheriff of Cleveland County. His cross-gable dwelling has a wraparound porch on Craftsman brick and wood supports. The porch has a porte cochere extension and a cornice ornamented with recessed panels. Other features of the house include interior and exterior chimneys and a low hipped dormer with casement windows. Nearby stands a versatile ca. 1920 frame outbuilding that alternately served as a smokehouse, garage, and storage shed and as a residence for Max Lattimore, who worked for Marion Jolley.

KINGS MOUNTAIN WATERWORKS

106 South Deal Street
Kings Mountain
Ca. 1920

This Colonial Revival–influenced two-story building has walls of stretcher-bond brick and a center entry with a six-light fanlight and a brick relieving arch with an inset keystone. To the sides are windows with keystones and brick lintels. Above the second-story windows is a circular decorative feature with floral ornament. The gable roof has a pronounced cornice and returns.

Kings Mountain Waterworks, top; detail, bottom (BRE)

New Prospect Baptist Church (BRE)

Pruett's Store (BRE)

Dan Moore House (BRE)

PAULINE MILLS CLUBHOUSE

227 Walker Street
Kings Mountain
Ca. 1920

This one-story building provided workers from the nearby Pauline textile mill with space for social gatherings. The building has a fieldstone facing, exterior and interior chimneys, and four-over-four and six-over-six windows.

APARTMENT HOUSE

211 West Mountain Street
Kings Mountain
Ca. 1920

This two-story stone apartment house features a three-bay facade. Centered on the roof is a low hipped dormer with multilight casement windows. A one-story porch shelters the center bay, and a wrought-iron railing defines an open portico above. A four-car stone garage with a hip roof stands to the rear.

PRUETT'S STORE

721 McBrayer Homestead Road (SR 1161)
Boiling Springs vicinity
Ca. 1920

This small one-story frame building has a front-gable roof behind a false front. The center entry is flanked by six-over-six windows, and its screen door is adorned with spindles; all are sheltered by a full-length porch. John Pruett operated his general store in the front of the building. The rear contained a barbershop run by Hubert Addington, and a separate entry allowed patrons to visit the barbershop without having to use the front door.

DAN MOORE HOUSE

1331 College Avenue (NC 150)
Boiling Springs vicinity
1921

J. F. Moore and Dan Moore Sr. built this Craftsman bungalow for Dan and his family. The house has remained in the family's possession and is currently occupied by one of Dan's daughters. The full-length recessed porch is supported by square wood columns and is screened in. A central hipped dormer dominates the roof, and cedar shakes cover the exterior. A porte cochere extends from the east elevation, and windows have two-over-two, four-over-four, and six-over-six sash. A board-and-batten shed stands nearby.

JOE BOYLES & SONS STORE

6457 Fallston Road (NC 18)
Belwood vicinity
Ca. 1921

This rectangular-plan one-story frame store features a side-gable roof and a recessed entrance with double-leaf doors. Built by Joe Boyles and his sons Carme and Roland, the store sold clothing, food, and other necessities to its rural clientele. In addition to their general mercantile enterprise, the store housed the Boyles' undertaking business. (It was a common practice in the early twentieth century to combine such diverse business ventures under one roof.) The store closed in the mid-1970s.

GROVER COMMERCIAL DISTRICT

The Piedmont Air Line, later known as the Atlanta & Charlotte Air Line, reached the Grover area in the early 1870s, and by the beginning of the twentieth century Grover's merchants had erected a cluster of brick commercial buildings at the community's heart. These buildings, many of which survive today, feature segmental-arched door and window openings and decorative corbeling in parapets.

EARL COMMERCIAL BUILDINGS

A pair of commercial buildings represents the historic commercial core of the village of Earl. The Bettis Store is a brick building dating to the early 1900s. Early partners in the enterprise included Joe Austell, Forest Austell, and Baxter and Will Bettis. Next door stands the ca. 1920 Webber General Store, a concrete block building owned and operated by Andrell Webber. Webber's store went out of business about 1923 due to the competition next door. Both buildings have similar one-story forms with stepped side parapets and storefronts in varying states of preservation.

J. D. AND JOHNYE ELLIOTT FARM

738 East College Avenue (NC 150)
Shelby vicinity
1922

Carpenter Rochel Hendricks built this frame one-and-a-half-story bungalow for cotton farmers and orchardists J. D. and Johnye Elliott. The roof is dominated by front and rear dormers, and a porte cochere extends from the west elevation. Other features include a front porch, exposed rafter ends, exterior and interior chimneys, and a shed addition. Most of the household and farm buildings date to the early twentieth century. Behind the house are a frame smokehouse, a grape arbor, and a concrete block flowerhouse. The farm buildings include a barn, a corncrib, two tractor sheds, and a storage shed. A small brick wellhouse stands at the edge of the farmyard.

NEWTON-ALLEN FARM

Rollingbrook Road (SR 2015)
Kings Mountain vicinity
Early 1920s

Andy Newton built this stretcher-bond brick bungalow along with a brick smokehouse, a frame corncrib, and a large frame potato house. Newton served as Cleveland County's

J. D. and Johnye Elliott House (BRE)

Newton-Allen House (BRE)

Joe Boyles & Sons Store (BRE)

Selected Inventory 253

register of deeds for many years, and he raised potatoes, cotton, corn, and wheat on his farm. In the 1930s he sold the property to Irvin Allen, a Cleveland County sheriff whose son Haywood was also a sheriff. H. O. (Toby) Williams bought the house in 1953, and the property remains in the Williams family. The house has a low hip roof with exposed rafter ends and a front porch supported by square-section brick pillars. Four-over-one windows, a back porch with brick enclosure, and exterior and interior chimneys are its other features.

D. C. Wright Store (BRE)

Byron and Mae Davis House (BRE)

D. C. WRIGHT STORE

312 West Main Street
Mooresboro
1924

Wright's General Store provided Mooresboro-area residents with staple items ranging from canned goods to fresh meat. Wright operated on credit, since many farmers had large amounts of cash on hand only after harvests. Wright lived in the DePriest House, which stands next door. In 1940 he sold the hip-roofed brick store to a Mr. Williamson, who later sold it to Reid Blackburn. Blackburn ran the business until 1971. Original features include built-in shelving units along the walls, a large showroom, and a rear storage room. A fourteen-light transom rests on top of the front door, flanked on either side by casement windows. Exposed pipes and pump bases are all that remain of the gas pumps.

BYRON AND MAE DAVIS FARM

252 Davis Road (SR 1107)
Earl vicinity
1924–25

Byron Davis commissioned Charlie Mintz to build this Craftsman bungalow in 1924, and he moved in with his wife Mae in 1925. The Davises grew cotton and raised chickens for the eggs; in fact, Mae Davis raises chickens there to this day. The bungalow has a large central dormer, an original pressed-tin roof, a wraparound front porch, and an enclosed back porch. The three-over-one and four-over-one windows are original. The seven-room interior features French doors, built-in cabinets, swinging doors between the kitchen and dining room, and beautifully carved mantels. Beyond the house are four sheds, a transverse mule barn, and two corncribs, all frame and all dating to the late 1920s.

KINGS MOUNTAIN SOUTHERN RAILWAY PASSENGER STATION

201 North Battleground Avenue
Kings Mountain
1925

Remodeled by the City of Kings Mountain in 1977, the depot now serves as a community center. The one-story brick building has a low hip roof with decorative knee braces and vergeboards in the eaves. During the 1977 modernization, new glass and aluminum doors were installed and an addition was constructed. Much of the original flooring remains intact; so do some interior space divisions.

GULF OIL COMPANY DISTRIBUTORSHIP

720 South Lafayette Street
Shelby
1925

Located in Shelby's early-twentieth-century industrial corridor, the Gulf Oil Company Distributorship was begun by Dr. Stephen S. Royster and his sons, D. W. and H. R. Royster. The business benefited from its proximity to the Southern rail line and utilized rail service until the mid-1970s. The distributorship is composed of two brick buildings with arched roofs that were built according to a design

Kings Mountain Southern Railway Passenger Station, left (BRE); bracket detail, above (JDP)

Gulf Oil Company Distributorship, above; interior, left (BRE)

used for all Gulf Oil facilities during the period. The building farthest from the railroad was originally a garage that was later converted to a warehouse. The other building served primarily for product distribution. Features common to both include continuous rows of casement windows running just below the roofline, and large freight doors that once facilitated the transfer of petroleum products from boxcars to trucks.

PLATO ALLISON FARM

2110 Camp Creek Church Road
(SR 1202)
Boiling Springs vicinity
1925

In 1925 Plato Allison (1884–1960) hired Grover Hamrick to build the one-story frame farmhouse that stands at the core of this relatively complete early-twentieth-century farm. The house has a T-plan form, with interior and exterior chimneys and original four-over-four double-hung sash windows. Changes include the addition of a front porch with jalousie windows and a small deck. Nearby stand several domestic and agricultural outbuildings. To the northeast are a saddle-notched log smokehouse and an early garden. A corn house and a cotton house, both frame, and a transverse saddle-notched log cow and mule barn complete the ensemble. Allison raised cotton, corn, wheat, cattle, and hogs on the property. Later Allison's foster grandson Ben A. (Jack) Holder lived here.

S. H. C. and Elsie DePriest House mantel (BRE)

Rush McCraw House (BRE)

MILLS AND HESTER CLINE FARM

1901 Fallston Road (NC 18)
Shelby vicinity
1925

A Mr. Branton built this brick Foursquare house, and Flay Cabaniss laid the brick. Shortly after the house was finished, David Mills Cline (1886–1954) and Hester Cabaniss Cline (1886–1955) moved in. The Clines were farmers who concentrated on cotton production but also grew wheat, corn, and vegetables for sale and personal consumption. The farm was one of the first in the county with a John Deere tractor (purchased in 1926 or 1927). The house is currently owned and inhabited by their son, John Cline.

The house has a low-pitched hip roof from which project two interior chimneys. A wraparound Craftsman-style porch terminates in a porch room on the south elevation and a porte cochere on the north elevation. A two-story brick ell extends off the south elevation, and at the rear of the house is a full-length frame shed addition that leads to the kitchen. The first floor has a center circulation hall flanked by a living room, a kitchen, a bathroom (later addition), and a single bedroom. The second floor consists of four bedrooms connected by a common hallway.

S. H. C. AND ELSIE DEPRIEST HOUSE

322 West Main Street
Mooresboro
1920s

The DePriest House is a typical Craftsman bungalow. The front porch is supported by square wood posts on brick piers. The five-bay facade has Craftsman four-over-one windows. A porte cochere extends from the east side, and a wraparound porch occupies all of the north elevation and half of the east elevation. Two interior chimneys are situated along the low hip roof, which is covered with shingle-pattern pressed metal. The interior features wainscoting topped with a chair rail and original doors. East of the house is a small frame chickenhouse.

RUSH MCCRAW HOUSE

2624 Wood Road (SR 1207)
Boiling Springs vicinity
1920s

Cotton farmer Robert Ed McCraw built this gable-fronted dwelling for his son Rush and his family. Rush farmed the property and earned additional income working at Duke Power's Cliffside Steam Station. The rectangular-plan house has a front porch supported on rough-hewn posts; interior chimneys; and six-over-six windows. North of the house are remnants of the original farm complex, including a frame smokehouse, a tractor shed, and a saddle-notched log corncrib. A grove of mature cherry and peach trees separates the dwelling from the outbuildings.

OVELLA AND LIZZIE GIBSON HOUSE

2408 South Post Road (SR 1107)
Earl vicinity
1920s

The residence of the Gibson sisters Ovella and Lizzie is typical of the Craftsman-style Foursquare house type. The hip roof is covered with Spanish tiles, and one of the two interior chimneys has a corbeled cap. Other features include an enclosed wraparound porch, six-over-one windows, and a kitchen ell with a stove tower topped by Spanish roof tiles.

GRAHAM ELEMENTARY SCHOOL

701 West Oak Street
Shelby
1920s

Following Shelby's annexation of South Shelby in the mid-1920s, four schools were planned and built: South Shelby, Jefferson, Graham, and Zoar. Graham School served first through seventh graders (eventually the seventh grade was transferred out). In 1979 it became Twelve Oaks Academy, a private school with a kindergarten through twelfth-grade curriculum. The front facade of the Colonial Revival building has recessed entries with multilight transoms flanking three sets of nine-over-nine windows, each set under a gabled dormer with a decorative window. The cross-gable roof has clipped gables. To the rear is a two-story flat-roofed brick addition dating to 1956.

BRIDGES & HOLLAND STORE

221 Flint Hill Church Road (SR 1148)
Boiling Springs
1920s

The Bridges & Holland Store is one of the county's best-preserved early-twentieth-century country stores. General stores such as this one were

Graham Elementary School (BRE)

Ovella and Lizzie Gibson House, left; rear elevation with stove tower, above (BRE)

Selected Inventory 257

once profitable financial enterprises as well as social centers for their communities. In the 1940s Xenophen Bridges (1892–1976) and Williamson Holland moved their business into Boiling Springs. The building features rough-hewn porch supports and unpainted weatherboard siding. Exposed rafter ends project from the eaves of the main roof and the attached hip-roofed metal canopy. A cookhouse attached to the east elevation was used to prepare food for sale. Nearby stands a large stock barn that rests on stone piers and has a metal roof and some metal walls. Behind the barn is a frame privy.

JOHN AND EDITH SAIN FARM

1273 Belwood-Lawndale Road
(SR 1612)
Belwood vicinity
1926

John and Edith Sain hired Sam Upton to build the modest brick Craftsman bungalow on this farm. John Sain assisted Upton in the construction. The house has a recessed porch supported by square columns on brick plinths, a low hip roof, and a small rear addition with a flat roof. Behind the house are several 1920s frame outbuildings situated in an orderly and efficient fashion. Southwest of the house are a car and tractor shed, a smokehouse, and a granary, and northwest of these is a frame transverse mule barn with shed additions. Across the farmyard stands a shed-roofed chickenhouse on stone foundation piers.

HUGH AND VIVIAN HOYLE HOUSE

204 Old Belwood Road (SR 1612)
Belwood vicinity
1926

Hugh Dixon Hoyle (1891–1980) built this modest bungalow on the site of the 1880s Belwood Institute, which was destroyed by fire in 1925. Hoyle bought the vacant lot from the county and proceeded to build his home using molded concrete blocks manufactured by John London and M. N. Gantt at Rockdale Mill, formerly a major producer of stone and block construction materials for upper Cleveland County. The sand used for mortar and cement came from a sandbar in Buffalo Creek. Hugh Hoyle and his wife Vivian (1897–1984) raised a family here and operated a harness shop (now deteriorated) nearby. The harness shop, opened by Hoyle in 1919, served Belwood until it closed in 1950. The Hoyles' one-and-a-half-story Craftsman bungalow has a prominent central dormer above a wraparound porch with round columns and a porch room illuminated by rows of four-over-four windows. A well originally associated with Belwood Institute is situated northwest of the house.

O. P. AND JESSIE HAMRICK HOUSE

328 North Main Street
Boiling Springs
1926

Oliver Paul Hamrick (1881–1968) and Jessie Teresa Pangle Hamrick (d. 1960) had this Craftsman bungalow built in 1926 using brick manufactured in Tennessee. O. P. Hamrick was the first principal of the Boiling Springs public high school, in addition to farming and serving as a Boiling Springs town commissioner. Jessie boarded Gardner-Webb University students and faculty in the house. The couple met in 1916, when Jessie came to Boiling Springs from Tennessee

Hugh and Vivian Hoyle House (BRE)

M. C. and Addie Whitworth House (BRE)

Cleveland Country Club (JDP)

cochere and a bay window with a shed roof. Small six-light casement windows are visible in the upper portions of the north and south elevations.

M. C. AND ADDIE WHITWORTH HOUSE

200 North Main Street
Waco
1927

Pink Miller, a prominent Waco cotton broker, built this frame Foursquare-form house for cotton farmer M. C. Whitworth in 1927. In this house Whitworth and his wife Addie provided lodging for ten teachers from nearby Waco School. Whitworth also ran a fertilizer and guano dealership and served as a Waco mayor. Following Addie's death in 1955 and M. C.'s death in 1964, the property was acquired by Coot and Frances Lutz. The center-passage-plan house has a hip roof with a hipped dormer and a one-story porch with a porte cochere extension. The one-story rear wings include a square-plan stove tower, and the windows are one-over-one or Craftsman three-over-one. Behind the house is a ca. 1965 garage, a transverse barn, two chickenhouses, and a smokehouse—all frame—and a hip-roofed brick pumphouse.

CLEVELAND COUNTRY CLUB

1360 East Marion Street
Shelby
1927

The recreational character of the area east of Shelby was established in the nineteenth century by the Cleveland

to teach art and expression. O. P. and Jessie wed the following year. O. P.'s autobiography, *Born at the Crossroads*, contains historical information on Boiling Springs and Gardner-Webb University.

The Hamrick House is a well-appointed example of the Craftsman bungalow idiom. Predominantly square in plan, with exterior end chimneys, the house has an engaged front porch supported by square brick columns with concrete adornments. The rear elevation may have had a similar treatment at one time but currently has brick infill and modern windows. The gable roof supports a large dormer, and on the side are a porte

Selected Inventory 259

Polkville High School Home Economics Building (BRE)

Marion Street Apartments (BRE)

Springs resort, and nearby the Cleveland Country Club was developed in the 1920s. The original portion of the present building is the east end, a two-story Colonial Revival building modeled on the plantation house ideal. The painted brick clubhouse features a two-story portico with monumental tapered and paneled square-section wood columns, originally topped off with a Chinese Chippendale railing. In the blind round arch over the front entry are a heraldic shield, wreath, and ribands, and in the gables flanking the chimneys are quarter-round windows. Later additions with a pyramidal-roofed porte cochere extend to the west, and the golf course spreads to the north and south of East Marion Street.

POLKVILLE HIGH SCHOOL HOME ECONOMICS BUILDING

Polkville Road (NC 226)
Polkville
Ca. 1927

Polkville High School was completed in 1927 and opened in 1928. The Colonial Revival hip-roofed brick school contained fourteen rooms and offered education through the eleventh grade. In 1967 the school was renamed Polkville Elementary, and recently it was demolished. Surviving, however, is the Home Economics Building, now owned by the Polkville Fire Department. The one-story brick Colonial Revival building has a low hip roof and three interior chimneys. The recessed central doorway has a pediment with cornice returns.

MARION STREET APARTMENTS

706 East Marion Street
Shelby
Ca. 1928

This large two-story brick building features double-tiered porticos and a central entrance. Other features include the low hip roof with beveled cornice and exterior end chimneys. A ca. 1928 brick garage stands to the rear.

W. J. EZELL HOUSE

1001 Frederick Street
Shelby
Late 1920s

When Dr. W. J. Ezell had this brick Tudor Revival residence constructed in 1928 or 1929, it was the first brick house built for an African American owner in Cleveland County. Ezell moved to Salisbury to practice medicine; the second owner was Barney Roberts, an educator who served as the principal of African American schools in Shelby and Charlotte. The contractor for the house is unknown but he is sure to have been black, as virtually all brickwork in Shelby was done by African American bricklayers during the period. The story-and-a-half house has the multiple steep gables and juxtaposed front entry vestibule and chimney of the simplified Tudor Revival style. Decorative accents include a round-arched front door, a small semicircular window in a side gable, and red and blond brickwork in the chimney.

W. J. Ezell House (TJF)

DeWitt M. and Essie Harrill House (BRE)

gable roof with a prominent front gable, stretcher-bond brick walls, and a small porch supported by brick arches. The front chimney has an S-shaped iron ornament or tie-rod plate on its face (whether the "S" has any meaning as an initial is unknown). Behind the house is a large frame garage with exposed rafter ends.

DEWITT M. AND ESSIE HARRILL HOUSE

3419 Yates Road (SR 1821)
Lawndale vicinity
1920s–1930s

This Colonial Revival dwelling was originally the home of cotton farmers DeWitt and Essie Harrill. It was built in the 1920s and remodeled in the 1930s. The two-story frame house features a three-bay facade and a large Craftsman-style ell. The two-story front porch stands on paired square columns and is crowned with a balustrade. The north elevation has a square bay, a Craftsman-style porch dominates the rear of the house, and the south elevation has a one-story screen porch. Near the house is a frame transverse barn adjoined by a covered well.

Norman and Iva Lee House (BRE)

NORMAN AND IVA LEE HOUSE

208 West Lee Street (SR 1161)
Lattimore
1929

Dr. L. V. Lee built this house for his son Norman Lee (1902–76) and daughter-in-law Margaret Iva Sperling Lee (b. 1901) in 1929 while the newlyweds were honeymooning in Europe. The Lees received the house as a wedding gift upon their return to Lattimore. The Tudor Revival cottage is an excellent example of how the style could be adapted on a modest scale. The dwelling has a steep side-

Patterson Grove School, above; classroom interior, right (BRE)

HOWARD HERNDON FARM

4909 East Dixon Boulevard (US 74)
Kings Mountain vicinity
Ca. 1930

Cotton farmer Howard Herndon had this one-and-a-half-story Craftsman bungalow erected about 1930, and the house and surrounding farm remain in Herndon family ownership. A wraparound engaged porch supported by square wood posts on brick pedestals shelters a center entry flanked by four-over-one windows. Above is a large shed dormer with three four-over-one windows. An exterior chimney rises on one side next to a projecting eave, and a small ell projects to the rear. Nearby stands a large gambrel-roofed transverse stock barn with shed additions on each side. Near the barn are a metal-sided frame tractor shed and large frame corncrib. Other outbuildings include a ca. 1955 workshop of concrete block construction and a modern frame garage with a gambrel roof.

Howard Herndon Farm scene (BRE)

PATTERSON GROVE SCHOOL

309 Oak Grove Road (SR 2035)
Kings Mountain vicinity
1931

Patterson Grove School served the community as a first- through seventh-grade elementary school. Two of the first teachers at the school were Mrs. J. K. Willis (who was also the principal) and Mrs. Kenneth Crook. Patterson Grove School follows a standard institutional plan for early-twentieth-century schools. Rectangular in plan,

Shelby Supply Company (former) (JDP)

Mooresboro School (BRE)

with stretcher bond brick walls, the school has a low hip roof with interior chimneys and exposed rafter ends. A small porch shelters the front entry; to each side are banks of five six-over-six windows. The rear elevation has similar windows, which provided ample light and ventilation before electricity was introduced to the area in 1936. The interior is largely intact and consists of a central hall that connects two large classrooms. Two panel doors at the end of the hallway lead to a combination auditorium and classroom. The entire school has beaded matchboard walls, hardwood floors, and many original light fixtures. A pot-bellied stove still sits in the west classroom.

MOORESBORO SCHOOL

4710 Mooresboro Road (SR 1327)
Mooresboro vicinity
Ca. 1931

The one-story frame Mooresboro School is one of Cleveland County's few surviving African American schools. The building has been vinyl-sided, and the original banks of classroom windows have been removed, but the outlines of the windows are still visible around the modern replacement sash. Several five-panel doors from the 1930s survive. The interior preserves a center partition with a two-sided blackboard that could be raised and lowered, allowing the space to be combined into one room or divided into two. Similar movable partitions were common in the standardized schools built with support from the Rosenwald Fund during the period. Modern partitions now divide the interior into four rooms. Former students and longtime local residents recall the ball field that extended below the school, and some claim that the lumber used in the school's construction was reused from an earlier black school in the area.

SHELBY SUPPLY COMPANY (FORMER)

222 North Lafayette Street
Shelby
1932, 1948–49

A recent rehabilitation has preserved the clean utilitarian character of this two-story brick building. The firm was established in 1922 by Charles Gerald Morgan and originally occupied a building across the street. The firm distributed mill supplies and hardware throughout the Carolinas. The north section of the present building was erected in 1932, and an extension on the south side in 1948–49 doubled the building's size to 36,000 square feet. The building features a plain parapet with a ceramic coping, industrial-type steel-frame windows, and anodized aluminum-frame display windows and recessed entries that evoke the originals.

WILLIAM AND NORA
LEICESTER HOUSE

250 East Main Street
Mooresboro
Early 1930s

Built by John Martin for William and Nora Leicester, this house is a fine example of a Craftsman bungalow. Typical of the type are the house's varying roof pitches, and a prominent front gable with bracketed eaves contains an upstairs bedroom. A front porch extends at each end to form porte cocheres. The house has a brick foundation and metal roofing. A frame shed stands behind.

KOURIS WAREHOUSE
(MORGAN & COMPANY
BUILDING)

200 West Warren Street
Shelby
Early 1930s

The Shelby architectural firm V. W. Breeze may have designed this two-story brick building, originally used as a wholesale fruit and vegetable market. The principal decorative treatment of the otherwise utilitarian building are the accent blocks that define the corners of the parapet panels and that form the ends of soldier-course lintels over the building's many large windows. The southeast corner office has plate glass windows with transoms, and the east elevation has freight doors that face the railroad tracks. In the 1950s the building was used by Morgan & Company. Organized in 1935 by O. Z. Morgan, Morgan & Company operated two cotton gins, and it advertised itself as a wholesaler and retailer in feeds, seeds, insecticides, and fertilizers. The building has served as Shelby's farmers market since at least the early 1980s.

BETHLEHEM SCHOOL

1012 Bethlehem Road (SR 2245)
Kings Mountain vicinity
1930s

Bethlehem School served its community until the late 1940s, when it was purchased by Bethlehem Baptist Church for use as a fellowship hall. The original teachers for this school were Letha Morris (first and second grades), Piccola Blalock (third and fourth grades), and Kate Willis (fifth, sixth, and seventh grades). The brick used in the construction of this one-story rectangular-plan building came from Gaffney, South Carolina. A gable-on-hip roof caps the building, and two chimneys rise from the interior. A small hip-roofed stoop marks the main entrance, and there is evidence on each elevation of the original banks of windows.

MAURICE AND ANNIE
WEATHERS HOUSE

1440 East Marion Street
Shelby
1930s

Shelby attorney Maurice Weathers built this one-story Mission-style house with stucco for the walls and foundation supplied by Maurice's brother, the owner of Weathers Concrete Company. Maurice and his wife Annie Wilson Weathers lived here until the early 1940s. Herman and

Bethlehem School (BRE)

Kouris Warehouse (BRE)

Tallulah Mauney then bought the house and resided here until about 1950. A hair and nail salon now occupies the building. A defining feature of the house is the Spanish tile pent roof, which runs below shaped parapets concealing a flat roof. The front entry is sheltered by an arched stoop with a hip roof and adjoined by an exterior chimney. Windows display a variety of sash arrangements, such as four-over-one, three-over-one, one-over-one, and six-over-six. Although the interior has been modified to suit its present commercial use, it retains an original cast-concrete mantel with a triangular keystone and broad pillars.

KADESH METHODIST CHURCH

208 Kadesh Church Road (SR 1612)
Belwood vicinity
1935

Founded in 1833, Kadesh Methodist Church has been an important institution in the Fallston area for nearly two centuries. The present brick-veneer building is the fourth church erected on the site. A portico supported by paired columns shelters double-leaf panel doors with a round-arched stained glass transom. Both the transom and the round arches over the side stained glass windows have white keystones and imposts. A two-story classroom and administrative wing extends to the rear, and a modern spire rises above the roof. The adjoining cemetery contains several notable graves from the Civil War and World War II. The church takes its name from a Hebrew word meaning "sacred."

DOVER SCHOOL

409 Polkville Road (NC 226)
Shelby vicinity
Ca. 1935–36

Built as a school for the children of the Dover mill village, Dover School was a kindergarten-through-sixth-grade facility. Students continued their schooling at either Shelby Junior High School or Lattimore School. The one-story Colonial Revival school has a T plan and, on the facade, a double door flanked by paired lights. Directly above the door is a small pedimented dormer, and banks of windows pierce the north and south elevations. Over the basement entry is a brick relieving arch, and an entry on the north elevation has a decorative transom. The school now serves as the Grace Fellowship Worship Center.

W. C. EDWARDS HOUSE (MAIE AND REID WILSON HOUSE)

232 Old Belwood Road (SR 1612)
Belwood vicinity
1936

W. C. Edwards built this Craftsman bungalow; later his daughter Maie and her husband Reid Wilson lived in the house. The farm on which the house stands once encompassed approximately 1,000 acres, much of it devoted to cotton. The Edwardses and Wilsons also operated a lumber mill on the property and managed a fertilizer company. The Wilson House has a clipped gable roof with a large front and rear dormers. A porte cochere extends off the front porch

Dover School (BRE)

Maurice and Annie Weathers House (BRE)

and is supported by brick columns. The interior retains much of the original woodwork and mantels. Behind the house is a frame shed, and just west of the house is a frame transverse stock barn with a clipped gable roof.

PAUL M. NEISLER HOUSE

110 North Gaston Street
Kings Mountain
1938

Paul Mauney Neisler, a son of Charles E. Neisler Sr. and treasurer of Neisler Mills, Inc., designed and built this two-story Classical Revival residence. The brick house features a monumental portico and Georgian Revival detail.

SHARON UNITED METHODIST CHURCH

867 College Avenue (NC 150)
Shelby vicinity
1939–40 (core, 1910s)

Originally known as Sharon Methodist Episcopal Church, the congregation was organized in 1851 as a result of a merger between Lee's Chapel and Poplar Springs Church. The original part of the present church building, the rear, was built in the 1910s (possibly in 1910) as a weatherboarded frame chapel. In 1939–40 a major addition was made to the front, and the entire church received a brick veneer. In its present form the building is entered through a vestibule with a lancet-arched entry and paneled double-leaf doors. Above the entry is a bell tower topped by a pyramidal roof with a cross finial. There are paired leaded glass casement windows on the north and south elevations. Next to the church is a one-story brick-veneer Tudor Revival parsonage built in 1948, and across College Avenue is the church cemetery.

W. C. Edwards House (Maie and Reid Wilson House) (BRE)

LUTZ-AUSTELL FUNERAL HOME CHAPEL

409 West Marion Street
Shelby
1940 (core, 1902)

In 1940 Shelby's Episcopal chapel, the Church of the Holy Redeemer, was moved to West Marion Street from its original site on South Lafayette Street to serve as a funeral and wedding chapel for the Lutz-Austell Funeral Home. In 1940 the originally wood-sided frame chapel was given a brick veneer that features a diamond-shaped diapered motif in the gable and a round-arched vestibule entry. The Episcopalians continued to use the chapel until 1951, when a new facility was erected on Sumter Street.

ISAAC AND EDNA MCGILL FARM

310 Saint Lukes Church Road
(SR 2008)
Kings Mountain vicinity
1940

Isaac Abernathy McGill (b. 1908) and his wife Edna Grant McGill commissioned W. D. Weaver to build this T-plan brick Craftsman bungalow. The house has a clipped gable roof with shingle-pattern pressed-metal sheathing and two interior chimneys. The recessed front porch stands on Craftsman brick and wood supports, and a front wing has a secondary entrance under a bracketed stoop. Windows have four-over-one sash. Isaac McGill and his brother William Fulton McGill (b. 1904) started the McGill Brothers Dairy in 1957. Their primary customer was Dairymans Inc., based in Bristol, Virginia. The sleeping barn and milking parlor associated with this dairy are now gone, but the property retains a frame smokehouse, a large transverse mule and feed barn, a tractor shed, a small chickenhouse, and a garage. The McGill brothers also operated a sawmill and earthmoving business.

STOWE AND FLORENCE HENDRICK HOUSE

West Zion Church Road (SR 1337)
Lattimore vicinity
1940

Stowe Hendrick hired Harlan McDaniel and Fonz White to assist him with the framing of this modest one-story house. After the frame was up, Hendrick hired a Spindale stonemason named Foster and a crew of sixteen helpers to face the house with stone. The house has multiple steeply pitched gables, a front stoop, and a recessed porch supported by stone arches. A brick *H* is embedded in the chimney, and the house is illuminated by three-, six-, eight-, nine-, and twelve-light casement windows. The rear of the dwelling has a shed roof and a full basement, and there is a small patio along the south elevation.

GOFORTH BROTHERS (CHURCHHILL DOWNS GRANDSTAND)

1840 East Dixon Boulevard
Shelby
20th century

The crowds at the 1937 Kentucky Derby cheered on War Admiral from this building, which originally served as a grandstand at Churchill Downs. As built in 1913, the grandstand had bleachers at the front and two levels of betting rooms to the rear. The grandstand was acquired by Cleveland County's own Dr. J. S. Dorton and in 1939 was moved to Charlotte, where it was used as bleachers and an exhibit hall for the Southern States Fair. The fair closed in 1960, and the grandstand was purchased by Joe A. Goforth, who with his brothers reassembled it in Shelby over the next four years. Goforth Brothers, now known as Southco Industries, uses the building to assemble chassis for tree-trimming trucks. The original wooden roof trusses have been replaced with metal trusses, and a brick entrance has been added. Materials discarded from the building during remodeling have been incorporated into farm buildings throughout the county.

EARL MORRIS HOUSE

2045 Shelby Road (US 74)
Kings Mountain
Ca. 1940

Earl Morris built this Tudor Revival dwelling and operated a scrap metal business on the adjacent property. Olden Horn executed the interior brickwork for Morris, and an unidentified mason finished the exterior brickwork. Notable exterior features include false half-timbering in the gables, a beautifully crafted arched lintel doorway with a keystone, and decorative chimney brickwork. The house has stretcher-bond brick walls, asphalt-shingle roofing, interior chimneys, and a full-length enclosed back porch. The seven-room interior contains two bedrooms, two living rooms, a dining room, a kitchen, and a bathroom. Original interior features include molded baseboards, chair rails, and brick mantels. The house still belongs to the Morris family.

LILY MILL CLUBHOUSE

Morton and Morgan Streets
Shelby
Ca. 1940

This brick-veneer rectangular-plan structure served as a clubhouse and meeting hall for employees of the Lily Mill & Power Company. The hip-

Stowe and Florence Hendrick House (BRE)

roofed clubhouse has a three-bay facade with a hip-roofed stoop, eight-over-eight and six-over-six windows, and a small rear stoop.

CHESLEY AND ADDIE DALTON HOUSE

2500 New Prospect Church Road (SR 1908)
Shelby vicinity
1941

Members of the Dalton family have lived at this location for over a hundred years. Chesley Amzi Dalton (1895–1953) and Addie Harrelson Dalton built the two-story stone veneer Colonial Revival house and moved in on Thanksgiving Day 1941. The front entry has a surround of fluted pilasters and a frieze with six evenly spaced triglyphs. Black keystones punctuate the window heads on the front, and a porte cochere with a wood roof balustrade extends from the north elevation. Behind the house are three apparently original outbuildings, including a stone pumphouse, a concrete block smokehouse, and a frame and metal corncrib and shed.

NORMAN'S GROVE BAPTIST CHURCH

206 Carpenters Grove Church Road (1614)
Belwood
1943

Founded in 1910 by the Reverend Frank Newton, Norman's Grove took its name from the Norman family, who donated the land for the church. Charter members of the congregation included D. M. Norman, Julius Norman, Mrs. John Boggs, and Mr. and Mrs. Julius Buff. The present church building features a portico with a round vent in the gable. A multisided steeple rises from a square weatherboarded base on the roof ridge, and stained glass windows ornament the side elevations.

HUDSON HOSIERY MILL

732 Grover Street
Shelby
Ca. 1945–46

The Hudson Hosiery Mill was a major manufacturer of textiles in Shelby for many years. The mill was later ac-

Chesley and Addie Dalton House (BRE)

Hudson Hosiery Mill (BRE)

268 Architectural Perspectives of Cleveland County

Dwight Hamrick House (BRE)

Kate and Paul Holland House (BRE)

Ernest V. Phillips Mill (BRE)

quired by the Chadborn Company, and in 1973 the Bernhardt Furniture Company moved into the streamlined building. A notable exterior feature is the large projecting bay with curved walls of glass block. The projection's center entry has a glass and metal door with plate glass sidelights and transom. The remainder of the flat-roofed building is strictly utilitarian in design.

DWIGHT HAMRICK HOUSE (THE ROCK HOUSE)

1203 Mount Pleasant Church Road (SR 1186)
Boiling Springs vicinity
1940s

Aaron Bonner Hamrick built this one-story dwelling for his son, Dwight Hamrick, using stone that the latter transported to the site from Spartanburg, South Carolina. Originally the house was the center of a small family farm that concentrated on cotton and corn production. The house retains much of its original character, but the arched front porch was enclosed in the 1960s and fitted with modern Palladian windows. Notable features include a limestone *H* on the chimney and an original stairway and stone mantel.

ERNEST V. PHILLIPS MILL

111 Flint Hill Church Road (SR 1148)
Boiling Springs
1947

Ernet Phillips built this unassuming molded concrete block gristmill in 1947. The gable-fronted building has a number of doors and windows. It was originally used as a slaughterhouse as well.

KATE AND PAUL HOLLAND FARM

108 West Lee Street (SR 1161)
Lattimore vicinity
1947

Kate and Paul Holland commissioned Wilbur Cabiness to build this stone

Selected Inventory 269

Tudor Revival dwelling. The Hollands lived here for the remainder of their lives, and now their daughter resides in the house with her husband. The one-and-a-half-story house features a recessed and arched front entry with finely crafted stonework. Similar stonework appears in a recessed front porch and on a side entry. Over the front porch is an iron balustrade, and above the roof rise interior and exterior chimneys. Original outbuildings include a concrete block chickenhouse and a flowerhouse with three four-over-four windows.

WACO HIGH SCHOOL AGRICULTURE BUILDING

200 A. W. Black Street
Waco
Ca. 1947

Constructed of brick laid in Flemish bond, this otherwise utilitarian building features a hip roof, banks of nine-over-nine windows, and several casement windows. Here students at Waco High School learned horticulture, farming techniques, farm equipment repair, and the construction of basic farm items such as hog feeders. Large wooden doors on the back of the building allowed equipment to be moved in and out. When Waco School closed in the 1960s, the agricultural department closed as well. The building now serves as Waco City Hall, and the adjacent school has been made Macedonia Baptist Church.

KARL AND YVONNE JORDAN HOUSE

1002 Steel Bridge Road (SR 1003)
Boiling Springs vicinity
1948

This stone-faced Tudor Revival house was designed by Yvonne Jordan. Her husband Karl hired Bennie McCall to blast the stone out of mountains near Linville Caverns, and Karl, his son Karl Jr., and Willie Pruitt hauled 120 tons of stone to the building site. Albert Glenn, owner of Glenn Lumber Company, used a portable sawmill to cut lumber for the house. The foot-thick walls consist of 6 inches of concrete with a 6-inch stone facing that give the one-story house a massive appearance. The front elevation features a single-shouldered chimney and a prominent front gable with a recessed entry and portico to one side. The windows are of the casement variety, one with as many as twenty-four panes. A small connecting wing links to a two-car garage. Other features include a side porch and a rear shed addition. A frame transverse stock barn and shed stand nearby.

MOTEL ROYAL

1709 Shelby Road (US 74 Business)
Kings Mountain
1940s

This example of roadside architecture is associated with the opening of Highway 74 in the mid-twentieth century. Historic features include stretcher-bond brick construction, the metal backing of a neon "Motel Royal" sign, original rooms and doors,

Waco High School Agriculture Building (BRE)

Karl and Yvonne Jordan House (BRE)

and an office at the east end of the L-form complex.

THOMAS AND VERDIE DEDMON FARM

1511 McBrayer Springs Road (SR 1827)
Shelby vicinity
Ca. 1948

This two-story Colonial Revival house of brick-veneer frame construction was the home of Thomas Lawson Dedmon (1889–1956) and his wife Verdie Mae Horn Dedmon (1893–1990). The Dedmons married in 1919, shortly after Tom's return from service with the Eighty-second Field Artillery in World War I. After their wedding they bought this farm, where they raised cotton and cattle. As their farm became more successful, they were able to build the present house. Today, the property is owned by their son, Roy, who raises purebred shorthorn cattle.

The gable-roofed house features a two-story porch; its balustrade is adorned with the letter *D*. Supported by paired square posts, the porch shelters a front entry with sidelights and a false fanlight recessed into a concrete panel. There are interior and exterior gable-end chimneys, a one-story enclosed porch on the south elevation, and a full-length brick addition across the rear of the house. The first-floor interior has a two-room plan. Mantels feature fluted pilasters, tile facings, and brick fireboxes. The second floor has a center-passage plan with three bedrooms on the south side, two bedrooms on the north side, and a sitting room at the end of the passage. To the northeast of the house stand a frame corncrib and barn.

WILLIE CARPENTER HOUSE

142 Carpenters Grove Church Road (SR 1614)
Belwood
1948–49

Willie Carpenter, a local stonemason, built this stone dwelling for himself in 1948–49. The side-gable one-story house features a prominent chimney and stone arches in the front porch (which has been enclosed). A single gable on the facade has a rectangular vent in its center. A frame shed sits behind the house, and a frame garage is located just west of it. Most of the rock used in the house came from Acre Rock, a rock quarry located in the upper end of Cleveland County. Carpenter also executed the stonework on the nearby Forrest and Ruby Carpenter House, completed in 1950.

DIXON PRESBYTERIAN CHURCH

602 Dixon School Road (SR 2283)
Kings Mountain vicinity
1948–49

Founders' Day for the Dixon Presbyterian Church is February 6, 1944, but

Thomas and Verdie Dedmon House (BRE)

Dixon Presbyterian Church (BRE)

the congregation met for several years before that in various churches and schools of the vicinity. The official establishment for the church took place at the Dixon School just across the road. A large portion of the congregation came from the First Presbyterian Church in Kings Mountain. The brick-veneered frame church features Gothic Revival elements such as blind lancet-arched transoms over windows. A modern portico defines the main entrance, and the interior has exposed rafters and original pews and ceiling.

Lawndale First Baptist Church (former) (BRE)

LAWNDALE FIRST BAPTIST CHURCH (FORMER)

138 Gold Street (SR 1814)
1948–49

The cornerstone on this imposing stone church identifies its architect as F. M. Pullen and lists the Reverend W. L. Johnson and a numbr of deacons. The original congregation met in a one-story frame house rented from Huss Cline for four dollars a month. The church's founder and first deacon was Benny Wray. The front of the present building features two stout corner towers that flank three paneled doorways set in stone arches. The towers have stained glass windows on the first story and louvered vents above. Centered in the gable end above the doors is a Palladian window. Stone buttresses support the side elevations, and stained glass windows fall between them. The congregation was organized, and built an earlier church building, in 1924.

Carolina Dairy, above; delivery truck, below (BRE)

CAROLINA DAIRY

804 Grover Street
Shelby
1940s–1950s

In 1925 Coleman Blanton joined other dairy farmers to form the Shelby Milk Plant, which became the Carolina Dairy in 1934. In 1940 the distributorship was purchased by John Burn, who moved it to the present location on

Forrest and Ruby Carpenter House (BRE)

WOHS, above (JDP); the Sisk Quartet performs at WOHS, below. Courtesy of the Uptown Shelby Association.

Grover Street. By the early 1950s the plant employed over thirty workers and produced butter, cottage cheese, and FlavorRich Ice Cream in addition to milk. The main section is a 1940s brick structure with a flat roof. Other parts of the plant included an ice cream store (later used by the All-Da BBQ restaurant) and a boiler room and warehouse.

WOHS RADIO STATION

1511 West Dixon Boulevard (US 74)
Shelby
1945–46

WOHS went on air in this modernist one-story brick building in August 1946. The building features flat and parapeted roof planes, a metal awning supported by slender steel poles, and a window-wall entry. About 1960 the building was painted white, but soon thereafter it was returned to its original red brick appearance.

HOLLY OAK PARK

809 Holly Oak Drive
Shelby
Mid-20th century

Holly Oak Park was established on the former Arey horse farm as a recreational amenity for the area's African American population. The park's "Old Center" began life as a stable, then was used as an overflow classroom building for the Hunter School, and now serves as a meeting place. The steel and concrete block "New Center" was built in 1959 by the Shelby firm Van Wageningen & Cothran. In its day, Holly Oak Park was considered one of the largest parks for blacks in western North Carolina.

FORREST AND RUBY CARPENTER HOUSE

1072 Belwood Lawndale Road
(SR 1612)
Belwood vicinity
1950

Shortly after finishing his own house in 1948–49, Willie Carpenter, a

Selected Inventory 273

Reciprocity Lodge No. 693 (JDP)

Sunset Drive-In Theatre, middle; concession stand, bottom (BRE)

Washington Theater showing Quonset hut auditorium (JDP)

Belwood stonemason, executed the stonework at this dwelling. Willie's brother, Robert Carpenter, and Forrest and Ruby Carpenter's son, Gordon, assisted Willie with the construction of the house. The stone came from Acre Rock, a large outcropping in the area. This house features a gable roof with two end dormers and a stoop porch. A stone and brick archway occupies the facade's east bay, while the center bay features a projecting arched entry. The east elevation has a stone chimney with a castellated coping of angular rocks. Nearby is a ca. 1950 frame barn.

RECIPROCITY LODGE NO. 693

Buffalo Street
Shelby
Ca. 1950

IBPOEW Reciprocity Lodge No. 693 is the local lodge of the Improved Benevolent and Protective Order of Elks, Worldwide, the African American Elks fraternal organization. The two-story cinder block building has a brick front veneer, glass block windows, and a front entry porch.

WASHINGTON THEATER

Buffalo Street
Shelby
Ca. 1950

An army surplus Quonset hut forms the auditorium of Shelby's historic African American movie house. A Dr. Sherer is thought to have started the theater about 1950, perhaps in 1948 or 1949. To the barrel-vaulted steel Quonset hut was added a two-story brick front with a recessed entry under a prow-like metal marquee formerly outlined with incandescent light bulbs. The theater now serves as storage for nearby Dockery's Funeral Home.

SUNSET DRIVE-IN THEATRE

3935 West Dixon Boulevard (US 74)
Shelby vicinity
Ca. 1950

The Sunset Drive-in Theatre is a rare survivor in this era of air-conditioned multiplexes. The teardrop concrete

Polkville Methodist Church (BRE)

Episcopal Church of the Redeemer (JDP)

foundations of the speaker poles have streamlined styling. An entrance sign informs moviegoers that the theater has "radio sound FM" and asks that patrons "dim lights." The ticket booth and concession stand have flat roofs, and small metal lights line the access drive. Sunset Drive-In still operates during the summer.

EPISCOPAL CHURCH OF THE REDEEMER

510 West Sumter Street
Shelby
1951, 2002

The original part of this brick church shows the influence of the Parish Church genre of Episcopal church design, first popularized in the nineteenth century. The low proportions, stubby buttresses, and rows of small peaked windows evoked the simple medieval parish churches of the English countryside. In 2002 a large addition designed by the Shelby architectural firm Martin Boal Anthony & Johnson was added to the original building. The addition, which now serves as the sanctuary, harmonizes with the original through its gable-fronted nave form, buttresses, and brick construction. A porch with lancet-arched openings projects from the front, and lancet-arched windows extend down the sides.

POLKVILLE METHODIST CHURCH

219 Church Drive
Polkville
1952

This site has had a church on it since the erection of the first Polkville Methodist Church in 1896. In 1922 the congregation rebuilt, and in 1952 the present stone church was erected. Horace Covington supplied the stone from a source on Patty's Creek in McDowell County, and Rile Watts executed the masonry. Gothic in inspiration, the church features a center projecting tower with battlements and pinnacles at its four corners. At the tower's base is an arched entry with a pair of panel doors and a stained glass transom. Paired round-arched stained glass windows run the length of the north and south elevations. A large two-story classroom and administration addition adjoins the rear of the sanctuary. A one-story stretcher-bond brick building attaches to the south elevation.

KNOB CREEK METHODIST CHURCH

226 Carpenters Grove Church Road
(SR 1614)
Belwood
1953

The Boggs family donated the land for this church about 1800. The founding members were Elizabeth Richard, Nancy Hartman, A. Noah Boggs, and A. E. Boggs, and the first pastor was a Reverend Boyce. A log church, a schoolhouse, and a parish house stood here in 1869. The present Gothic-influenced building, completed in 1953, is the fourth church on the site. The congregation chose to build it out of stone quarried in Georgia rather than the local Acre Rock stone. The church features a central bell tower with an entry at its base, louvered belfry openings, and a parapet pierced with lancet-arched openings. Lancet-arched stained glass windows extend along the side elevations. A two-story classroom wing with a low hip roof brings up the rear. The earliest known grave in the adjacent cemetery belongs to James S. Pauley, who died in 1809.

PHILADELPHIA METHODIST CHURCH

2848 Philadelphia Road (SR 1801)
Fallston vicinity
1954

The poor freedmen who organized Philadelphia Church about 1884 depended on assistance from their white neighbors to build the first church. They went to the elders of Salem Church, a white congregation, to inquire about starting up a church, and they asked the white landowners of the area to donate pine logs. The donated logs had to be hauled to the sawmill at night, since the church members needed to work during the day. The first church, built by a Mr. Matton for twenty-five dollars, was "very small, planked up and down outside, and never [sheathed on the interior]." A second church and then a third, in 1906, followed. The present brick building was erected in early 1954 during the pastorate of Rev. C. E. Strickland using materials salvaged from the 1906 building. Philadelphia Church has a gabled L-shaped plan with the entry at the angle of the L. The entry has a simple peaked surround and is situated under a small belfry with an arched opening for the bell. The mostly blank gable end of the sanctuary has a small round window and cornice returns supported on paired polelike columns.

NUMBER 3 EGG PRODUCERS

2505 South Post Road (NC 180)
Earl vicinity
Ca. 1955

In the early 1950s J. D Ellis and Carver Bridges organized what came to be known as Number 3 Egg Producers. The numeric portion of the name refers to the enterprise's location: Number 3 township of Cleveland County. Bridges organized local farmers to supply eggs to the Community Cash Grocery Store in Spartanburg, South Carolina, a business that soon expanded to Community Cash stores in other towns. The operation became so prosperous that Bridges needed a central distributorship, and about 1955 he built this rectangular one-story building for the purpose. The building has a flat roof, casement windows, loading docks, and two original signs. One sign has "No. 3 Egg Producers" in cursive script; the other features an image of eggs frying in a pan and urges passersby, "Eat More Eggs."

Knob Creek Methodist Church (BRE)

Number 3 Egg Producers (BRE)

Macedonia Baptist Church (JDP)

Kings Mountain Country Club (TJF)

MACEDONIA BAPTIST CHURCH

1101 South Battleground Avenue
(NC 216)
Kings Mountain vicinity
1956

The Macedonia Baptist congregation was organized in 1920 and built this Romanesque-influenced church in 1956. The church was built by Webber & Sons Construction, headed by Ralph Furman Webber (1903–72). The building is constructed of textured tan brick, with salmon brick in a round-arched entry recess that contains a large round window. Round-arched stained glass windows, a gable roof, a modillion cornice, and a freestanding bell tower with a cruciform plan are other features.

KINGS MOUNTAIN COUNTRY CLUB

Country Club Road
Kings Mountain
1961

The influence of Frank Lloyd Wright can be seen in the horizontal massing and anchoring chimney of this one-story tan brick building, designed by Shelby architects Breeze, Holland & Riviere in 1960 and probably completed the following year. Stacked like building blocks at the base of the chimney and under the end of a front porte cochere and rectangular masses of brick—some serving as planters—that give the building a studied informality. A swimming pool and bathhouse project to one side. The country club formerly used a converted house, which burned shortly before the present facility was constructed.

CLEVELAND SAVINGS & LOAN BUILDING

131 North Lafayette Street
Shelby
1962

This glass- and marble-faced building is one of the county's best examples of the International style, corporate America's style of choice for a generation after World War II. The marble is white and gray veining; the window walls flood the banking floor and office mezzanine level with cool northern light. Designed by local architect L. Pegram Holland Jr. of

Selected Inventory 277

Holland & Riviere, the building is now occupied by RBC Centura.

CAMP CALL LODGE NO. 534

3801 Polkville Road (NC 226)
Polkville
1969

Architect Fred M. Simmons, a Polkville resident, conceived this simple two-story lodge building of modernist character. The arcaded front was intended to evoke the architecture of the Holy Land and is one element of what was originally a more ambitious design. Pre-stressed concrete columns support round concrete arches that were poured on the ground and lifted into place by crane. Behind the arches is a stuccoed cinder block wall with a single entry opening; this wall was (and is) painted off-white to conrast with the white of the arches. The other exterior walls are brick and are devoid of windows; inside, an assembly rooms occupies the first floor, and a lodge room occupies the second floor.

CLEVELAND COUNTY MEMORIAL LIBRARY

104 Howie Drive
Shelby
1971, ca. 1990

The original library at this location near the city park was built in 1971 according to a design by architect Crawford Murphy with the Shelby firm Holland & Riviere. As originally designed, the library was modern in style, with walls of handmade brick. O. Stanhope Anthony of the Shelby architectural firm Martin Boal Anthony & Johnson designed a major expansion and renovation, completed about 1990. Anthony's Postmodern design reoriented the building to face the city park across Sumter Street, and it created a civic appearance through the use of symmetry, columns, arches, and a pedimented entry portico.

Cleveland Savings & Loan north elevation (JDP)

Camp Call Lodge No. 534 (JDP)

WEST CLEVELAND OFFICE OF FIRST NATIONAL BANK

208 North Main Street
Boiling Springs
1994

Norman "Bud" Talley of the Shelby firm Talley & Smith Architecture designed this brick bank, a modern

West Cleveland Office of First National Bank. Courtesy of Normal Talley.

AGI (TJF)

AGI

790 South Battleground Avenue (US 29)
Grover vicinity
1997–98

A sleek wedge of blue glass and yellow-painted steel projects from the front of this large plant, built for the printing of paper inserts for compact disc jewel cases. The building has precast concrete front and side elevations—the front with a facing of tan brick in alternating sizes—and a corrugated steel rear elevation to facilitate future expansion. AGI began as Album Graphics, Inc., a producer of record jackets for phonograph albums. The Grover area was chosen as the location for the plant because of its proximity to Universal Music & Logistics, one of the nation's largest compact disc pressing facilities. Eckenhoff Saunders Architects of Chicago designed the plant, Bovis Construction of Charlotte built it, and Freya Black Design of New York City provided interior design.

interpretation of the Colonial Revival style built by the Morrison Construction Company of Shelby. The building's intersecting gables end in pediment-like-parapets with large circular louvered vents and stout Doric columns underneath. An octagonal cupola, a drive-through on Doric columns, and windows with jack-arched heads are other features. The building was designed to harmonize with the Colonial Revival campus of Gardner-Webb University, located nearby.

Downtown Kings Mountain. 1940s photo courtesy of the Kings Mountain Historical Museum.

REFERENCES

APPENDIX: *National Register and Study List Properties*

The National Register of Historic Places includes buildings, structures, objects, sites, and districts that are significant in American history, architecture, archaeology, engineering, and culture. The National Register is maintained by the National Park Service. The Study List is a roster of properties that warrant consideration for listing in the National Register. The Study List is maintained by the North Carolina Historic Preservation Office, a branch of the state's Office of Archives and History. Properties are continually added to (and sometimes removed from) the National Register and the Study List. The lists presented here are current as of November 2002. One property—Webbley—is also designated a National Historic Landmark. Note: Property names are given as they appear in the official listing; secondary names or property names as they appear in this book, if substantially different, follow in parentheses.

National Register of Historic Places

The Banker's House
Joshua Beam House
Central School Historic District
Central Shelby Historic District (original and expansion)
Cleveland County Courthouse
East Marion-Belvedere Park Historic District
E. B. Hamrick Hall
James Hayward Hull House (Hudson-Hull House)
Irvin-Hamrick Log House
John Lattimore House (Lattimore House)
Dr. Victor McBrayer House (Victor and Esther McBrayer House)
Masonic Temple Building
Smith-Suttle House (Twin Chimneys)
George Sperling House and Outbuildings (George and Mary Jane Sperling Farm)
Webbley (Governor O. Max Gardner House)

Study List

- John Frank Beam House
- Big Hill Methodist Church
- Burwell Blanton Farm
- Coleman Blanton Farm
- Brackett House
- J. W. and Maude Brackett Farm
- Broad River Academy
- Clifton Davis Farm
- Dover Mill Overhead Bridge
- Dover School
- El Bethel United Methodist Church
- El Nido
- Elliot's Church (Elliott Chapel)
- Ellis Ferry House (Grambling House)
- First Broad River Bridge
- Garrett House (I. Walton Garrett House)
- Grover Historic District
- Gulf Oil Distributorship
- G. L. Hamrick and Son Dairy Farm
- (former) Hudson Hosiery Mills Building
- King Street Overhead Bridge
- (former) Kings Mountain Post Office
- Lattimore Historic District
- Lee's Chapel
- Logan-Harrill House
- Margrace Mill Village Historic District
- William Martin Farm
- McBrayer House
- John McBrayer Barn
- Will McBrayer Farm
- Mooresboro Historic District
- Morgan Street Historic District
- Mount Harmony Methodist Church
- Newton House
- William Oats Jr. House
- Plonk Farm
- Rufus and Kathleen Plonk Farm
- Philip Ramsour House (Ramseur-Sarratt House)
- (former) Saint Mary's Catholic Church
- Earl Scruggs Birthplace (George and Lula Scruggs House)
- Seaboard Railway Freight Depot
- 31RF 16, 19, 39, 40, 47 & 51 Second Broad River Watershed District (archaeological sites)
- (former) Shelby Armory
- (former) Shelby Cotton Mills Building
- Shiloh Presbyterian Church Cemetery
- Southern Railway Freight Depot
- Southern Railway Trestle
- Southern Railway Trestle & Bridge
- Stice Shoals Power Plant
- Frank and Bonnie Mauney Summers House
- Sunset Cemetery
- Sunset Drive-In Theatre
- Carl and Elva Thompson House
- Warren Street Historic District
- Waters Library
- Richard Meredith White House
- Zion School

GLOSSARY

APSE A semicircular or polygonal projection on a church.

ARCH A curved structural element that spans an opening. An arch is usually of masonry construction and, in some examples, has a specialized *keystone* at the top of the curve. An *impost* block sometimes appears at the springing point or foot of the arch, and the blocks between the imposts and keystone may be referred to as *voussoir* blocks. A *jack arch* is flat and is often supported by a concealed lintel. A *round arch* is semicircular. A *segmental arch* consists of a curved segment that is less than a semicircle, bow-shaped. A *lancet arch,* characteristic of the Gothic Revival style, is composed of two curved sections that meet at a point. A *Tudor arch,* characteristic of the Tudor Revival style, is a flattened form of the lancet arch.

ARCHITRAVE A molded surround around a fireplace or a molded lintel over a window.

BALUSTER/BALUSTRADE A turned or sawn element that supports a stair or porch railing. A balustrade is a series of balusters.

BARGEBOARD A decorative border suspended from the eaves of a roof. Also known as a VERGEBOARD.

BATTEN DOOR/SHUTTER A door or shutter constructed of vertical boards held in place by horizontal battens. Usually of cruder construction than panel doors and shutters.

BAY A horizontal division of an elevation. For example, a house with a front door flanked by two windows would be described as having a three-bay facade.

ARCHES

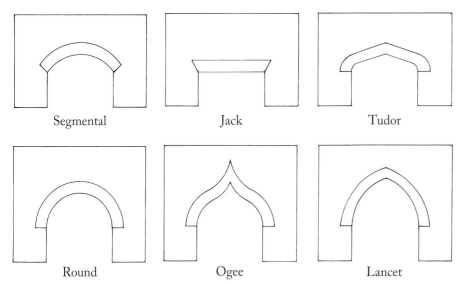

BRICKS

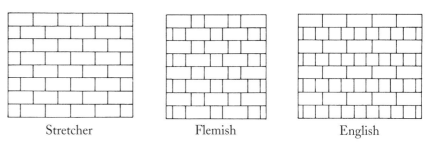

Stretcher   Flemish   English

BAY WINDOW *See* WINDOW.

BEAD A simple round molding, usually cut into the lower edge of a weatherboard or the edges of a tongue-and-groove board. *See also* MATCHBOARD.

BOND *See* BRICK.

BOWSTRING ROOF *See* ROOF.

BOXED STAIR A stair with a board enclosure, also known as an enclosed stair.

BREEZEWAY A short open-air passageway connecting a house to a dependency, usually a kitchen.

BRICK A clay (or shale) masonry unit, solid or partly hollow, that is formed in a mold and fired until hard. When laid in a wall so that its long side is visible, referred to as a *stretcher brick*. When laid so that its short end is visible, referred to as a *header brick*. A *closer brick* is a partial brick used at the end of a course to even it up. A *gauged brick* is a brick that has been shaped to form part of a jack arch. (Gauged and closer bricks are associated with early brickwork.) The coursing or pattern of bricks in a wall is referred to as the *bond,* and the divisions between bricks and courses are referred to as *mortar joints*. *Stretcher bond* is composed exclusively of stretcher bricks. *Flemish bond* is composed of alternating stretcher and header bricks and is associated with early and Colonial Revival brickwork. *English bond* is composed of courses of stretcher bricks alternating with courses of header bricks. *American bond* has two or more courses of stretcher bricks alternating with header bricks. *Dogtooth* refers to bricks set at an angle, creating a sawtooth appearance, and is sometimes referred to as *hound's-tooth brickwork*. *Paving* refers to bricks used like pavers to cover the sloped shoulders of early chimneys.

BUNGALOW A one-story or story-and-a-half house typically detailed in the Craftsman style and most popular in Cleveland County from the 1910s through the 1930s. *See also* CRAFTSMAN STYLE, GABLE-FRONTED BUNGALOW.

CAPITAL The top section of a column, often decorative. *See also* ORDER.

CARBIDE LIGHTING Lighting produced from carbide gas. Popular in the early 1900s before rural electrification.

CARRARA GLASS Colored opaque glass typically used as a storefront material in the mid–twentieth century. Also known as structural glass.

CARTOUCHE A plaquelike ornament, often richly decorated.

CASTELLATION Decorative battlementlike elements at the top of a parapet or chimney (also known as crenelation).

CENTER HALL PLAN *See* PLAN.

CHAIR RAIL A trim board, often molded, attached to an interior wall several feet above the floor.

CHAMFER The beveled edge or corner of a beam or post.

CIRCULAR-SAWN Sawn with a mechanical circular saw, creating curved saw marks.

CLASSICAL Architectural forms derived from classical Greek and Roman architecture.

CLASSICAL REVIVAL STYLE An architectural style characterized by the use of classical Greek and Roman forms and ornament, especially monumental porticoes. Also known as the Neoclassical style.

CLIPPED GABLE ROOF *See* ROOF.

CLOSER *See* BRICK.

COLLAR BEAM A structural member that links a rafter couple (like the cross line in the letter *A*).

COLONIAL REVIVAL STYLE An architectural style characterized by the use of classical forms and detailing (or, in more academic examples, allusions to Colonial- or Early National–period American architecture) and symmetrical composition. Some examples are referred to as the Georgian Revival style.

COLONNETTE A small, slender column often used decoratively in mantels from the late 1800s and early 1900s.

CORBEL An outward stepping of bricks, stones, or other masonry units used decoratively or to support an overhanging element.

CORINTHIAN *See* ORDER.

CORNER BLOCK A decorative blocklike element used to define the corner of a door or window surround.

CORNICE An exterior crowning element, often ornamented, at the top of a wall but below a parapet. *Cornice returns* are sections of cornice in a gable or on the end of a building. On the interior a cornice is a molding that runs at the juncture of a wall and ceiling.

CRAFTSMAN STYLE An architectural style characterized in Cleveland County domestic architecture by the use of broad, spreading forms; low-pitched gable or hip roofs, often with gable and eaves brackets; and decorative windows and other details. Most popular locally from the 1910s through the 1930s. The bungalow and Foursquare house forms are associated with the style. A Craftsman porch is usually supported by tapered wood columns on brick bases. *See also* BUNGALOW, FOURSQUARE.

CRENELATION *See* CASTELLATION.

CRESTING An ornamental projection on a roof, parapet, or other element.

CUPOLA A small dome or domelike element on a roof.

DENTIL A small blocklike element used repetitively as a molding in classical and classically derived architecture.

DOGTOOTH *See* BRICK.

DORIC *See* ORDER.

DOUBLE-SHOULDERED *See* SHOULDER.

DOVETAIL NOTCHING *See* LOG CONSTRUCTION.

EASTLAKE STYLE *See* VICTORIAN.

ENGLISH BOND *See* BRICK.

FACADE The front or principal side of a building.

FEDERAL STYLE An architectural style encountered in Cleveland County houses of the early 1800s and characterized by delicately rendered classical forms, intricate ornament, and typically three-part mantel compositions.

FINIAL A terminal or topmost element on a newel post, roof peak, etc.

FLEMISH BOND *See* BRICK.

FLUTING Vertical concave indentations along the length of a column, giving the surface a rippled or scalloped appearance.

FOURSQUARE A house form of the early 1900s characterized by a boxy, cubic massing, often with a hip roof, four-room plan, and Craftsman-style detail. *See also* CRAFTSMAN STYLE.

FRIEZE The horizontal section at the top of a wall or a range of columns, piers, or pilasters but below the cornice, or the horizontal section of a mantel that spans across the fireplace and is visually supported by pilasters on the sides of the fireplace, as in most Greek Revival mantels. *See also* POST-AND-LINTEL.

GABLE ROOF *See* ROOF.

GABLE-FRONTED BUNGALOW A dwelling type popular during the first half of the twentieth century in rural Cleveland County with its front entry on its gable end.

GAMBREL ROOF *See* ROOF.

GAUGED *See* BRICK.

GEORGIAN REVIVAL STYLE *See* COLONIAL REVIVAL STYLE.

GEORGIAN STYLE An architectural style characterized by the use of classical forms and detailing and symmetrical compositions. Rarely survives in Cleveland County from the early 1800s.

GOTHIC REVIVAL STYLE An architectural style characterized by allusions to medieval Gothic architecture: lancet-arched openings, peaked mantel frieze profiles, vertical detailing and composition. In Cleveland County the style is most often seen in church architecture from the late nineteenth century to the present.

GRAINING The painted simulation of wood grain.

GREEK REVIVAL STYLE An architectural style that emulated the simplicity and purity of classical Greek architecture as typified by the Greek temple. Most popular in Cleveland County during the mid-1800s.

HALF-DOVETAIL NOTCHING *See* LOG CONSTRUCTION.

HALL-PARLOR PLAN *See* PLAN.

HEADER *See* BRICK.

HIP ROOF *See* ROOF.

HL HINGE An early hinge type composed of iron shapes resembling the letters *H* and *L* side by side.

HYPHEN A connecting element between two sections of a building.

I-HOUSE A two-story house type, often with a center-passage plan.

IMPOST *See* ARCH.

IONIC *See* ORDER.

ITALIANATE STYLE An architectural style characterized in Cleveland County domestic architecture by cornice brackets and arched door panels. Popular locally during the second half of the nineteenth century.

JACK ARCH *See* ARCH.

JALOUSIE WINDOW *See* WINDOW.

KEYSTONE *See* ARCH.

LANCET ARCH *See* ARCH.

LOG CONSTRUCTION A traditional form of building in which logs are stacked horizontally to form building enclosures. *Notching* is the technique by which logs are

LOG CONSTRUCTION

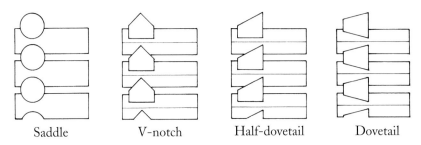

Saddle   V-notch   Half-dovetail   Dovetail

joined together at their ends. *Saddle-notching* is the simplest form, with crudely scalloped notches. In *half-dovetail notching* the top of the end of the log is sloped and the bottom is squared. In *dovetail notching* both the top and bottom of the log are sloped. In *V-notching* the top of the end of the log is given a tentlike or inverted V form.

LOTIFORM Resembling lotus buds or flowers.

LUNETTE *See* WINDOW.

MANSARD ROOF *See* ROOF.

MARBLING The painted simulation of marble.

MATCHBOARD Boards joined together with tongue-and-groove edges. Beaded matchboard sheathing consists of narrow boards decorated with one or more rows of beading. Matchboard sheathing was mass-produced during the late 1800s and early 1900s. *See also* BEAD.

MERLON A toothlike projection in a battlement, separated from other merlons by gaps.

MODERNE A modernistic style popular locally during the 1930s and 1940s characterized by streamlined forms and a general lack of ornamentation.

MODILLION A blocklike element in a cornice under the eaves of a roof.

MORTAR JOINTS *See* BRICK.

MORTISE-AND-TENON CONSTRUCTION A construction technique in which framing members are joined together with a projecting tenon and a slotlike mortise and generally held together with a wooden peg. Mortise-and-tenon heavy frame construction eventually gave way to light nailed frame construction in Cleveland County.

ONE-ROOM PLAN *See* PLAN.

ORDER In classical and classically derived architecture, the style or system of proportion and detail of a column and related elements. There are three principal orders of classical Greek and Roman architecture. The *Doric Order* is characterized by simplicity, with a molded column capital. The *Ionic Order* has capitals with dominant

ORDER

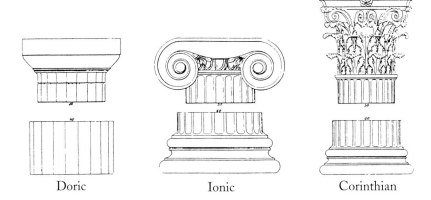

Doric   Ionic   Corinthian

volutes (spiraled, cushionlike elements). The *Corinthian Order*, the most ornate, is characterized by delicate leaflike ornament and small volutes.

OUTBUILDING An auxiliary building in a domestic or agricultural complex.

OVERMANTEL The section of a mantel over the mantel shelf. Georgian and Colonial Revival–style overmantels are often composed of panels. Victorian and Craftsman overmantels often feature mirrors, colonnettes, and other ornament.

PALLADIAN WINDOW *See* WINDOW.

PATERAE Round ornaments.

PAVED *See* BRICK.

PEAKED Denoting a pointed profile suggestive of a pediment or a lancet arch.

PEDIMENT In classical and classically derived architecture, the triangular end of a gable roof, defined by cornices. Used as a decorative element above a door or window opening in Colonial Revival architecture, sometimes broken and/or scrolled at the center.

PERGOLA A garden structure with an open roof structure. Some porches, especially on Craftsman-style examples, have pergola effects.

PILASTER An engaged column, or a columnlike element that visually supports the frieze in a Greek Revival mantel. *See also* POST-AND-LINTEL.

PINTEL The pin on which a shutter swings.

PLAN The interior layout of a house or building. Traditional Cleveland County dwellings are characterized by a small set of recurring plans. The *one-room plan* is the most basic, consisting of a single unpartitioned space. The *hall-parlor plan* (sometimes referred to as the hall and parlor plan) has two rooms of unequal size; the larger room is referred to as the hall, and the smaller as the parlor (not to be confused with the parlor—or best room—of a Victorian house). The *center-passage plan* (sometimes

PLAN TYPES

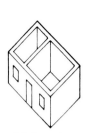
Hall-parlor

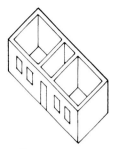
Center-passage

referred to as the center-hall plan) features two rooms or two pairs of rooms of nearly equal size separated and served by a center passage.

PORCH ROOM A small room partitioned off from one end of a porch, typically used as a spare bedroom. Known colloquially as a "pizer room" (from piazza, or porch).

PORTE COCHERE A covered area in which to park a carriage or automobile or load and unload passengers, often treated as an extension of a porch.

PORTICO A porch, usually one that is classically detailed and imposing in size.

POST-AND-LINTEL Used to describe a standard nineteenth-century Greek Revival and Victorian mantel form with a lintel (or frieze) visually supported by posts (pilasters). *See also* FRIEZE, PILASTER.

PUNCHWORK Federal-style decoration with deeply recessed or "punched" patterns.

PYRAMIDAL ROOF *See* ROOF.

QUEEN ANNE STYLE *See* VICTORIAN.

QUOIN A usually decorative corner treatment in stone or projecting brickwork.

RAKE BOARD/RAKING CORNICE A board or cornice running along the edge of a gable.

REEDING Delicate parallel convex moldings or beading that create a corrugated appearance.

ROOF The cover of a building. A *shed roof* is a single-sloped roof. A *gable roof* is a double-sloped roof with a triangular or A-shaped section. A *clipped gable roof* has a small hip at the apex of the gable; also called a jerkinhead roof. A *gambrel roof* is a double-sloped roof with a double-sloped pitch to each slope, associated in Cleveland County with dairy barns and certain Colonial Revival houses. A *hip roof* has four slopes; a *pyramidal roof* is a form of hip roof in which the four roof slopes meet at a single point. A *mansard roof* is similar to a truncated pyramid in form; occasionally it has concave or convex sides. A *bowstring roof* has a bowed or curved surface created by a bowstring truss understructure. The roofs of Craftsman and Colonial Revival

ROOF TYPES

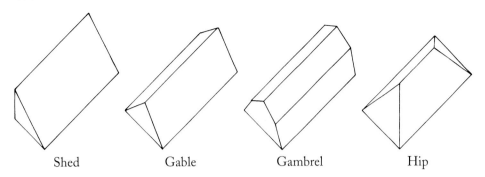

Shed   Gable   Gambrel   Hip

houses often feature *dormers,* windows that project from the slope of the roof and that can have gable, pedimented gable, shed, or hip roofs.

SADDLE NOTCHING   *See* LOG CONSTRUCTION.

SASH   *See* WINDOW.

SEGMENTAL ARCH   *See* ARCH.

SHED ROOF   *See* ROOF.

SHOULDER   The point at which the body of a chimney narrows, usually at the level of the eaves. Most chimney shoulders are stepped; some are paved. Some early chimneys are double-shouldered, with shoulders above the fireplaces at the first- and second-story levels. *See also* BRICK.

SPANDREL   The triangular section of wall under a flight of steps, or the section of wall that spans between windows on consecutive stories of a facade.

SPINDLE   A small turned piece of wood used decoratively in Victorian architecture, sometimes used repetitively under the eaves of a porch roof as a spindle frieze.

STRETCHER   *See* BRICK.

STYLE   A fashion or mode of architecture.

TONGUE-AND-GROOVE   *See* MATCHBOARD.

TRACERY   *See* WINDOW.

TRIGLYPH   A blocklike frieze ornament.

TRIPLE-A   Describes a side-gable roof with a third gable centered over the front elevation. Also describes a house with this kind of roof.

TUDOR ARCH   *See* ARCH.

TUDOR REVIVAL STYLE   A style derived from the architecture of Medieval and Early Modern England characterized by asymmetrical compositions. Akin to the Gothic Revival style.

TYMPANUM The face of a pediment.

V-NOTCHING *See* LOG CONSTRUCTION.

VERGEBOARD *See* BARGEBOARD.

VICTORIAN Architecture from the late 1800s and early 1900s characterized by asymmetrical composition, complex massing and roof lines, architectural details that distantly reflect medieval prototypes, and the liberal use of machined ornament. Typical Victorian features include hip-and-gable roofs, bay windows, porches supported by chamfered or turned posts with sawn brackets, wood-shingle sheathing, decorative roof vents, and intricate mantels. The *Queen Anne style* is a particularly elaborate form of Victorian styling. The *Eastlake style* is another variant.

VOUSSOIR *See* ARCH.

WAINSCOT Paneling or other wood facing at the base of an interior wall. Sometimes referred to as a dado.

WINDER A triangular or wedge-shaped step used to turn a corner in a stair.

WINDOW An opening in a wall that provides light and ventilation to the interior of a building. Most historic Cleveland County buildings have double-hung sash windows; in the text, the number of panes of glass in each sash is referred to numerically. For example, a window with nine panes in the upper sash and six panes in the lower sash is referred to as a nine-over-six-sash window. A *bay window* projects from the wall of a building and is often made up of several individual windows. Polygonal bay windows of one or more stories in height are associated with Victorian domestic architecture. A *jalousie window* has multiple operable glass slats. A *Palladian window* (after the sixteenth-century Venetian architect Andrea Palladio) consists of three windows: a central round-arched window flanked by lower square-headed windows. A *lunette* is a semicircular window, usually in a gable. *Tracery* is a decorative pattern of wood or stone muntins and is characteristic of Gothic Revival lancet-arched windows.

WRAPAROUND PORCH A porch that extends to two or more sides of a building, characteristic of Victorian architecture.

BIBLIOGRAPHY

Alexander, W. Ted. "The Renovation of a Landmark." *Energy Manager* (June 2000): 22–24.

Bishir, Catherine W. *North Carolina Architecture.* Raleigh, N.C.: Historic Preservation Foundation of North Carolina, Inc., 1990.

Bishir, Catherine W., and Michael T. Southern. *A Guide to the Historic Architecture of Piedmont North Carolina.* Chapel Hill, N.C.: The University of North Carolina Press, 2003.

Bowers, Sybil Argintar. "East Marion–Belvedere Park Historic District." National Register of Historic Places Registration Form, 2002.

———. "Sperling, George, House and Outbuildings." National Register of Historic Places Registration Form, 2001.

Brewer, Priscilla J. *From Fireplace to Cookstove: Technology and the Domestic Ideal in America.* Syracuse, N.Y.: Syracuse University Press, 2000.

Bridges, Ezra A., and Cothenia Jolley. "A 2002 Search in Cleveland County for the Works of Julius Rosenwald."

Bridges, Jackie. "Historic Treasures: Tour Celebrates and Helps Preserve Kings Mountain Landmarks." *Shelby Star,* April 21, 2002.

Brown, Brenda Mauney, comp. "Douglas High School." Report for the Lawndale Historical Society, n.d.

Bumgarner, Matthew C., Ladley Burn, Thomas J. Forney Jr., and R. Douglas Walker. *The Lawndale Railway & Industrial Company with the Southern & Western Air Line.* Hickory, N.C.: N.C. Railroad Heritage Publishing Co., 1999.

Caldwell, Wilber W. *The Courthouse and the Depot.* Macon, Ga.: Mercer University Press, 2001.

Cass, E. H. Lawndale Railway Drawings. 1953. Cleveland County Historical Museum Collection. Shelby, N.C.

Cimino, Karen. "Area Got Its Start As a Resort Town." *Shelby Star,* February 25, 1997.

Clayton, Bruce. *W. J. Cash: A Life.* Baton Rouge: Louisiana State University Press, 1991.

"Cleveland County Courthouse." Entry in thematic nomination of North Carolina courthouses.

Cleveland County deed and commissioners minute book records. Shelby, N.C.

Cleveland County Historical Museum Collection. Shelby, N.C.

Cleveland Mills. Lawndale, N.C.: Cleveland Mills, ca. 1985.

Cleveland Star. Shelby, N.C.

Copeland, Melvin Thomas. *The Cotton Manufacturing Industry in the United States.* Cambridge, Mass.: Harvard University, 1912.

"County's Mineral Springs Recall Colorful Era." Undated clipping in the Cleveland County Museum Collection.

Cross, Jerry L., and Michael Southern. "Joshua Beam House." National Register of Historic Places Inventory-Nomination Form, 1980.

———. "Irvin-Hamrick Log House." National Register of Historic Places Inventory-Nomination Form, ca. 1980.

———. "Webbley." National Register of Historic Places Inventory-Nomination Form, 1980.

Davis, Burke. *The Southern Railway: Road of Innovators.* Chapel Hill, N.C.: The University of North Carolina Press, 1985.

DePriest, Joe. "Historic Find: House Survives Years." *Shelby Star,* January 25, 1984.

———. "Textiles in Transition." *Shelby Star,* February 18–23, 1985 (special section).

"Dockery's Funeral Home, Inc." Poster, 1981.

Draper, E. S. "Village Plan for Eastside Mfg. Co. Shelby NC." 1919. Photographic copy in the North Carolina Collection, Wilson Library, University of North Carolina, Chapel Hill.

Eades, Brian R. "The History and Architecture of Cleveland County, North Carolina." Manuscript, 1998.

Eades, Brian R., and Megan Eades. "Central School Historic District." National Register of Historic Places Registration Form, 2001.

Ebeltoft, Elizabeth. "Shelby as Resort." Presentation to the Ishpening Club, 1916. In the Cleveland County Historical Museum Collection.

Fore, George. "Historic Finishes Analysis for the Rogers Theatre." 2002.

Gardner, O. Max, III. "Historic Webbley." Brochure, ca. 1990.

Glisson, Linda S. "Main Street: Open for Business." Washington, D.C.: National Main Street Center, 1984.

Goforth, Michael. "Lawndale Center Opens Sunday." *Shelby Star,* September 11, 1987.

Hambright, Sarah, and Ola Pruette. "The Bicentennial History of Shiloh Presbyterian Church, Grover, North Carolina, 1780–1980." Ca. 1980.

Hamrick, George W. *History of the Oil Mill at Lattimore, North Carolina.* 1998.

Hanchett, Thomas W. "The Rosenwald Schools and Black Education in North Carolina." *North Carolina Historical Review* 65, no. 4 (October 1988): 387–444.

Hargrove, Thomas, and Michael Hammond. "Dan River Basin Cultural Resources Study." Chapel Hill, N.C.: Archaeological Research Consultants, 1981.

Heath, Betty Rose. "Hudson-Hull House." Report, 1998.

Henry, Michael. "A Piece of Churchill Downs Houses Southco." *Shelby Star,* July 26, 2003.

The Heritage of Cleveland County, Volume I — 1982. Shelby, N.C.: Cleveland County Historical Association, 1982.

Herring, Harriet L. *Welfare Work in Mill Villages.* Chapel Hill: University of North Carolina Press, 1929.

Hilgard, Eugene W. *Report of Cotton Production in the United States.* Part 2. Washington, D.C.: Government Printing Office, 1884.

Howe, Claudia. "Folks Still Swear by Lithia Water." *Charlotte Observer,* September 19, 1971.

Hoyle, Jack. "Belwood School and Other Schools in #10 Township." Report, 1997.

Hutchison, Janet, and Jerry L. Cross. "John Lattimore House." National Register of Historic Places Inventory-Nomination Form, 1981.

Jolley, Jim. "Cleveland Has Western Carolina's Only Cottonseed Crushing Mill." *Shelby Daily Star*, January 21, 1960.

Jolley, Lansford. *Dreaming, Daring, Doing: The Story of Gardner-Webb University, 1907–1997*. Boiling Springs, N.C.: Gardner-Webb University, 1997.

Joyner, J. Y. *Plans for Public Schoolhouses*. Raleigh, N.C.: E. M. Uzzell & Co., 1911.

Keller, Genevieve, and Timothy Keller. "Central Shelby Historic District." National Register of Historic Places Inventory-Nomination Form, 1983.

Kings Mountain Historical Society Collection. Kings Mountain Historical Museum, Kings Mountain, N.C.

Land and Community Associates. "City of Shelby Architectural and Historic Inventory." Report, 1983.

Larimore, Denise, and Jennifer Kibby, comps. "Central Shelby Historic District Walking Tour." Brochure. Shelby, N.C.: Historic Shelby Foundation and Uptown Shelby Association, 1992.

Laughlin, Mike. "Kingstown Area Looks for Growth." *Shelby Star*, June 26, 1996.

Lefler, Hugh Talmage, and Albert Ray Newsome. *North Carolina: The History of a Southern State*. Chapel Hill: University of North Carolina Press, 1963.

Little, M. Ruth. *Sticks and Stones: Three Centuries of North Carolina Gravemarkers*. Chapel Hill: University of North Carolina Press, 1998.

Long, Brian, and April Long. *Spartan Mills, 100th Anniversary, 1890–1990*. Spartanburg, S.C.: Spartan Mills, 1990.

"Map of Kings Mountain, N.C." 1914 map in the Kings Mountain Historical Society Collection, Kings Mountain, N.C.

Michael, Michelle Ann. "The Rise of the Regional Architect in North Carolina as Seen through the Manufacturer's Record, 1890–1910." MHP thesis, University of Georgia, 1994.

Morrison, Joseph L. *Governor O. Max Gardner: A Power in North Carolina and New Deal Washington*. Chapel Hill: University of North Carolina Press, 1971.

———. *W. J. Cash: Southern Prophet*. New York, N.Y.: Alfred A. Knopf, 1967.

"New Joy Theatre Scheduled to Open Wednesday." *Kings Mountain Herald*, May 27, 1949.

Our Heritage: A History of Cleveland County. Shelby, N.C.: Shelby Daily Star, 1976.

Patterson, U. L. "Rusty," and Barry E. Hambright. *Shelby and Cleveland County, North Carolina*. Charleston, S.C.: Arcadia Publishing, 2000.

Perrin, Carol Carré. "Kings Mountain Historic Inventory Project Completion Report." 1980.

"Pictorial Review of Shelby and Cleveland County." *Shelby Daily Star*, 1953.

Poston, Lyda, ed. *History of Zion Church, 1816–1955*. Ca. 1955.

Rainey, Lee. "The Lawndale Dummy." 1983 article.

Rhyne, Jennings J. *Some Southern Cotton Mill Workers and Their Villages*. Chapel Hill: University of North Carolina Press, 1930.

Rounding Board (Newsletter of Shelby City Park Carrousel Friends, Inc., Shelby, N.C.).

Sanborn Map Company. Maps of Shelby, N.C.

Shelby Aurora (Shelby, N.C.).

Shelby Daily Star (Shelby, N.C.).

"The Shelby Oil Mill." *Cleveland Star,* October 31, 1916.

Simmons, Rika. "Remembering Matthew Mauney." *Shelby Star,* July 22, 2002.

Smith, John W. *Building a Railroad (1832–1952): The Seaboard Air Line, Its Beginnings and Its Contributions.* New York, N.Y.: The Newcomen Society in North America, 1952.

Southern, Michael, James Sumner, and Walter Best. "Dr. Victor McBrayer House." National Register of Historic Places Inventory-Nomination Form, 1979.

Spencer, Frank. "Cleveland County Dairy History." Speech transcript, 1995.

Sumner, James, and Michael Southern. "E. B. Hamrick Hall." National Register of Historic Places Inventory-Nomination Form, 1981.

———. "Joseph Suttle House." National Register of Historic Places Inventory-Nomination Form, 1980.

Survey and Planning Unit, Division of Archives and History. "Banker's House." National Register of Historic Places Inventory-Nomination Form, 1975.

Swaim, Douglas, Janet Hutchison, and James Sumner. "Masonic Temple Building." National Register of Historic Places Inventory-Nomination Form, 1981.

Tarpley, Cassie. "Carl Dockery Sr. Wasn't Afraid of New Frontiers." *Shelby Star,* September 17, 2001.

———. "A Home for History." *Shelby Star,* April 28, 1999.

Tarpley, Cassie, ed. *A History of Faith: A Collection of Stories on the Cleveland County Area's Oldest Congregations.* Shelby, N.C.: The Star, 2001.

Weathers, Lee B. *The Living Past of Cleveland County: A History.* Shelby, N.C.: Star Publishing Co., 1956.

Webb, Elizabeth Yates. "The Development of Industry in North Carolina: A Century of Textiles, 1830–1930." Ca. 1930 typescript at the North Carolina Collection, University of North Carolina, Chapel Hill, N.C.

Wilbor, A. G. "Cleveland Cotton Mills No. 2." Hartford, Conn.: Factory Insurance Association, 1898. Plan and isometric drawing on display at the Lawndale Historical Museum, Lawndale, N.C.

Wood, Amy Jo. "Renovation Showing at Rogers Theatre." *Our State* (November 2001): 70–72.

Carolina Motor Inn, a typical 1920s service station, Shelby. Photo courtesy of Iris Francis.

INDEX

31RF 16, 19, 39, 40, 47 & 51 Second Broad River Watershed District (archaeological sites), 284

A&P grocery store, 131
Acre Rock quarry, 49, 177, 193, 206, 271, 274, 276
Adams, L. L., 169
Adams family, 238
Addington, Hubert, 252
AGI, 53, 279
Album Graphics, Inc., 279
All-Day BBQ restaurant, 273
Allen, Haywood, 254
Allen, Irvin, 254
Allied Kentuckians, 159
Allison, Plato, 255
Allison, Plato, Farm, 255
Allison, Una Dean, 165
Ambassador Baptist College, 55, 191
America's 11 Most Endangered Properties, 198
American Treasure, 198
Andrews-Royster House, 43, 129
Anthony, J. A., 45, 124
Anthony, Jacob, 70
Anthony, Lloyd, 102
Anthony, O. Stanhope, 219, 278
Apartment House (211 W. Mountain, Kings Mountain), 252
Appleget, G. S. H., 24, 43, 84
Arey, Carole Suttle, 67
Arey, William Jackson, 67
Arey horse farm, 273
Art Metal Construction Company, 122
Artizan A-2 Military Band Organ, 212
Asbury, Louis H., 38
Atlanta & Charlotte Air Line (railroad), 15, 17, 82, 253
Atlanta & Charlotte division of the Richmond & Danville (railroad), 36
Austell, Bostick, 30, 138
Austell, Forest, 253
Austell, Joe, 253
Austell, Tom, 138
Aycock, Charles B., 38–39

Babington, Benjamin Boyer, 27
Babington, Thomas, 27
Babington, William, 27
Bailey, Anne Dover, Carousel Pavilion, 212
Balfour, R. J., 81
Banker's House, 23–24, 84–85, 283, plate 1
Barber, John, House, 202
Barrett & Thomson, 39
Barrett & Thomson Design No. 2, 39
Barrett's Salvage and Floor Covering, 169
Battle of Gaines Mill, 135
Battle of Kings Mountain, 8, 9, 61, 202
Battleground Avenue, 174
Beam, Aaron, 70
Beam, Elizabeth, 70
Beam, John F., House, 97, 284
Beam, John Frank, 97
Beam, John Teeter, 70, 250
Beam, John Teeter, grave, 250
Beam, Joshua, 10, 70
Beam, Joshua, & Company, 70
Beam, Joshua, House, 10–11, 58–59, 70–71, 283, plate 7
Beam, Joshua, ironworks, 70
Beam, Martin Francis, 97
Beam, Matilda (Mauney), 70
Beam, Susan (Heavner), 70
Beam Construction Company, 219
Beam's Mill, 97
Beason family, 233, 242
Beason House, 233
Beecher, Eunice, 27
Belk-Royster Building, 158
Belk-Stevens Building, 55, 158
Belk-Stevens Company, 158
Bell, Captain, 190
Belmont Abbey, 195
Belmont Cotton Mills, 18, 86
Belvedere Avenue, 49
Belvedere Park, 49, 151, plate 18
Belwood, N.C., 3
Belwood Institute, 38, 39, 258
Belwood Post Office, 12, 118
Belwood School, 167

Belwood School Teacherage, 167
Benedick, Dexter N., 219
Benjamin, Asher, 11
Benton, Charles C., 198
Bernhardt Furniture Company, 269
Besser, Charles S., Company, 213
Bethlehem Baptist Church, 181, 264
Bethlehem School, 264
"Better Acres Contest," 101
Bettis, Allen and Leola, House, 230
Bettis, Allen Erastus, 230, 242
Bettis, Baxter, 253
Bettis, Corrie Towery, 242
Bettis, Leola Austell, 230
Bettis, Will, 253
Bettis, William and Corrie, House, 242
Bettis, William French, 242
Bettis Store, 253
Big Hill Methodist Church, 240, 284
Bigham family, 14
Bingham, Cynthia Jane Brackett, 236
Bingham, Joseph and Jane, House, 236
Bingham, Joseph Pinkney, 236
Black, Freya, Design, 279
Blackburn, Reid, 254
Blackley, Fred B., 125
Blacksburg (South Carolina) Veterans Class, 76
Blalock, Piccola, 264
Bland, Frank, 141
Blanton, B., & Company, 84, 86, 108
Blanton, Burwell, 84, 86, 108
Blanton, Burwell, Farm, 86, 284, plate 2
Blanton, Charles, 66
Blanton, Charles Coleman, 84
Blanton, Coleman, 29, 241, 272
Blanton, Coleman, Farm, 29, 241–242, 284
Blanton, Frances Doggett, 86
Blanton, George Sr., 144
Blanton, George H. Jr., 84, 85
Blanton, J. B., 235
Blanton, J. B., House, 235
Blanton, Jewel, 78

299

Blanton, Mr., 256
Blanton, Nancy, 85
Blanton, Pattie, 84
Blanton Building, 108–109
Blanton family, 86
Bleynat, Albert, 49, 177, 206
Blue Grass Boys, 159
Blue Ridge Environmental Specialists, 195
Boggs, A. E., 275
Boggs, A. Noah, 275
Boggs, Bill, 237
Boggs, Bill and Melinda, Farm, 237
Boggs, Ella Spurling, 237
Boggs, John, 237
Boggs, Lloyd, 237
Boggs, Max, 209
Boggs, Melinda, 237
Boggs, Mrs. John, 268
Boggs, Vangie Mull, 237
Boggs Cotton Gin, 17, 209, plate 21
Boggs family, 275
Boiling Springs, N.C., 3, 55, 172, 259
Boiling Springs Baptist Church Cemetery, 28
Boiling Springs Community Fair Association, 160
Boiling Springs High School (private), 40, 170, 224
Boiling Springs High School (public), 55, 171–172, 258
Boiling Springs Post Office (former), 242
Boiling Springs Springhouse, 171
Boiling Springs to Lattimore Telephone Exchange, 229
Bonnie Mill Village, 21
Bonnie Mills, 18, 154
Borders, Bable, 188
Borders, Calb, 188
Borders, Filet, 188
Borders, G. B., 188
Borders, J. W., 188
Borders, J. W. and Mittie, House, 188
Borders, Miles, 188
Borders, Mills, 188
Borders, Mittie, 188
Bostic, N.C., 241
Bostic Brick Company, 241
Bovis Construction, 279
Bowen, Carrie Williamson, 244
Bowen, Elijah, 231

Bowen, Elijah and Margaret, House, 231–232
Bowen, Forrest, 232, 244
Bowen, Forrest and Carrie, House, 244
Bowen, Margaret, 231
Bowers Snuff & Tobacco Company, 126
Boyce, Rev., 275
Boyles, Carme, 252
Boyles, Joe, 252
Boyles, Joe, & Sons Store, 252
Boyles, Roland, 252
Brackett, J. H., 167
Brackett, J. W., 12, 118
Brackett, J. W. Jr., 118
Brackett, J. W. and Maude, Farm, 12, 30, 118, 284
Brackett, Maude, 118
Brackett family, 223
Brackett House, 223, 284
Branton, Augustus, 46, 150, 176
Breeze, Victor Winfred, 43–45, 196
Breeze, Victor Winfred, firm, 201, 264
Breeze, Holland & Riviere, 45, 50, 277
Bridges, Carver S., 215, 276
Bridges, Lyttle, 215
Bridges, Red, 215
Bridges, Xenophen, 258
Bridges & Holland Store, 257–258
Bridges Barbecue Lodge, 52, 215
Broad River, 3
Broad River Academy, 81, 284
Broad River Baptist Association, 250
Broad River Greenway, 7, 69
Broad River steel bridge, 43
Brooks, Grady, 187, 214
Brushy Creek Dairy Farm, 29, 241–242
Brushy Creek dam, 43
Bryant, Hal, 68
Buff, Julius, 268
Buff, Mrs. Julius, 268
Buffalo Creek, 3
Builders, architects, landscape architects, artists, tombstone carvers, and building tradesmen/women:
 Anthony, O. Stanhope, 219, 278
 Appleget, G. S. H., 24, 43, 84
 Asbury, Louis H., 38
 Barrett & Thomson, 39
 Beam Construction Company, 219

Benedick, Dexter N., 219
Benjamin, Asher, 11
Benton, Charles C., 198
Besser, Charles S., Company, 213
Bigham family, 14
Black, Freya, Design, 279
Blackley, Fred B., 125
Blanton, Mr., 256
Bleynat, Albert, 49, 177, 206
Borders, Filet, 188
Bovis Construction, 279
Brackett, J. H., 167
Branton, Augustus, 46, 150, 176
Breeze, Victor Winfred, 43–45, 196
Breeze, Victor Winfred, firm, 201, 264
Breeze, Holland & Riviere, 45, 50, 277
Brooks, Grady, 187, 214
Cabaniss, Flay, 256
Cabiness, Wilbur, 269
Carpenter, Willie, 271, 273–274
Caveny family, 14
Colyer, Leigh, 49
Crawford, Robert M., 14
Crawford, William N., 14
Crawford family, 14
Dameron, John, 9
Demmitt, Tim, 51
Draper, Earl S., 20
Eaker, John, 244
Eckenhoff Saunders Architects, 279
Elliott, Joe, 207
Evans, Gus, 152
Foothills Builders, 131
Foster (stonemason), 267
Fuller, Buckminster, 52
Gardner, J. A., & Co., 136
Goforth, John, 242
Hamrick, D. J., 28
Hamrick, Grover, 255
Harbin, W. Lee, 136
Harry, David F. C., 175
Haynes, Clive, 4
Hendricks, Rochel, 253
Holland, L. Pegram Jr., 201, 277
Holland & Riviere, 50, 278
Holland Hamrick & Patterson Architects, 45, 201, 212, 213
Hook, Charles Christian, 21
Hughes, W. Gordon, 189

300 Index

Johnson, Ralph, Associates, 51
Jones, Haynes F., 40
Jordan, Yvonne, 270
Korner, J. Gilmer, 136, 137
Little, John P., & Son, 155, 157
Lowery, W. B., 238
Lowman, R. Lee, 166, 184
McAllister, Junius, 170
McCall, Bennie, 270
McCulloch, John, 170
McCulloch-English Associates, 170
McDaniel, Harlan, 267
McIntyre, Virgil, 215
McMichael, J. M., 43, 129, 130, 155
McSwain, Lawson, 145
McSwain, Pete, 230
Marsh, M. R., 213
Martin, John, 264
Martin Boal Anthony & Johnson (MBAJ Architecture), 53, 131, 219, 275, 278
Matton (builder), 276
Mauney, Matthew Marcus, 42–43, 98, 105
Melick, Neal A., 202
Miller, Pink, 259
Mintz, Charlie, 254
Moore, Dan Sr., 252
Moore, J. F., 252
Moore, John F., 40
Morgan, Ron, 158
Morrison Construction Company, 279
Murphy, Crawford, 278
O'Brien, Michael, 158
Overcash-Demmitt Architects, 51
Parker, George, 223
Payne, George Hardy, Studio, 136
Pease, J. N., 50, 185
Phillip, W., 24
Pruett, Doug, 219
Pullen, F. M., 272
Ramsey, A. A., 180
Roberts Filter Manufacturing Company, 185
Rogers, Willard G., 43, 157
Rollins (builder), 110
Rudisill, Michael, 27, 42
Simmons, Fred M., 51, 278
Simon, Louis A., 202
Smith, George, 9

Smith, Lyle, 134, 135
Stockton, Robert L., 80
Summers, Bonnie E. Mauney, 183
Sunshine Construction Company, 134
Swanson, Aurelia, 150
Talley, Norman "Bud," 278
Talley & Smith Architecture, 278
Upton, Sam, 258
Van Wageningen, Fred, 44, 201
Van Wageningen & Cothran, 215, 273
Wall, Otis, 164
Watts, Rile, 275
Weaver, W. D., 266
Webber (possible builder), 120
Webber, Ralph Furman, 277
Webber & Sons Construction, 170, 277
Wetmore, James A., 250
Wheeler & Stern, 43, 136
White, A., & Sons, 170
White, David, 170
White, Fonz, 267
White, Hugh, 136
Wright, Frank Lloyd, 50–51, 156, 215, 277
Young, Lee, 250
Zourras (artist), 219
Burn, John, 272
Burnham family, 232
Burns Middle School, 167
Burrtown, N.C., 64
Burrus, H. C., 141
Burrus, Roy Grady, 146
Burrus, Roy Grady Jr., 146
Burrus & Bland tobacco factory, 141
Burrus Mill, 146
Burton, Augustus, 124
Burton, Cecil M., Funeral Home, 184

Cabaniss, Flay, 256
Cabarrus County Courthouse, 84
Cabiness, Wilbur, 269
Calton, William T., 26, 112, 116
Calton Lumber Yard, 116, 117
Calton-Martin House, 25–26, 116–117, plate 3
Camp Call Lodge No. 534, 278
Capernaum Arbor, 12, 247
Capernaum Baptist Church, 247

Capernaum Baptist Church Cemetery, 247
Capernaum Baptist congregation, 12
Captain Bell's Boys School, 38, 190
Carnation Dairy, 162
Carolina Central Railroad, 15, 91
Carolina Dairy, 272–273
Carolina Motor Inn, 298
Carolina Theatre, 249
Carpenter, Clora Louvenia, 235
Carpenter, Forrest, 49, 274
Carpenter, Forrest and Ruby, House, 49, 271, 273–274
Carpenter, Gordon, 274
Carpenter, Jacob, grave, 250
Carpenter, James and Clora, Farm, 235
Carpenter, James Buchanan, 235
Carpenter, John David Schenck, 93
Carpenter, Martha, grave, 250
Carpenter, Robert, 274
Carpenter, Ruby, 274
Carpenter, Schenck, 228
Carpenter, Will, 244
Carpenter, Will, Farm, 244
Carpenter, Will W., 235
Carpenter, Willie, 49, 271, 273–274
Carpenter, Willie, House, 49, 271, 273
Carpenter, Zoie Elam Lattimore, 93
Carpenter family, 93
Carraway, Gertrude S., Award of Merit, 125
Casar, N.C., 3, 164
Casar Baptist Church, 192
Casar Cash Grocery, 164
Casar Commercial District, 164
Casar High School, 165
Casar Methodist Church, 207
Casar Post Office, 164
Cash, Charles, 213
Cash, David, 213
Cash, Freemon, 231
Cash, Wilbur Joseph, 28, 170
Catawbas, 4
Causby, Harold and Mary Lou, 51
Caveny family, 14
Central Cleveland Junior High School, 40
Central High School, 190
Central Hotel, 35, 108–109
Central School Historic District, 283
Central Shelby Historic District, 55, 283

Central United Methodist Church, 43, 126, 155
Chadborn Company, 269
Champion, Carrie Alice (Crowder), 94
Champion, Clifton and Alice, House, 94, plate 30
Champion, Clifton Otis, 94
Charles, The, 109
Charlotte Section of the American Institute of Architects, 158
Cherokees, 4
Cherryville Manufacturing Company, 126
Childhood Education Center, 169
Church Spring, 171
Churchill Downs, 267
Churchill Downs Grandstand, 267
Civilian Defense bomb shelter, 202
Clark, John, 91
Cleaveland, Benjamin, 8
Cleaveland County, 8
Cleaveland Guards, 84
Cleveland, Grover, 8
Cleveland Bank & Trust Company, 151, 238
Cleveland Building & Loan Association, 151
Cleveland Community College, 68
Cleveland Cotton Mills, 42, 98
Cleveland Cotton Mills No. 2, 19
Cleveland Country Club, 47, 259–260
Cleveland County, 2–3, 5, 8, 70, 121, 124
Cleveland County Arts Council, 250
Cleveland County Board of Education, 134
Cleveland County Courthouse (1845 building), 9–10, 62, 121
Cleveland County Courthouse (former; 1907–8 building), frontispiece, 10, 47, 121–123, 283
Cleveland County Courthouse (present), 123, 219
Cleveland County Courthouse Springhouse, 123
Cleveland County Fair, 160, 176, 241
Cleveland County Fairgrounds, 160–161
Cleveland County Historic Preservation Taskforce, ix, x, xi

Cleveland County Historical Museum, 123
Cleveland County Justice Complex, 219
Cleveland County Memorial Library, 278
Cleveland County Negro Fair, 160
Cleveland County Township 3, 276
Cleveland County Township 4, 246
Cleveland Elementary School, 41
Cleveland Eye Clinic, 51
Cleveland Lodge of the Ancient, Free, and Accepted Masons of North Carolina, 157
Cleveland Mall, 53, 54, 158
Cleveland Memorial Park, 29
Cleveland Mill & Power Company, 98, 134, 147
Cleveland Mill & Power Company Store, 21, 22
Cleveland Mills, 16, 93, 98–99, 102, 152, plate 29
Cleveland Mills Company, 93
Cleveland Mills Union Church, 21, 22
Cleveland Oil Mill, 112
Cleveland Savings & Loan Association, 50, 67, 277
Cleveland Savings & Loan Building, 50, 277–278
Cleveland Springs, 35, 259–260
Cleveland Springs Hotel, 37
Cliffside Mills, 225
Cliffside Steam Station, 211, 256
Cline, David Mills, 256
Cline, Hester Cabaniss, 256
Cline, Huss, 272
Cline, John, 256
Cline, John and Mary, House, 224
Cline, John Franklin, 224
Cline, Mary Elizabeth Hoyle, 224
Cline, Mills and Hester, Farm, 256
Clover Hill United Methodist Church, 49, 193, 207
Clover Hill United Methodist Church cemetery, 193
Coca-Cola Distributing Plant, 204
Cogdell family, 227
College Farm, 76
Collins, Samuel, 139
Collins, "Sumul," 139
Collins Cemetery, 13
Colyer, Leigh, 49
Commercial Hotel, 33

Community Cash Grocery Store, 276
Compact School, 169, 246
Cone Mills, 225
Confederate States Army (CSA), 74, 76, 225
Confederate Memorial, 122, 123
Cora Mill Village, 20
Cora Mills, 18
Cornwell, George and Julia, House, 234
Cornwell, George L., 234
Cornwell, Julia Gold, 234
Cornwell, Lee, 208
Cornwell, Wilson, 208
Cornwell, Wilson, Cotton Gin, 208
Costner, Dwight, 194
Costner's Furniture No. 2 Building, 164
Country Music Hall of Fame, 159
County Training School No. 2, 41
Court of St. James, 124
Courtview Hotel, 33, 35
Covington, Horace, 275
Covington Mountain, 3
Crawford, Robert M., 14
Crawford, William N., 14
Crawford family, 14
Cromer, Ellison, 168
Crook, Mrs. Kenneth, 262
Crowder, Forrest, 90
CSX Corporation, 4, 91
Culp, Hill, 169

Dairymans Inc., 266
Dalton, Addie Harrelson, 268
Dalton, Chesley Amzi, 268
Dalton, Chesley and Addie, House, 268
Dalton family, 268
Dameron, John, 9
Davis, Byron, 254
Davis, Byron and Mae, Farm, 254
Davis, Clifton, 145
Davis, Clifton, Farm, 145, 284
Davis, Mae, 254
DeBerry family monument, 214
Dedmon, Roy, 271
Dedmon, Thomas and Verdie, Farm, 271
Dedmon, Thomas Lawson, 271
Dedmon, Verdie Mae Horn, 271
Dellinger, J. P., 235
Demmitt, Tim, 51

DePriest, S. H. C. and Elsie, House, 254, 256
Dickson, Edward, 64
Dilling, Charles A., 83
Dilling Mill, 18
Dilling Mill Village, 20, 21
Dixie-Home Supermarket, 157
Dixon, Thomas Jr., 250
Dixon, Thomas Sr., 66, 157, 250
Dixon, Thomas Sr., grave, 250
Dixon Presbyterian Church, 189, 271–272
Dixon School, 189, 272
Dockery, Alma Dwin, 168
Dockery, Carl James, 168
Dockery, Carl James Jr., 168
Dockery, Charlie, 168
Dockery's Funeral Home, 168, 274
Dockery's Mutual Burial Association, 168
Dora Mill, 148
Dorton, J. S., 160, 267
Double Shoals Baptist Church, 231
Double Shoals Company, Inc., 102
Double Shoals Cotton Mills, 102–103
Double Shoals Methodist/Baptist Cemetery, 28–29
Double Springs Baptist Church, 66
Douglas Academy, 40
Dover, Charles I., 148
Dover, Elizabeth, 13–14, 15
Dover, Elizabeth, tombstone 13–14, 15
Dover, John R., Memorial Library, 42
Dover, John Randolph, 18, 148
Dover, John Randolph Jr., 148
Dover Mill Overhead Bridge, 284
Dover Mill Village, 148, 265
Dover Mill, 148
Dover School, 265, 284
Downs, D. S., 192
Draper, Earl S., 20
Duke Power Company, 211, 240
Duke Power Clubhouse, 211
Duke Power Cliffside Steam Station and Clubhouse, 211
Durbro, N.C., 225
Durbro Post Office, 12, 225

Eagle Roller Mill, 91, 144
Eaker, John, 244
Earl, Abel, 72
Earl, Abel, distillery, 72

Earl, Abel and Mary, 72
Earl, Mary (Polly) Sepaugh, 72
Earl, N.C., 3, 253
Earl Commercial Buildings, 253
Earl School (black), 40
Earl School (white), 39, 40
Earl Southern Railway Depot, 92, 250
East Marion Street development, 49
East Marion-Belvedere Park Historic District, 283
Eastside Cemetery, 29
Eastside Manufacturing Company Mill Village, 20, 49
Eastside Mill, 20
Ebeltoft, T. E., 224
Ebenezer Baptist Church (former), 194
Eckenhoff Saunders Architects, 279
Eddins (teacher), 95
Edwards, Forrest, 49, 177, 206
Edwards, Hattie Ola Bingham, 177
Edwards, W. C., House (Maie and Reid Wilson House), 265–266
Edwards House and Clinic (Forrest Edwards House), 49, 177
El Bethel United Methodist Church, 139, 284
El Bethel United Methodist Church Cemetery, 14, 139
El Nido, 48, 150, 284, plate 37
Elks, 245, 274
Elks Club, 182
Ella Manufacturing Company, 148
Ella Mills, 18
Elliott, J. D., 253
Elliott, J. D. and Johnye, Farm, 253
Elliott, Jim, 78
Elliott, Joe, 207
Elliott, John, 239
Elliott, John Crenshaw, 80
Elliott, John Paxton, 223
Elliott, John Paxton, House, 223
Elliott, Johnye, 253
Elliott, Mary Donoho, 80
Elliott, Mildred, 239
Elliott, Nora, 78
Elliott, Oliver and Virginia, Farm, 222–223
Elliott, Oliver Beam, 222, 223
Elliott, Thomas, 222
Elliott, Virginia Ann (Stockton), 222
Elliott Chapel, 13, 80, 284
Elliott's Church, 13, 80, 284

Ellis, Benjamin, 8, 64
Ellis, Bill, 52
Ellis, Bill and Thelma, House, 52
Ellis, J. D., 276
Ellis, James, 64
Ellis, Rick, 64
Ellis, Thelma, 52
Ellis, Willis, 64
Ellis Ferry, 64
Ellis Ferry House, 8, 64, 284
Ellis Tavern, 64
Elmore, Decatur, 228
Enterprise Mill, 18
Episcopal Church of the Holy Redeemer, 266
Episcopal Church of the Redeemer, 275
Epps springs, 36
Esther Mill, 18, 20, 148
Europeans, 4
Evans, Gus, 152
Ezell, W. J., 260
Ezell, W. J., House, 260–261

Fairview School, 80
Falls, Benjamin, 228
Falls, Benjamin, House, 228
Falls, Cicero and Hattie, House, 127
Falls, Cicero Clemmie, 127
Falls, Hattie Maude Lattimore, 127
Falls, John Zemri, 127
Falls, Robert, House, 51
Falls City Construction Company, 121
Fallston, N.C., 3
Fancy Post Office, 74
Farmer's Bank of Rutherfordton, 112
Fielden & Allen, 122
First Baptist Church Kings Mountain (former), 140
First Baptist Church Kings Mountain (present), 140
First Baptist Church Shelby, 43, 136–137, plate 12
First Broad River, 3
First Broad River Bridge, 284
First National Bank (Kings Mountain), 183
First National Bank (Shelby), 53, 55, 86, 101, 108–109, 279
First Presbyterian Church, 272
Fite, Will, 112
Flatt, Lester, 159
Flick (theater), 200

Index 303

Foggy Mountain Boys, 159
Foothills Builders, 131
Forney, C. D. and Frances, House, 27
Forney, Peter, 169
Fortenberry, Charlie, 226
Fortenberry, Sudie Mae, 226
Foster (stonemason), 267
Froneberger, Sam, 29
Fulenwider, Eli, 224
Fulenwider-Ebeltoft House, 224
Fuller, Buckminster, 52

Gallery, The, 130
Gamble, Andrew J., 79
Gamble, Joseph Franklin, 79
Gamble, Laura Jane Watterson, 79
Gamble, Leonard, 79
Gamble, Ruth, 79
Gantt, M. N., 258
Garden of Memories, 29
Gardner, Fay Lamar (Webb), 124, 224
Gardner, J. A., & Co., 136
Gardner, Max III, 125
Gardner, Oliver Maxwell, 88, 124, 149, 157, 224
Gardner, O. Max, Memorial Student Union Building, 40, 42
Gardner, Ralph Webb, 124
Gardner Drug Store, 32
Gardner-Webb College, 40, 170
Gardner-Webb President's House, 170
Gardner-Webb University, 40, 42, 55, 76, 146, 170–172, 224, 258, 259, 279
Gardner-Webb University gymnasium (original), 229
Garrett, Frank, 83
Garrett, I. Walton, 24, 83
Garrett, I. Walton, House, 83, 284
Garrett, John, 83
Garrett, Richard, 83
Garrett House, 83, 284
Germans, 4
Gibbs, Emmett W., 150
Gibbs, Maude Sams, 48, 150
Gibbs, Ray, 150
Gibson, Lizzie, 257
Gibson, Ovella, 257
Gibson, Ovella and Lizzie, House, 257

Gingles, Cornelius F., 194
Glenn, Albert, 229, 270
Glenn family, 236
Glenn Lumber Company, 270
Glenn-Stamey House, 236
Gobber, Robert, 118
Goforth, Joe A., 267
Goforth, John, 242
Goforth, Preston, 139
Goforth Brothers, 267
Gold's General Store, 244–245
Goode, Essie and Everett, House, 246
Goode, Essie (Hamrick), House, 246
Goode, Everett, 246
Gordon family, 243
Gordon-Wilson House, 243
Grace Fellowship Worship Center, 265
Graham Elementary School, 257
Graham House, 23
Grambling House, 8, 284
Grayson, Lyn, 227
Great Gulf, Colorado & Santa Fe Railroad, 222
Green, George, 226
Green, Tom, 165
Green-Hoey House, 226
Greene, Reuben, 223
Greene, Reuben, House, 223
Grier, Thomas L., 162
Grover, N.C., 3, 15, 253
Grover Commercial District, 253, plate 28
Grover Historic District, 284
Grover School, 189, 246
Guffey, Mitchell, 222
Gulf Oil Company Distributorship, 254–255, 284
G.U.O of O.F., 245

Haas, Lucille Sarratt, 62
Hamilton, Joseph, 65
Hamilton, Joseph, grave, 65
Hamilton Doctor's Office, 6, 65
Hamilton-McBrayer Farm, 6, 65
Hamrick, Aaron Bonner, 269
Hamrick, Aubrey Yates, 142
Hamrick, Aubrey Yates, House, 142
Hamrick, C. J., 224
Hamrick, C. J., Store, 248
Hamrick, C. J. and Sarah, House, 25, 104, plate 6

Hamrick, Cameron Street, 60
Hamrick, Cameron Street, Memorial Association, 55
Hamrick, Charles Jefferson, 104, 112, 248
Hamrick, D. J., 28
Hamrick, Dwight, 269
Hamrick, Dwight, House (The Rock House), 269
Hamrick, E. B., Hall, 40, 170, 224, 283
Hamrick, E. B., House, 224
Hamrick, Elijah Bly, 224, 248
Hamrick, Elijah W., House, 227
Hamrick, Elijah Wright, 227
Hamrick, Elmira, 60
Hamrick, Frances, 228
Hamrick, Frankie, 60
Hamrick, G. L. & Son, Dairy Farm, 142–143, 284
Hamrick, George L., 142
Hamrick, George L., House, 142, 143
Hamrick, Grover, 255
Hamrick, Hubbard, 228
Hamrick, Jessie Teresa Pangle, 258
Hamrick, Landrum, 142
Hamrick, Leander, 228
Hamrick, Lester, 102
Hamrick, Max, 209
Hamrick, Max, Cotton Gin, 209
Hamrick, Noah, 246
Hamrick, O. P. and Jessie, House, 258–259
Hamrick, Oliver, 248
Hamrick, Oliver, House, 248–249
Hamrick, Oliver Paul, 258
Hamrick, Pinckney, 229
Hamrick, Pinckney, House, 104, 229
Hamrick, Sarah, 104
Hamrick, Sarah (1862–1955), 228
Hamrick, T. W., 238
Hamrick, Thomas, 225
Hamrick, Thomas, House, 225
Hamrick, Wiley, 225
Hamrick, Wiley, House, 225–226, 227
Hamrick family, 7, 54
Hamrick Family Reunion, 54
Hamrick Jewelers Building, 238
Harbin, W. Lee, 136
Harrill, Beulah Falls, 78
Harrill, DeWitt, 261
Harrill, DeWitt and Essie, House, 261

Harrill, Essie, 261
Harrill, Hattie, 95
Harrill, John A., 95
Harrill family, 95
Harris, Kenny, 101
Harris, Madge, 222
Harris, Rita, 101
Harris Children's Wing, 153
Harry, Charles and Effie, House, 173
Harry, Charles Franklin Sr., 18, 173
Harry, David F. C., 175
Harry, Effie Jeanette Holmes, 173
Harry, Jeanette, 18
Harry, Minnie, 18
Hartman, Nancy, 275
Hawkins, Arrie, 101
Hawkins, Barbara Gamble, 79
Hawkins, Beunah, 100
Hawkins, John, 101
Hawkins, Otho, 100
Hawkins, Preston Plato, 100
Hawkins, Ruth Weathers, 101
Hawkins, Susan Smith, 100
Hawkins, Yates, 100, 101
Hawkins Farm, 100
Haynes, Charlie, 88
Haynes, Clive, 4
Haynes Mills, 225
Heck-Andrews House, 84
Hege, Joe, 236
Hendrick, Chapel, 88
Hendrick, Maurice, 88
Hendrick, Stowe, 267
Hendrick, Stowe and Florence, House, 267
Hendrick family, 88
Hendrick-Meacham House, 88–89
Hendricks, Rochel, 253
Herndon, Arthur H., House, 228
Herndon, Arthur Henderson, 228
Herndon, George Carruth, House, 24
Herndon, Howard, 262
Herndon, Howard, Farm, 262
Herndon, Lester, 162
Herndon, Martha (Poston), 228
Herndon family, 262
Herschell-Spillman Company, 212
Hewitt, Robert, 112
Hicks, Dobbin, 239
Hicks, Dobbin and Jane, House, 239–240
Hicks, Jane, 239

Highway 74, 4
Historic Preservation Society of North Carolina, 109
Historic Shelby Foundation, 54
Hoey, Bess (Gardner), 149
Hoey, Clyde, 226
Hoey, Clyde R., House, 149
Hoey, Clyde Roark, 124, 149, 157
Hoey, Will, 226
Holder, Ben A. (Jack), 255
Holland, Kate, 269
Holland, Kate and Paul, Farm, 269–270
Holland, L. Pegram Jr., 201, 277
Holland, Oliver, 76, 77
Holland, Oliver and Rosannah, House, 76–77
Holland, Paul, 269
Holland, Ralph, 236
Holland, Ralph, House, 236
Holland, Rosannah, 76, 77
Holland, Williamson, 258
Holland & Riviere, 50, 278
Holland Hamrick & Patterson Architects, 45, 201, 212, 213
Hollifield, Abram, 192
Hollifield Carillon, 42
Holly Oak Park, 273
Homesley, Albert, 102
Hook, Charles Christian, 21
"Hoover rail," 98
Hopper, Buri, 240, 241
Hopper, C. F., 81
Hopper, Lance, 120
Hopper, Lance and Ollie, House, 120
Hopper, Ollie, 120
Hord, Carrie Belle White, 153
Hord, J. G. and Carrie, House, 46, 153
Hord, Jacob George Van Buren, 153
Horn, Olden, 267
Hotel Charles, 35, 55, 108–109
House (120 Pleasant Ridge Church Rd.), 143
House (121 Pleasant Ridge Church Rd.), 143
House (123 Pleasant Ridge Church Rd.), 143
House (Warren St., Shelby), 116
Howell, Robert, 81
Hoyle, Hugh and Vivian, House, 258

Hoyle, Hugh Dixon, 258
Hoyle, Hugh Dixon, Harness Shop, 118, 258
Hoyle, Lightfoot Williams Jr., 87
Hoyle, Theresa Self, 224
Hoyle, William, 224
Hoyle family, 97
Hoyle-Stroup House, 87, plate 17
Hoyle-Warlick House, 224
Hudson, Hillary, 126
Hudson, Mary T. Lee, 126
Hudson Hosiery Mill, 268–269, 284
Hudson-Hull House, 126, 283
Huggins-Curtis Building, 40, 42
Hughes, W. Gordon, 189
Hull, James Heyward, 126
Hull, James Heyward, House, 126, 283
Hull, Loula (Abernethy), 126
Hunt, Alma (Harrill), 187
Hunt, Robert and Alma, 187
Hunt, Robert Lee, 1, 112
Hunt, Tommy, 147
Hunt & Hewitt Store, 1, 112
Hunter School, 273
Hut, The, 206

IBPOEW Reciprocity Lodge No. 693, 274
Improved Benevolent and Protective Order of Elks, Worldwide, 274
International Downtown Association, 158
Interstate 85, 3, 53
Irvin, James, 6, 60
Irvin, Rebecca (Hardin), 60
Irvin-Hamrick House, 6, 7, 54, 55, 60, 283, plate 15
Irvinsville, N.C., 64
Ivester, Pam, 78
Ivester, Ronny, 78

Jackson, Abernathy, 102
Jackson, Delbert, 189
Jackson, Jessie, 243
Jackson, Lilly, 189
Jackson, Marion, 189
Jackson, Thomas R., 102
Jackson, Tildon, 243
Jefferson School, 257
Jenkins, Harriett (Brown), 84
Jenkins, J., & Company, 86, 108

Jenkins, J. Frank, 235
Jenkins, Jesse, 23, 84
Jenkins, Jesse, House, 84–85
John Deere dealership, 248
Johnson, Lady Bird, 124
Johnson, Ralph, Associates, 51
Johnson, W. L., 272
Jolley, Dovie Hopper, 251
Jolley, Marion and Dovie, House, 251
Jolley, Marion Augustus, 251
Jolley, P. G., 225
Jones, "Hatcher," 243
Jones, Haynes F., 40
Jones family monument, 214
Jones Hatchery, 243
Jordan, Karl, 270
Jordan, Karl and Yvonne, House, 270
Jordan, Karl Jr., 270
Jordan, Yvonne, 270
Joy Performance Center, 213
Joy Theatre, 35, 55, 213
Joyner, J. Y., 39

Kadesh Methodist Church, 265
Kadesh Methodist Church Cemetery, 265
Keeter's Department Store, 230
Kendrick, Lawson and Ponola, Farm, 234
Kendrick, Lawson "Loss" Irvin, 234
Kendrick, Zuar Ponola Camp, 234
Kentucky Derby, 267
King Street Overhead Bridge, 284, plate 25
Kings Mountain, 3, 4
Kings Mountain, City of, 153, 254
Kings Mountain, N.C., 3, 15, 18, 20, 55, 174, 225, 227, 230, 280–281
Kings Mountain Baptist Association, 40, 66, 170, 192
Kings Mountain Central Business District, 53, 280–281
Kings Mountain City Hall (former), 46, 47
Kings Mountain City Hall (present), 202
Kings Mountain Commercial District, 174
Kings Mountain Country Club, 50, 277

Kings Mountain Historic Home Preservation Inc., 82
Kings Mountain Historical Museum, 202
Kings Mountain Historical Society, 202
Kings Mountain Landmarks Commission, x
Kings Mountain Manufacturing Company (KMMC), 18, 154, 230, 247, 251
Kings Mountain Military School, 38, 190
Kings Mountain Post Office (former), 202, 284
Kings Mountain Neisler Company, 103
Kings Mountain school system, 246
Kings Mountain Southern Railway Depot, 254, 255
Kings Mountain Waterworks, 251
Kings Mountain Womans Club, 154
Kingstown, N.C., 3
Kiser, Larkin A., 154
Knob Creek Methodist Church, 275–276
Knob Creek Methodist Church Cemetery, 276
Korner, J. Gilmer, 136, 137
Kouris Warehouse (Morgan & Company Building), 264
Kyzer map, 5

Lackey, Josephine, 74
Lackey, Phate, 74
Lafayette Place, 158
Lanier, Sidney, 35
Larkin Building, 156
Lattimore, Ann, 229
Lattimore, Audley and Mary Jane, House, 229
Lattimore, Audley Martin, 114, 229
Lattimore, Charles, 207
Lattimore, Daniel, 63
Lattimore, Isabella (Carson), 63
Lattimore, J. B., Store, 112, 113, 241
Lattimore, John, 111
Lattimore, John, House, 7, 8, 63, 283
Lattimore, John and Vertie, House, 26–27, 111
Lattimore, John "Big John," 63
Lattimore, John Broadus, 112, 241

Lattimore, John L., 63
Lattimore, Mary Jane Hamrick, 229
Lattimore, Max, 251
Lattimore, Sunie Jones, 241
Lattimore, Tom, 229
Lattimore, Vertie (Mauney), 111
Lattimore, N.C., 3, 55, 112–113, 114, 229, 241
Lattimore Baptist Church, 187, 214
Lattimore Baptist Church Cemetery, 214
Lattimore Commercial District, 112
Lattimore Historic District, 284
Lattimore House, 7, 8, 63, 283, plate 16
Lattimore Oil Company, 112
Lattimore School, 78, 191, 265
Lattimore Seaboard Air Line Railroad Depot, 90, 241
Lattimore spec housing, 187
Lattimore Telephone Company, 94
Lattimore Town Hall, 113
Lavender, Bessie Sue, 120
Lavender, Claude Lee, 120
Lawndale, N.C., 3, 16, 18, 55, 98
Lawndale, Town of, 134
Lawndale Dummy, 16
Lawndale First Baptist Church, 40
Lawndale First Baptist Church (former), 272, plate 22
Lawndale Historical Museum, 16, 135
Lawndale Historical Society, 135, 147
Lawndale Junction, 147
Lawndale Railway, 16, 99, 147
Lawndale Railway & Industrial Company, 16, 147
Lawndale Railway & Industrial Company Engine House, 16, 147
Lawndale Railway & Industrial Company Locomotive Number 5, 16, 147
Lawndale Railway boxcar, 135
Lee, Gamie, 233
Lee, Gamie, House, 233
Lee, H. DeKalb, 84
Lee, L. V. and Susan, Farm, 114
Lee, Lawrence Victor, 112, 114, 261
Lee, Margaret Iva Sperling, 261
Lee, Norman, 261
Lee, Sarah, 84
Lee, Susan C. Lattimore, 114

Lee House, 47
Lee's Chapel Methodist Church, 207, 227–228, 266, 284
LeGrand House, 45
Leicester, Nora, 264
Leicester, William, 264
Leicester, William and Nora, House, 264, plate 5
Lewman, Harry L., 121, 123
Lewman, M. T., 121
Lily Mill & Power Company, 152, 239, 267
Lily Mill, 18, 102, 152, 239
Lily Mill Clubhouse, 22, 267–268
Lineberger, John Dixon Jr., 47, 182
Lineberger, Mattie Flack, 151
Lineberger, Nannie Belle Sherrill, 47, 182
Lineberger, William and Mattie, House, 151
Lineberger, William Mundy, 49, 151
Lineberger Brothers, 182
Lineberger family, 151
Little, John P., & Son, 155, 157
Logan, Benjamin Franklin, 95
Logan, Elizabeth Jane "Jennie" (Hogue), 95
Logan, John Pinckney, 95
Logan, Marilyn, 95
Logan-Harrill House, 95, 284
London, John, 258
London, Morgan, 207
Lovelace, Jonas A., House, 246
Lovelace, Jonas Alvin, 246
Lowe, L. Vincent, Business Award, 109
Lowery, W. B., 238
Lowman, R. Lee, 166, 184
Loy's Mens Shop, 33, 34, 130
Lucas, R. D., 194
Lucky Strike Yarn Mill, 103
Lula Mills, 18
Lutheran church, 250
Lutz, Carl, 168
Lutz, Coot, 259
Lutz, Frances, 259
Lutz-Austell Funeral Home Chapel, 266

Macedonia Baptist Church, 270, 277
Magness, J. H., 192
Main Street communities, 54

Margrace Mill Village, 20, 251, plate 19
Margrace Mill Village Historic District, 284
Margrace Mills, 18, 247
Margrace Mills Clubhouse, 251
Marin County Courthouse, 51
Marion Street Apartments, 260
Marsh, M. R., 213
Martin, Byron, 75
Martin, Donnis Magness, 116
Martin, James Wyatt, 112, 116
Martin, John, 264
Martin, John Thomas, 75
Martin, Julius C., 116
Martin, Lillie Angeline Walker, 116
Martin, Lydia, 14, 15
Martin, Lydia, tombstone, 14, 15
Martin, William A., 75
Martin, William A., Farm, 75, 284
Martin Boal Anthony & Johnson (MBAJ Architecture), 53, 131, 219, 275, 278
Martin Building, 112
Martin family, 75
Mason Square, 157
Masonic Temple Building, 43, 55, 156–157, 283, plate 9
Masons, 156–157, 245
Matton (builder), 276
Mauney, Bessie Miller (Frantz), 115
Mauney, Dorris (Dorus) Carl, 154
Mauney, Dorus and Sarah, House, 154
Mauney, Herman, 264–265
Mauney, Jacob and Margaret, House, 230
Mauney, Jacob S., Memorial Library, 46, 153, 230
Mauney, Jacob Simri, 18, 230
Mauney, John and Bessie, House, 115
Mauney, John David, 115
Mauney, Margaret Juletta (Julia) Rudisill, 230
Mauney, Matthew Marcus, 42–43, 98, 105
Mauney, Sarah (Sadie) Elizabeth Fisher, 154
Mauney, Tallulah, 265
Mauney, William A., House, 230, plate 13

Mauney, William Andrew, 18, 32, 79, 82, 183, 230, 251
Mauney, William Andrew, Store, 230
Mauney Brothers, 82
Mauney family, 153, 251
Mauney House, 32, 55, 82, plate 36
Mauney Steel Company, 154
Mauney Store, 32
Mauney Mausoleum, 28
Mauney Mills, 18
McAllister, Junius, 170
McBrayer, David, 225
McBrayer, David and Martha, House, 225
McBrayer, Dr. Victor, House, 25, 106–107, 283
McBrayer, Esther (Suttle), 106
McBrayer, John, Barn, 29, 180, 284
McBrayer, John Albert, 180
McBrayer, John E., 65
McBrayer, John Z., 132
McBrayer, Martha Ann (Blanton), 225
McBrayer, Reuben H., 106
McBrayer, Robert, 65
McBrayer, Victor, 106
McBrayer, Victor and Esther, House, 25, 106–107, 283, plate 4
McBrayer, Will, 132
McBrayer, Will, Farm, 132–133, 284
McBrayer family, 65
McBrayer House, 284
McBrayer School, 145
McCall, Bennie, 270
McCombs, Robert L., 29
McCraw, Robert Ed, 256
McCraw, Rush, 256
McCraw, Rush, House, 256
McCulloch, John, 170
McCulloch-English Associates, 170
McDaniel, Glenn, 247
McDaniel, Glenn, House, 247–248
McDaniel, Harlan, 267
McEntyre, A. A., 128
McEntyre, Avro, 128
McEntyre, Avro and Laura, House, 128
McGill, Edna Grant, 266
McGill, Isaac Abernathy, 266
McGill, Isaac and Edna, Farm, 266–267
McGill, William Fulton, 266

McGill Brothers Dairy, 266, 267
McIntyre, Virgil, 215
McMichael, J. M., 43, 129, 130, 155
McMurray, J. J., 235
McMurry, A. W., 102
McMurry, J. J., & Company, 126
McMurry-Beam Building, 112
McSwain, Lawson, 145
McSwain, Pete, 230
Meacham, Earl, 88
Meacham, Mrs. Earl, 88
Melick, Neal A., 202
Merchant Mills, 227
Metal Post Office, 233
Metcalfe, Gene, 147
Metcalfe, Irma, 147
Metcalfe, Quincy Hague, 147
Metcalfe, N.C., 16
Metcalfe Station, 16, 147, plate 26
Miller, A. C., 86
Miller, Lost John, 159
Miller, Pink, 259
Miller Apartments, 45
Minette Mills, 18, 21–22, 173, 226
Mintz, Charlie, 254
Miracle Farm, 76–77
Miracle Farm Day, 76, 77
Monroe, Bill, 159
Moore, Dan, 252
Moore, Dan, House, 252
Moore, Dan Sr., 252
Moore, J. F., 233, 252
Moore, J. F., House, 233–234
Moore, John, 65
Moore, John F., 40
Moore, Lem, 141
Moore, Mr., 228
Moore, Tom, 102
Moore-Hamrick House, 228–229
Mooresboro, N.C., 3, 141
Mooresboro Bank, 94
Mooresboro Commercial District, 141, plate 20
Mooresboro Cotton Oil Mill, 94
Mooresboro Creamery, 141
Mooresboro Historic District, 284
Mooresboro Masonic Lodge, 141
Mooresboro Oil Mill, 141
Mooresboro School, 263
Morgan, Charles Gerald, 263
Morgan, E. A., 102
Morgan, Fred, 102

Morgan, O. Z., 264
Morgan, Ron, 158
Morgan, Cline & Company, 105
Morgan & Company, 264
Morgan & Company Building, 264
Morgan Street Historic District, 284
Morris, Earl, 267
Morris, Earl, House, 267
Morris, Letha, 264
Morris Brothers, 159
Morris family, 267
Morrison Construction Company, 279
Morton (industrialist), 152
Moss, Alice Runyon, 240
Moss, John, Store, 237
Moss, Merrimon T., 240
Moss, Thomas, 250
Moss family, 250
Moss-Hopper House, 240–241
Motel Royal, 270–271
Mount Harmony Methodist Church, 207, 284, plate 24
Mount Harmony Methodist Church Cemetery, 207
"Mountain Music," 159
Mountain Rest Cemetery, 28
Mountain View Hotel, 25
Mull, O. M., 88
Murphy, Crawford, 278
Murray, W. M., 194

National Historic Landmark, 125, 283
National Main Street Program, 54
National Park Service, 283
National Register of Historic Places, 55, 283
National Trust for Historic Preservation, 55, 198
National Youth Administration, 135, 203
Native Americans, 4
Neisler, Charles E. Sr., 251, 266
Neisler, Charles Eugene, 18, 247
Neisler, Ida Pauline Mauney, 247
Neisler, Laura Grace, 18, 251
Neisler, Margaret Sue, 18, 251
Neisler, Mary, 82
Neisler, Paul M., House, 266
Neisler, Paul Mauney, 266
Neisler family, 18, 103, 247, 251
Neisler Mills Inc., 266

New Bethel Baptist Church, 66
New Hope Baptist Church, 120
New Prospect Baptist Church, 250
New Prospect Baptist Church Cemetery, 250
New York to Jacksonville highway, 36
Newton, Andy, 253
Newton, Ellen, 192
Newton, Frank, 268
Newton, J. A., 192
Newton family, 229
Newton House, 26, 229, 284
Newton-Allen Farm, 253–254
Nicholsonville, N.C., 225
Nicholsonville Cotton Mill, 225
Noel Hall, 42
Norman, D. M., 268
Norman, Julius, 268
Norman family, 268
Norman's Grove Baptist Church, 268
North Carolina Historic Preservation Office, 283
North Carolina Office of Archives and History, 283
North Carolina State Fair, 160
North Cleveland Junior High School, 167
Number 3 Egg Producers, 249, 276
NuWay Spinning Company, 176

Oates, Rush, 86
Oates, Sarah Ann Kiser, 74
Oates, Thomas and Sarah, House, 74
Oates, Thomas Milton Addison, 74
Oates, William Jr., House, 284
Oates General Store, 74
Oates Store, 11
O'Brien, Michael, 158
Odd Fellows, 245
Office of War Mobilization, 124
Olive, Ed, 250
Olive, Ed and Edith, House, 250
Olive, Edith, 250
Ora Mills, 18, 148
Osborne, Joseph Cullen, 93
Osborne, Margaret Schenck, 93
Osborne-Carpenter House, 27, 93, plate 32
Overcash-Demmitt Architects, 51

Paine Mountain, 3
Park Grace School, 246
Parker, George, 223
Parker, Joe, Store, 192
Patricia Mills, 18, 247
Patterson, Robert and Nancy, House, 202
Patterson, William George, 36
Patterson Grove School, 262–263
Patterson Springs, N.C., 3, 35
Patterson Springs Hotel, 36
Patterson Springs resort, 36
Pauley, James S., grave, 276
Pauline mill houses, 20
Pauline Mills, 18, 247, 252
Pauline Mills Clubhouse, 22, 252
Payne, George Hardy, Studio, 136
Pearl Post Office, 12, 232
Pease, J. N., 50, 185
Peeler House, 160, 161
Peelers Mill, 161
Peoples Bank, 233
People's Drug Store, 240
Perry, Dwight, 103
Phenix Mill, 20
Phenix Mill Village, 20
Phifer, John, 69
Phifer, Martin, 69
Phifer family, 69
Phifer House, 7, 69
Philadelphia Methodist Church, 276
Philbeck, Gaither, 227
Philbeck, Gaither, Farm, 227
Phillip, W., 24
Phillips, Ernest, 269
Phillips, Ernest V., Mill, 269
Phillips 66 Station (Shelby), 52
Piedmont Air Line (railroad), 15, 253
Piedmont Elementary School, 134
Piedmont School, 16, 24, 38, 55, 134–135, 228, plate 35
Piedmont School Agriculture and Home Economics Building, 134
Pisgah Lodge 9080, 245
Pittsburgh Plate Glass, 218
Plonk, Bill, 210
Plonk, Clarence and Ellen, Farm, 242–243
Plonk, Clarence Sloan, 242, 243
Plonk, Ellen Patterson, 242
Plonk, Mary Kathleen McGill, 210
Plonk, Rufus and Kathleen, Farm, 30, 210, 284

Plonk, Rufus Lawrence, 210
Plonk Building, 174
Plonk family, 210
Plonk Farm, 284
Polkville, N.C., 3
Polkville Elementary School, 260
Polkville Fire Department, 260
Polkville High School, 41, 260
Polkville High School Home Economics Building, 260
Polkville Methodist Church, 207, 275
Poplar Springs Methodist Church, 266
Post Office Annex, 250
Poston, Rachel (King), 222
Poston, Samuel, 222
Poston Cemetery, 28
Poston House, 222
PPG Industries, 218
Presbyterian Manse (former; Shelby), 42
Preservation North Carolina, 85, 125, 150
Princess Theatre, 249
Pruett, Doug, 219
Pruett, John, 252
Pruett family, 236
Pruett's Grocery, 164
Pruett's Store, 252
Pruitt, Willie, 270
Pullen, F. M., 272
Putnam, Baxter and Ida, Farm, 166
Putnam, Baxter Cleveland, 166
Putnam, Ida Hamrick, 166
Putnam family, 238
Putnam-Adams House, 238–239

Quonset hut, 274

Ramseur, David, 62
Ramseur, Frederick, 62
Ramseur, Phillip, 8, 62
Ramseur family, 62
Ramseur-Sarratt House, 8, 9, 62, 284, plate 31
Ramsey, A. A., 180
Ramsour, Philip, House, 284
Randall, Elias, 81
RBC Centura, 278
Reciprocity Lodge No. 693, 274
Rehobeth Methodist Church, 207
Rhyne, Mrs. C. Q., 154

Richard, Elizabeth, 275
Richmond & Danville (railroad), 15, 36
Roark, James Alex, 162
Roark, Margaret Avalona Earle, 162
Roark-Grier House, 162
Roberts, Barney, 260
Roberts, J. F., 122
Roberts, John M., House, 73
Roberts, John Miller, 73
Roberts, L. M. H., 225
Roberts, Vernon, 73
Roberts Farm, 231
Roberts Filter Manufacturing Company, 185
Roberts-Cash House, 231
Rockdale Mill, 258
Rogers, Robert Hamer, 198
Rogers, Willard G., 43, 157
Rogers Ford dealership, 198
Rogers Motors, 198
Rogers Theatre, vi, 49–50, 55, 198–199
Rogers Theatre Consortium, 198
Rollins (builder), 110
Rollins, V. G., 81
Roosevelt, Franklin Delano, 124
Rose Hill, 24, 88–89
Rose Hill Restaurant, 88
Rosenwald, Julius, 40
Rosenwald Fund, 40, 169, 263
Rosenwald Schools, 40
Ross Grove Baptist Church, 176
Ross Grove Baptist congregation, 12
Rotary Special, 212
Royster, David Wyeth, 129, 254
Royster, H. R., 254
Royster, Olive Bruce McBrayer, 129
Royster, Ralph, 102
Royster, Stephen and Olive, House, 43, 129
Royster, Stephen Sampson, 43, 129, 130, 158, 212, 254
Royster Building, 33, 34, 43, 129, 130, plate 27
Rudisill, Michael, 27, 42
Rudisill, Michael, planing mill, 42
Ruppe, Daniel, 68
Ruppe family, 68
Rural Electrification Administration, 110
Rutherford Electric Co-op, 110

s & w Cafeteria chain, 182
Sadie Mill Village, 20
Sadie Mills, 18, 154
Sain, Edith, 258
Sain, John, 258
Sain, John and Edith, Farm, 258
St. Mary's Catholic Church (former), 195, 284
St. Matthew's Lutheran Church, 216–217, plate 11
St. Peter's United Methodist Church, 49, 193, 206
Salem Church, 276
Sandy Run Baptist Association, 40, 170
Sandy Run Baptist Church, 12
Sarratt, Leonora (Ramseur), 62
Sarratt, Obadiah, 62
Sarratt, Wellington, 62
Sarratt Cotton Gin, 242
Schenck, Evelyn Pyle, 152
Schenck, Henry Franklin, 16, 18, 93, 98, 134
Schenck, Jean, 152
Schenck, John F., 18
Schenck, John Franklin Jr., 152
Schenck, John Jr. and Evelyn, House, 152
Schenck, Lily Moore, 152
Schenck family, 102–103
Schenck Hall, 134
School of Divinity, 42
Schwab Safe Company, 202
Scism, Amanda, 231
Scism, Clyde, 208
Scism, Mindy, 231
Scism, W. C., 231
Scism's Store, 231
Scots-Irish, 4
Scott, Kerr, 76
Scott, W. L., 207
Scruggs, Earl, 159
Scruggs, Earl, Birthplace, 159, 284
Scruggs, Earl, Review, 159
Scruggs, Gary, 159
Scruggs, George and Lula, House (Earl Scruggs Birthplace), 159, 284
Scruggs, George Elam, 159
Scruggs, Lula, 159
Scruggs, Randy, 159
Scruggs family, 159
Seaboard Air Line Railroad, 4, 16, 90, 91, 112, 141, 211, 218

Seaboard Railway Freight Depot, 284
Seal Wire Company, 112
Sharon Methodist Episcopal Church, 266
Sharon United Methodist Church, 145, 266
Sharon United Methodist Church Cemetery, 266
Shelby, Isaac, 9
Shelby, City of, 212, 218, 239, 257
Shelby, N.C., 3, 8–9, 15, 18, 33, 54–55, 121, 225
Shelby Armory (former), 50, 205, 284
Shelby Bonded Warehouse, 17
Shelby Building & Loan Building, 51
Shelby building and loan associations, 228
Shelby Cafe, 249
Shelby Cafe Block, 249
Shelby Central Business District, frontispiece, 53, 54, 121
Shelby City Cemetery, 28
Shelby City Hall (former), 131, plate 10
Shelby City Hall (present), 44, 47, 201
Shelby City Park, 212
Shelby City Park Carousel, 212
Shelby Cotton Mills, 18, 42, 105, 284
Shelby Cotton Mills Village, 105
Shelby Cotton Seed Oil Mill, 235
Shelby Daily Star Building, 44–45
Shelby Dynasty, 124, 149, 250
Shelby Economic Development Commission, 54
Shelby Farm and Garden Supply Store, 186
Shelby Female Academy, 201
Shelby High School (former), 44, 196
Shelby Junior High School, 265
Shelby Kiwanis Club, 160
Shelby Lions Club, 76
Shelby Middle School, 196
Shelby Milk Plant, 272
Shelby Post Office (former), 250
Shelby Savings Bank, 51
Shelby Seaboard Air Line Railroad Depot, 91
Shelby Southern Railway Freight Depot (1929 building), 186

Shelby Southern Railway Freight Depot (19th century building), 186
Shelby Supply Company (former), 263
Shelby Tabernacle, 12
Shelby Waterworks, 50, 185
Sherer, Dr., 274
Shiloh Presbyterian Church, 12, 175
Shiloh Presbyterian Church Cemetery, 13, 14, 284
Simmons, Fred M., 51, 278
Simmons, George and Josephine, House, 12, 232–233
Simmons, George Hampton "Hapt," 12, 232
Simmons, Josephine Perlina Martin, 232
Simmons, Margaret Louise Mauney, 232
Simmons, Wilbur, 232
Simmons family, 232
Simon, Louis A., 202
Sisk Quartet, 273
Slater, Al, 103
Slater family, 103
Smart, W. W. G., 91
Smith, Caroline Jane, 66
Smith, George, 9
Smith, Jane Berry, 66
Smith, Lyle, 134, 135
Smith, Minor W., 66
Smith-Suttle family cemetery, 67
Smith-Suttle House, 66–67, 283
Software Training Service, 224
South Mountains, 3
South Shelby, N.C., 257
South Shelby School, 257
Southeast Saturday Night FM Network radio show, 198
Southern Association of Colleges and Schools, 170
Southern Cotton Oil Mill, 235–236
Southern Railway, 4, 15–16, 92, 112, 141, 174, 254
Southern Railway Freight Depot, 284
Southern Railway Trestle, 284
Southern Railway Trestle & Bridge, 284
Southern States Fair, 267
Spangler, Abson Dixon "Dick," 238
Spangler, C. D. and Veva C. Yelton, Library, 134
Spangler, Daisy Beam, 238

Spangler, Dick and Patience, Farm, 238
Spangler, E. Yates, 238
Spangler, Nannie Patience "Patie" Green, 238
Spartan Mills, 99
Sperling, George, House and Outbuildings, 30, 46, 176, 283
Sperling, George and Mary Jane, Barn, 30
Sperling, George and Mary Jane, Farm, 30, 46, 176, 283
Sperling, George Elzie, 46, 176
Sperling, Mary Jane Justice, 46, 176
Sperling House, 176
Spurlin, Elijah, 14, 139
Spurlin, Elijah, tombstone, 14, 139
Spurlin, Susanah, 139
Stamey, Annie Alexander, 236
Stamey, Clarence, 178
Stamey, Frank, 236
Stamey, Thomas, 178
Stamey Brothers, 178
Stamey Brothers Store, 178
Stamey Farm, 179, plate 14
Stamey Stores Inc., 178
State Theatre, 49, 200, 220–221
Sterchis Store, 44
Stice Shoals Dam, 239
Stice Shoals Dam and Power Plant, 239
Stice Shoals Power Plant, 239, 284
Stockton, George Robert, 231
Stockton, Robert L., 80
Stockton-Scism House, 231
Strickland, C. E., 276
Stroud family monument, 214
Stroud, Biddie Jones, 245
Stroud, Biddie Jones, Farm, 245–246
Stroud, William, 245
Stroup, Daniel Boyd, 87
Stroup, Eura, 87
Study List, 283, 284
Summers, Bonnie E. Mauney, 183
Summers, Frank and Bonnie, House, 47, 183, 284
Summers, Frank Rickert, 183
Summers Drug Store, 183
Sun Ra, 156
Sunrise Dairy, 210
Sunset Cemetery, 14, 28, 284, plate 23

Sunset Drive-In Theatre, 274–275, 284
Sunshine Construction Company, 134
Superintendent of Public Instruction, 39
Suttle, Elvira (Blanton), 66
Suttle, Joseph, 66
Suttle, Joseph Linton Jr., 66–67, 149
Suttle, Sarah McFarland (Mrs. J. L. Jr.), 67, 149
Swanson, Aurelia, 150

Talley, Norman "Bud," 278
Talley & Smith Architecture, 278
Tate, Annie Bridges, 240
Tate, Fannie Ellis, 240
Tate, Mannasseh Masshaw, 240
Tate, Roland Clifton, 240
Tate House, 240
Texaco service station, 147
Thompson, Carl, 184
Thompson, Carl and Elva, House, 184, 284
Thompson, Elva, 184
Thompson, W. H., Factory, 23
Thompson Lumber Company, 184
Thursday Afternoon Book Club, 154
Tompkins, Daniel A., 21
Truman, Harry S., 124
Twelve Oaks Academy, 257
Twin Chimneys, 66–67, 283, plate 33

Union Community Fair, 160
United States Gypsum Company, 247
Unity Church, 156
Universal Music & Logistics, 279
Upper Cleveland Office of First National Bank, 53
Upton, Sam, 258
Uptown Shelby, 33, 34, 55, 123
Uptown Shelby Association (USA), 54–55, 198
Usonian house designs, 50

Van Wageningen, Fred, 44, 201
Van Wageningen & Cothran, 215, 273
Vauxhall, 47, 182
Vauxhall Gardens, 182
Verner Oil Company, 112, 116

Waco, N.C., 3, 233, 259
Waco Baptist Church, 247
Waco City Hall, 270
Waco High School, 203, 259, 270
Waco High School Agriculture Building, 270
Waco Post Office (former), 233
Waco Women's Club (Waco Community Building), 203
Waldenses, 49
Wall, Otis, 164
War Admiral (horse), 267
Ware, Beth, School, 246
Ware, Moffat, 227
Ware, William Alexander, 227
Ware, William O., House, 227
Ware, William Oates, 227
Warlick, A. A., & Co. Store, 164
Warlick, Decatur, 96
Warlick, Decatur and Mittie, House, 96
Warlick, Henry, 234
Warlick, Henry and Susan, House, 234–235
Warlick, Mittie, 96
Warlick, Susan, 234
Warlick, Theodore, 224
Warlick family, 96, 224
Warlick general store, 164
Warren Street Historic District, 284
Washburn, Hone I., 112
Washburn, Hone I., Store, 112
Washburn Block, 238
Washburn Hardware Building, 238
Washburn Library, 40
Washington, Booker T., 40
Washington Missionary Church, 247
Washington School, 188
Washington Theater, 274
Waters, A. G., 135
Waters Library, 24, 55, 134–135, 284, plate 35
Watts, Rile, 275
Weare, Boyce, 79
Weare-Gamble House, 79
Weathers, Annie Wilson, 264
Weathers, Maurice, 264
Weathers, Maurice and Annie, House, 48, 264
Weathers, William, 9
Weathers, William, House, 9

Index 311

Weathers Concrete Company, 264
Weaver, W. D., 266
Webb, Edwin Yates, 250
Webb, James L., 124, 157, 224
Webb, James Milton, 137
Webb, Kansas "Kans," 124
Webb Chapel, 137
Webber (possible builder), 120
Webber, Andrell, 138, 253
Webber, Eva, 138
Webber, Ralph Furman, 277
Webber & Sons Construction, 170, 277
Webber General Store, 253
Webber-Austell Farm, 30, 138
Webbley (Governor O. Max Gardner House), 45–46, 124–125, 224, 283, plate 8
Wells, Anne Gladden, 61
Wells, Isaac, 61
Wells, J. K., House, 223
Wells, John, 61
Wells, John, House 61
Wells, Lucinda Gladden, 61
Wells, Mary H., tombstone, 207
Wells, Nick, 147
Wells, Robert H., 61
West Cleveland Office of First National Bank, 278–279
Westinghouse air-conditioning unit, 213
Wetmore, James A., 250
WGWG radio station, 171
Wheeler & Stern, 43, 136

Whisnant, Abraham, 232
Whisnant, John O., 232
Whisnant House, 232
White, A., & Sons, 170
White, David, 170
White, Fonz, 267
White, Hugh, 136
White, Richard M., House, 119
White, Richard Meredith, 119, 284
White family, 163
White House, 163
White Plains, N.C., 174
White Plains Post Office, 79
Whitney, Eli, 209
Whitworth, Addie, 259
Whitworth, M. C., 259
Whitworth, M. C. and Addie, House, 259
Wilbor, A. G., plan, 19
Williams, H. O. (Toby), 254
Williams family, 254
Williamson, Mr., 254
Willis, Addie (Alexander), 110
Willis, Joseph Gallashaw, 110
Willis, Kate, 264
Willis, Mary (Wilson), 110
Willis, Mrs. J. K., 262
Willis, Thomas Jacob, 110
Willis, Tommy, 207
Willis House, 110
Wilmington, Charlotte & Rutherford Railroad, 15
Wilson, D. C., 194
Wilson, Jack, 208

Wilson, Maie and Reid, House, 265–266
Wilson, Thomas, 36
Wilson Building, 238
Wilson family, 243
WOHS Radio Station, 273
Wood, Michael Thomas, 149
Wood, Millie Arey, 149
Woods Meeting House, 171
Works Progress Administration (WPA), 44, 191, 201, 202, 205
Worthington, M. S., 27
Wray, A. V., & 6 Sons Department Store, 33
Wray, Benny, 272
Wray Building, 33
Wright, D. C., 254
Wright, D. C., Store, 254
Wright, Dorsey Hoyle, 243
Wright, Frank Lloyd, 50–51, 156, 215, 277
Wright, John 243
Wright, Voidrey, 243
Wright, Voidrey and Dorsey, Farm, 243–244

Young, Lee, 250
Young, Samuel, House, 222

Zion Baptist congregation, 12
Zion School, 78, 284, plate 34
Zoar School, 257
Zourras (artist), 219